C000260859

A Path of Love

My Soul's Journey in this Body

SONELLE EUSKERA

Copyright © 2022 Sonelle Euskera.

All rights reserved. No part of this book may be used or reproduced by any means, graphic, electronic, or mechanical, including photocopying, recording, taping or by any information storage retrieval system without the written permission of the author except in the case of brief quotations embodied in critical articles and reviews.

Balboa Press books may be ordered through booksellers or by contacting:

Balboa Press
A Division of Hay House
1663 Liberty Drive
Bloomington, IN 47403
www.balboapress.co.uk
UK TFN: 0800 0148647 (Toll Free inside the UK)
UK Local: 02036 956325 (+44 20 3695 6325 from outside the UK)

Because of the dynamic nature of the Internet, any web addresses or links contained in this book may have changed since publication and may no longer be valid. The views expressed in this work are solely those of the author and do not necessarily reflect the views of the publisher, and the publisher hereby disclaims any responsibility for them.

Any people depicted in stock imagery provided by Getty Images are models, and such images are being used for illustrative purposes only.
Certain stock imagery © Getty Images.

ISBN: 978-1-9822-8641-5 (sc)
ISBN: 978-1-9822-8640-8 (e)

Print information available on the last page.

Balboa Press rev. date: 11/12/2022

Contents

My Soul's Journey in this Body 1

Chapter 1 Forgiveness 9

Chapter 2 Purpose 49

Chapter 3 One Hundred percent Responsible 138

Overview of what I have realized on the Journey 212

A Path of Love

My Soul's Journey in this Body

My open-hearted gratitude, as an avid reader, to all the writers who have enriched & inspired my imagination. I offer this, my first completed book, in all humility, all compassion, in honour of every soul on this Earth-life journey. I am hoping that some will be stirred, to open more deeply, into acceptance & love, of all of Nature's creations, as well as Self-love, and beyond, realizing our true multi-dimensional nature. In fact, only from this realization, of the truth of our origin, can one know that Self, is part of all 'Other'! I believe all, is being birthed from a vast multi-dimensional void, including our Earth hologram, thus allowing, our human free will experiment. Despite every holocaust, all suffering, acknowledging too, every act of, greatness & Love, it is all a perfect Experiment. If you allow, that no doubt, every one of us has played both 'hateful', ugly, miserable roles, feeling ourselves as pitiful victims, being selfish, or uncaring, as well as more enlightened selves, this has been a perfect part of our learning. I am grateful that Life has asked me, to write this book, trusting somehow it plays its part, in Love's Web.

I have loved so many books, writers like Ella Lee, in her "Wild Courage," Jeff Brown in his "Soul Shaping," with his depth, exposure, charge, authentic nakedness and powerful vocabulary. More recently, I was inspired by two books gifted to me by one of my sisters, on my 81st birthday, 'The Salt Path' & 'The Wild Silence' by Raynor Winn, which share their deep connection with, & boundless love of the natural world of land, sea, rivers, woods, - all wild life. It was an honour, to be invited to share their journeys.

I believe they may have enjoyed better health if, they had lived on raw organic food but, though they lost their farm, their income, their land, which had sheltered generations of their family, their journeying was magic.

I also was given a book written by Peter Wohlleben, 'The Hidden Life of Trees,' teaching me in greater depth, about how species of trees support each other. Important too, in this time when those who should be safe-guarding, our wild heritage, such as ancient irreplaceable woodlands, are so short-sightedly ignorant & greedy, for quick profit, hearts closed to the magic, that feeds us, spiritually as well as physically, beyond monetary value. Important to emphasize how 'Irreplaceable' - the Fight to Save our Wild Places,' by Julian Hoffman, is a book which should not be ignored, nor under-estimated, when making decisions which, really can lead to, irreplaceable loss of, a vast network of plants, insects & places of deep tranquillity, for those sensitive & humble enough, to recognize the true gauge of 'worth! I read too, his 2nd book, 'Taming the Flood'. More alarming, even than Elizabeth Kolbert's book, 'Field Notes from a Catastrophe - A frontline report on Climate change,' where she mentions the 8 Arctic Nations, the U.S.A., Russia, Finland and Iceland, Canada, Norway, Denmark and Sweden, - 'In a meeting attended in the year 2000, by nearly 300 scientists and native arctic residents, -reindeer herders, subsistence hunters, and representatives of groups like the Inuvialuit Game Council and, men with the brightly coloured tunics of the Sami, plus several others wearing sealskin vests, mentioning change at an unpredicted rate, - shrinking sea ice, receding glaciers, thawing permafrost, the Arctic Climate warming rapidly <u>now</u>. Particularly alarming the most recent data from Greenland, showing the ice sheet melting much faster, than predicted even 10yrs. ago. The study's executive summary stated unequivocally, that human beings had become the 'dominant factor' influencing the climate. <u>Not</u> just a natural process. The policy document remained unfinished because <u>American</u> negotiators, had rejected much of the language, proposed by the seven other Arctic nations. (A few weeks later the United States agreed to a vaguely worded statement calling for 'effective' - but not obligatory - actions to combat the problem…etc.) Her book 'The Prophet of Love' - and other tales of power and deceit, tell of U.S.A. political shenanigans. Unless Human beings learn, greater humility and wisdom, reading her book 'Under a White Sky,' I am beginning to change my mind, about re-incarnating, after this life, on Earth, with arrogant, clueless 'human' beings, trying to do a better job, than Nature, in her wisdom! Or at least I will wait, until 2025 onwards, when 'human' Beings may have bowed, to Nature's superior knowing.

I am delighted, to have discovered the existence of, an organization called 'Buglife,' I had never heard of, supporting the insects I so honour!! I thought I was in a minority, being fascinated with the beauty, and diversity of insects. Every life-form, has its perfect role here, …Human beings not apparently so!

*

I am someone, who reads voraciously, and deeply enjoys too, so much 'Fiction,' from writers whose stories, are the distillation, of the lessons learnt, from their experience of Life's passions, losses, challenges, pains and, joys. So much courage! I see these books being, as spiritual as the non-fiction, as every life-story is being created every moment, with every thought and action, a living fiction. I could name so very many writers, William Horwood, J. Allen Boone, Louise Hays, JZ Knight, Derek Gow, Cha Zay, Machaelle Small Wright, Michael Roads, James Twyman, Jean M. Auel, Jeremy Purseglove, Julian Hoffman, Michelle Paver, & such prolific popular fiction stars, as Danielle Steel, & Nora Roberts too, whose highly creative, independent, strong, passionate women, meet seemingly incompatible men with similar traits, leading to the grand, once in a life-time, true love and marriage, so many women yearn for. Heart-weary cynics may see only an oft-repeated formula, drawing in the gullible, but I see human beings, women especially, yearning for harmony, love, happiness - the happy 'ending.' Surely every writer, no matter what the surface motivation for writing a book, is looking for the same, - to live in Joyful connection with Infinite Love, wherever found. Whichever names I have written, they represent too, so very many unmentioned, yet enjoyed, with new ones, ever coming my way. (More added on Resources pages).

I recall how, before fully forgiving my father, for our ongoing discord, I had read his memoirs, which tell his life story up to about 1949, & I was still so critical, judging what he shared, for lack of emotional depth. Once my heart was full of Love for him, it was like reading a different story. I know now, if we meet in a 'future' life, our relationship will be truly harmonious, since I learned, after much inner processing, to really love him. Two or three years ago, Cristina, asked me if I would translate my parents' many War-time letters, 1937-1946, which led me, to read many related books, listed on the Resources page, of 'Mama y Papa' - my completed translations, tales of Holocaust, genocide, the horrors humans unleash on each other & all other beings, sharing our planet - by Paul Preston, Laurie Lee, Slavomir Rawicz, Misha Defonseca & others I will add.

Also though, may I be at least, a half-adequate voice, for the many voices, though so few mentioned, in my Resources section, lamenting our disregard, cruelty, greed, lack of compassion or true vision, short-sighted closed minds and hearts, concerning our precious fellow inheritors, of an Ecological Wonderland!

It has brought me to tears, realizing the depth of courage called for, in every one of us, to make sense of finding ourselves, in what has seemed like, a loveless world or, rationed love at best.

Thank you, all beings whose inspiration and interaction, have contributed to my evolution. I am grateful to my parents in this life, of previous lives too, however testing, or abusive, the experience may have been in some lives, to my sisters Carmen and Cristina, my lovely, capable, dog-loving - (especially rottweilers!) daughter, Samantha, & gentle-natured, equally capable son Rammiel, their fathers, to all who have most impacted me, in the learning and recognizing of my life's lessons, and for the fun, love and friendship shared. I honour Jungleyes, & his family, also my 'legal' ex-husbands, first Berris, and later Sam, all my close women & men friends, Parvati, Pete, Hari Sudha, Durgadas, Gopal Hari & family, Verity, Jonah, Louise, Vijaya, local friends, Judith, (plus for a while, our Women's group), Jane and family, (my erstwhile neighbours, - despite, territorial battles, with Maurice! - though I hear he now misses me)! Widdy, Ish and Daxa, Thrisha and family, plus many more in the Stroud Community. Sandra, is my brave adventure friend, my childhood best friends Elaine, & later Claire, new friends, Patricia, more recently, Penny & Guy, with special dog Boosh, & dear cat friend Beatrice, whose home, I was recently so blessed to share for about a year. Earlier deepening connections, included our Women's group, who supported one another to live from the fullness of our potential. Also, Max, Mu, & all 'lovers.' All have shown how little I knew of love, every hidden pain, fear & feeling of inadequacy triggered, whatever was not love so, needed to be brought to light, awareness and healing. What a gift we've all been to each other, navigating our way in the world of Polarity and apparently dense matter.

I am grateful for my global spiritual teachers both incarnate, in this life-time, such as Osho, Babaji, & other, many-dimensional beings, who entered my life, and are significant at key times, Gezra, & Lu Yin, Ja-Karuk - (as spelled by the artist medium who drew his portrait 18yrs. ago, in pastels, for me, and wrote his wise message), only days ago (2022), recently heard & felt, strongly impacting in my heart & 'whoosh', grounding me into Earth, in perfect timing)! Alicia Power with her 'Creator Beings,' - also Ammaji, Michael Roads, Rikka, Jean Houston, Edwige Bingue, Esther Hicks, and most significantly these recent months, - Prageet & Julieanne, via such a deepening with their channel Alcazar group of Masters. So many inspired luminaries, inner helpers & guides, Pan, who oversees the Nature Beings' kingdom, Melchizadek, (I had been told, very soon after I had met him in a meditation, is my overseeing guide), St. Germain with his purple healing light, Tara, Archangels Rafael & Michael, Metatron, Gabriel, my Guardian Angels & wild Golden Goddess, my Sophia Dragon Kaia Ra tribe & Star families, Kasey Brad (via channel Julius), & of course, my own multi-dimensional Being &, so many more. So much inspiration & help, showering on us, currently, as we approach, a more enlightened civilization! Still much awakening to happen, from mechanistic Science. I have been deeply blessed & guided, throughout my life.

Truthfully, these recent months, it has predominantly been the daily channelled guidance, from 'Alcazar,' in daily meditations, via Prageet & 'Jules,'- '(Stargate Academy),' into an increasingly deep awareness, of a bigger story, of the Void, multiverses, the Quantum Field, from which our holographic human &, all other Mother Earth reality, is born, which has opened my heart & being into permanently radiating Love/Joy. Sometimes meditations & inspiration, via Kryon & Asil Toksal too, supported increasingly by the Elohim, & beings from so many dimensions. Increasingly I feel deep Gratitude, for their encouragement. Huge shifts have happened, & are accelerating, between the birth of this book in 2011, up until this year 2022. Recently, a depth of expansion has been happening for so many of us in this Stargate Community. For weeks now, since the last days of Alcazar's teachings in 'Becoming Superconscious' and the ensuing weeks of 'Into the Void' I feel an ever-present deep warm glow in my heart and throat, from my creative centre, which I visualise expanding through my crown, despite my active mind! This makes me wonder, if I will be called on to communicate more widely, beyond present comfort limits! I am glad this radiating love, has now moved down deeply, through the sacral centre & only recently, down from my knees too, I sensed needed strengthening. In any case, knowing myself as this heart-warm Joy, which had before now, always felt so elusive, I am so grateful for Existence and, feel deeply exhilarated, that this love is beaming out to all of Life. I was blessed also, to attend, such a powerful, love-filled two-day live Stargate event with Prageet, Jules, Eugenia & Siri, in London, shortly before New Year's Day 2022. Siri is what I believe is called a Sangoma, after an empowering initiation, she underwent in Africa. She mentioned that some of the seers in Africa, have recently been seeing geometric structures emerging, out of the Earth. We were working through Eugenia, with Ley lines from St. Michael's Mount & also with the Mary Line weaving together, connecting too with the Cathars in France, plus a mass of other ley lines. Julieanne says she can also sense the connection with the Celtic beings in Ireland. The wonderful musician Robert Cox, was playing his music, to accompany us too.

Thousands of us, world-wide, who focus daily, on raising our collective vibration, are a great contrast, to the spread of fear, fostered by controlling, restrictive powers, introducing too, pharmaceutical measures, and attempting to foist these unnatural potions & pills, sometimes via vaccinations, on our children, our older men, women and on or into, every other life form Every-one of us, is born, vulnerable, without possessions, into a world where, there are established controls, accepted beliefs, ready to be foisted on many, by the few. Wide-spread advertising, attempts to persuade people, as to what to buy or believe. Fortunately, freedom of belief is allowed, more so in some environments than others. Sometimes control on how many children can be born, and which sex is preferable in the interest of 'important,' or 'upper-class' interests. Control of the land with fences, barbed wire, hedges, with governmental subsidies maybe encouraging the use of, poisonous pesticides, or the sowing of favoured food crops. Also guarded frontiers or borders, control of every physical thing, through accumulation & control of money. Governments or banks, could phase out physical money, increase or decrease, the worth of private funds, plus control people's financial wealth, monitoring bank accounts electronically. Control of health & disease, through vaccination programmes, control of beliefs through biased education, with some countries allowing greater freedoms than others.

Fortunately, there are many alternative healing modalities, & many. more enlightened beings, broadcasting enlightened teachings & practices. The Stargate Academy channelled teachings, have accelerated inner growth & multi-dimensional awareness & expansion. Such a power-house of Love & Light beaming out, & I have personally, received so much love & generosity from so many dear ones. Many have been feeling my energy, across the room & reflecting this back to me, what I have so strongly, recently especially, been feeling myself. - Thank you, my beautiful guides, in every form. This has been strongly confirming, the changes I have been going through, thanks to the Alcazar group of 'Higher' wisdom Masters, channelled through Prageet & Julieanne, including Julieanne's 'Essence of Life' initiations, with Michelle. Alcazar tells us, they are not 'higher', they are simply on a different plane with <u>their</u> learning.

Going now to my past, since many of my earlier, deepest shifts & changes in my life, came through 'The Journey,' I acknowledge my deep gratitude, for Brandon Bays &, my 'Journey family,' who have helped me so much, with inner child, from Nov. 2003-2019, until this Covid ban on Humans coming together! 'The Journey' recently gifted me, with a 'zoom' 'Enneagram & Abundance' 3day work-shop &, I was pleasantly surprised to find our process sessions with partners, as powerful, as when we come together physically!

I will be describing in these chapters, some of my key 'journeys,' resulting in some of my pivotal life changes. This book has not been written to promote 'The Journey,' though so instrumental, the last 18yrs. & more, in my inner delving, showing me the preciousness of Life &, of every one of us, expanding too, my vision of what is possible. We all have our individual paths, carefully chosen beforehand.

(I had transferred Chapter 1 onto computer, (& my typing skills are somewhat slow), yet due to my lack, of great computer expertise, it resulted in my losing the whole chapter! I thought O.K., that is how it is, I will just retype the written paper version. However, my confidence shaken, (especially as one friend's response was, maybe you will do it even better the 2nd time!) finally, after many days of avoidance, I admitted my 'writer's block,' but then, was inspired to write instead, this acknowledgement section, expressing gratitude for so much and so many, in my life. Words then flowed again, & in my surrender to Life, I accepted I am going through, huge shifts of consciousness, & great expansion, like so many of us at this time).

Having listened to meditations throughout many years, with inspirational, loving teachers such as Matt Kahn, Maureen Moss, Dr. Edwige Bingue, Richard Gordon, Patricia Cote Robles, Kaia Ra, Jo Dunning, Gerald O'Donnell, Panache Desai, Isira Sananda, Amean Hameed, Robert Potter, Emmanuel Dahger, Arielle Indigo, Asara Lovejoy, Michael Beckwith, though these days most often, meditations channelling Alcazar, via Prageet & Julieanne, & sometimes Kryon, or Asil Toksal & the Elohim Council; Meg Benedicte, Rikka Zimmerman, Alicia Power & of course, ongoing training, as a Journey Practitioner, with Brandon Bays & the Journey team, plus so many, many heart-open interdimensional wise beings, showering us, with so much healing & energy, my trust continues to deepen, thus, I'm controlling my life less & less, from mind, living more fully in my heart-space, in more earthed, full embodiment. I honour the Sun fire, Earth lush richness, (more so when humans refrain from so much slaughter & depletion of all we have been gifted with), Air Life-currents, Water flow, sustaining so many forms, more so, when we live in right relationship with all. I am re-connecting more deeply with my essential being, who is fully loved & enough, with nothing to prove. Thus, if my book is in some ways, as I once judged my father's memoirs to be, i.e., maybe lacking in excitement, sensuality, fun & richness, I can feel fulfilled just to write it, as best I can, letting go of judgement of myself or anyone, including any possible detractors & judges! My parents were both teachers &, I went through, what felt like a somewhat alien, academic, fear-fuelled, educational system, yet that & my love of reading, (other than during the first 3 years, following the academic-filled University years, when I could not face more books), has given me an extensive vocabulary &, a strong mind. I am fortunate to have, a 'Public library,' close to my home!

I honour the flow of life, within all created Being, in heart-open welcome, an Earth full of Love, with compassion towards self, & every other being, including Nature's trees, stones, the crystal, plant, animal, insect, bird, & fish worlds, or any other realms, blessing & enjoying Harmony, Peace, Sensuality, Beauty, Passion, & Creative Energy! The multi-dimensional potential, behind every transient form. Insects! Their vital life purpose, in harmony with Nature & each doing no harm, in its proper place, on our precious Earth. May we human beings, remember our true potential for good, & raise the vibration enough, to welcome back Unicorns, & friendly Dragons & other blessings. So be It!

After the August 17th 2012 new moon, I went through a deeper transition, helped by words of wisdom reaching me, from my evolutionary helpers & friends. Thank you from my open Heart to my Loving guides, Light Beings, my Soul Wisdom, also to all the human beings, & all created life form with whom I share this Magic Planet Earth journey. My friend, who, among other names, liked to be called Jungleyes, had a beauty of being that shone out from his eyes. In the years, he was bed-bound, we spent many hours reading to each other, often stories for children. I love stories, even am addicted to them, simply, clearly told, & firing my imagination in a much richer way than a film. So, when it has come to me to write this book, I choose to do it through stories from my life. What I learn relates to every or anyone.

****

A Path of Love

Chapter 1

Forgiveness

It was at the Winter Solstice 2011, I was shown in a dream, the book I was to write; not only that, but I was given the 3 Chapter headings too, for this small book. It was one of those dreams, I have felt guided to pay attention to, as, from time to time, I am shown future events, or voices give me messages. By the daytime, I had forgotten one heading, but the dream repeated the next night so, I was able to memorize, the same message as in the 1st dream. Thus, Forgiveness is the theme of this first chapter story. We human Beings have much for which to be forgiven, in our interaction with all Earth beings, on the ground, in the air, & in the Oceans too. Around that time too, during some early morning 'connecting with me' time, I had stood at my altar and declared out aloud, both my heartfelt intent to partner with Life, and had called to, "whichever beings are waiting to work through me, in service of all earth-created beings, - I'm ready." Since I had had no recent thoughts of writing a book, surely this book project must be one consequence of this prayer. I have been entering a deeper trust, knowing my own essence to be one and the same, as this immense potential from which everything is forever being born, in the quantum field. Also, following that prayer, Lu Yin & Gezra, made themselves known to me, from wherever they are: they, plus Haidakhandi Babaji, also St. Germaine, felt to be my closest overseeing guides. Though in more recent years, I have connected with feminine guides too, Quan Yin, Tara, & one whose name I do not know, staying in total equanimity, plus a golden goddess, who whirled me into a mad, fast dance.

With the lockdown on free movement, I had had little physical contact with my 'Journey' friends, since 2019, other than my local friend Judith, with whom I recently went walking. My dear friend Judit(h), - (Austrian pronunciation), was my main swap partner since 2005 supporting, each other, for 10years approx., in powerful inner Journeys. "The Journey's," been particularly relevant, from 2003 to 2019, in my own shift from judgement & blame, to real forgiveness, of every soul, playing a role in my life dramas, albeit unconsciously. I now know every being is essentially innocent, most of us caught more, or less, in the delusion of separation. I have retained my Practitioner status, this year 2022, thanks to interacting through Zoom. Recently, as I have been living since November 2020, so, approaching **2 years**, on a very reduced income, having to be helped by my friends & family, I was unexpectedly gifted with a 'zoom' online 'Enneagram & Abundance' 3day Journey event, & to my surprise, found that the processes we swapped every day, were equally as powerful as, 'in the flesh'.

Prageet & Julieanne (Jules), through their channel Alcazar, already mentioned, have been my more recent daily, inspiration, through increasingly deepening communications, over many years, (these days, with a global Community of thousands of us, from 70 countries). What I find most painful in these times, is the lack of compassion & such shockingly cruel treatment, by so many, deliberately causing harm, in murderous ways, seemingly divorced from any feeling of empathy.

The 1947 Agriculture Act, following the War, was the start of pressure on Nature, to the detriment of diversity, to feed human beings, despite the slaughter of so many men, set in motion by politicians, who would demand conscription of able men, while they stayed out of the firing lines. In fact, in my meditation this morning, I was suddenly in tears, as I both feel joyous warmth and love in my being, yet also want to hear and read about people's holocaust stories, and the horrors we unleash on all other life forms, thus I found myself in deep sorrowful tears, at the brutality inflicted on each other and everything else. In truth it is all one, appearing as the many.

It seems the deeper the love flow in my body, the more I can feel for those suffering from human inflicted terrors and horror. (I never watch thrillers, rarely watch any News, but choose not to turn away, from knowing of the wars, inflicted usually by power despots, more often men, acting out their hatred often, on the unarmed women & children). It seems our politicians or political power-structures, are granted almost 'carte blanche' or world-wide, killing power, in their human interactions, with Nature; our food sources, with animals, insects, the Earth and Oceans with their plants and species, on our own doorstep, as well as any 'Foreign' countries, with any natural assets, worth exploiting.

Shell Oil, notwithstanding the damage to our Earth/Sea planet, still greedy for profit, at the expense of all other. I drive my car much less, these last couple of years, aware of the impact of being dependent on petrol & oil, via Shell, Esso, etc. etc. The only car I read about years ago, which interested me from an ethical stand-point, was one being developed in France, running on air. They did not seem to communicate in English & I have not followed this up recently. Their email address was cqfd.be@infonie.fr. - in Brignoles. I did meet some new friends, in the December 2021 London Stargate 2 day gathering, I recently attended, mentioning a new energy, (Innovation-T LLC.), being developed in the U.S.A. I believe. I hope there are indeed, new technologies, enhancing all life on this planet. I have heard that engines which run on water, are now being developed. I hope this would be a good invention.

Reading 'Irreplaceable' by Julian Hoffman, of all the books warning us human beings, about our shockingly destructive effect, on Planet Earth, his book is the most shocking one yet. Every chapter, details more of the devastation and death, we are causing to so many beings. I was deeply touched by his account of Henry Beston, (whose book I have read), who lived a year in a self-built cabin, on the outer shores of Cape Cod, watching the struggles of, the creatures surviving in extreme conditions, of 'fierce storms,' ice, 'pillaging winds' etc. and subsequently wrote a book called, 'The Outermost House' Julian H. describes as, 'beautifully luminous.' Julian Hoffman paints a very detailed and clear picture, of the damage happening, throughout our beleaguered world. (I have added more near the start of Chapter 2). Difficult for me, to read books like 'Bringing back the Beaver.' Men, bloodthirsty farmers, occasional women too, shooting animals in the face, and other terrors. Since I was a child, I have loved close interaction with insects, animals, wild plants and, the fungal, or mushroom life, earth worms and all.

I have heard, via someone who sees other realities, that every animal etc. that has ever existed, can be found in Telos, an other-dimensional place deep under Mount Shasta; maybe the appropriate equivalent, to our 'after-death' worlds.

*

I will be writing about "The Journey." evolved & given birth by Brandon Bays, (born in New York,) & describing, the actual 'Journey process' I received, 4 or 5 days, before my book dream on December 17th. This happened, when she was faced with a growing melon-sized tumour in her belly, in the processes which, she and her team then evolved, over the years. Her experimental bid to heal herself quickly, avoided the assault of surgery etc. on her body, & the first 'Journey' took shape.

Finding herself tumour-free in 6-7 wks., in her generosity of heart and spirit, she began sharing her method, with friends looking for emotional resolution, to their own distress, whatever the cause. The fruitful results of this, led her to put out a greater prayer and intent, to serve growing numbers of people, and so her vision found form, and is realizing itself in every Continent, in at least 45 countries, attracting men as well as women, and serving children too.

I was 63yrs.old when I came to 'The Journey,' as conceived by Brandon, in late 2003. Now, as I am re-editing this book, (hopefully the last re-edit!!), in 2022, I feel deep gratitude to her and, the whole Journey family, for this that was shared with me, & so many others. I have been propelled into a deeper, soul engaging, heart-opening connection, with myself, than I'd so far experienced, through all my erstwhile spiritual explorations, in short, they have been a journey to Love. I will explain briefly what Journey 'processes' are, hoping, that the inner, usually visual or, kinaesthetic experiences, I describe, will seem like fascinating inner adventures. Being very visual, I get very fascinated, exploring the details, on each guided journey, into my body & emotions, so, will describe what I feel, or see, wherever I land, - usually a staircase, taking me deep inside. As I travel deeper down, feeling which emotion makes itself felt, I am curious as to how deep I, & in turn, the partner with whom, I may exchange a session, will be willing to go, also what kind of Mentor/helpers we will meet on, the other side of the doorway, through which we usually pass, on our way to connect with, one's Soul or higher self, plus other players on our stage! What vehicle will show up, to transport me, to wherever I land in my body, and what will it be like in there? Which emotional issue, will show up for healing? All memories good or bad, all traumas we have experienced, were stored within the body, in our cell receptors, & the deeper down we stored our pain, the more this led to contraction, or shutting down, our remembering. Each journey into the body, takes us to the relevant area, allowing access that day, to memories, which yield fresh insights. This leads to much 'inner child' healing, with more, or less, inner resistance, allowing release of, an emotional memory, which has held the soul back, on its evolutionary journey, at some key moment, in time, allowing deepening forgiveness. It is best to always trust body/soul wisdom, welcoming the feelings and memories which show up. It all tends to play out in unexpectedly wise, & coherent ways.

The 'Emotional Journey,' tends to be more challenging, inviting us to let go resistance, control, self-judgement and, defensive ego-armour, as we meet the 'not O.K.' aspects and feelings we pushed away more deeply. Not however by judging these, rather by embracing whatever feeling shows up, so it dissolves in acceptance & love. So much energy is used in not facing our demons! Everything others did not approve of, so we preferred not to see in ourselves. No wonder we have often felt so inadequate or unworthy maybe, or opted to numb ourselves, slowly or quickly, or became more rigid, belligerent, or whatever.

We end up with much less alive, fluid emotions, or less joyful, a very slow death! Easier to see what is 'shut-down' in others! In avoiding our own pain & shadows however, we ended up avoiding & missing a miracle Love affair with ourselves, which would allow us rich, potent, full Life expression. Not enough energy nor motivation left! But at what cost?

*

I have always loved, every 'outer' kind of journey, whether on foot, (much more walking during the Covid19 panic & so, much less use of my car), driving, cycling, by train, ship, aeroplane, but so many 'inner' voyages too, first with L.S.D. in the sixties, later travel into other realms through shamanism, ayahuasca ceremonies, and psychotropic fungi. The Rebirthing training & sessions I received, made me decide I would find my way, to the truth of reality through spiritual exploration, that did not depend on any outside agent or laboratory. I have trained too, with hypnotherapy, past life regression and many other of the emerging therapies of the 70's onwards, exploring inner territory.

****

I want now, to assure my readers, I lost my zeal long ago for converting others to 'my way,' left behind largely after my first year as a student, age 19. I'd gone in the face of, my father's belief in the perniciousness of Religion, but required at 17yrs.old, his permission, to convert to Catholicism. He said "It'll kill you or cure you." So, I was running the University Catholic book stall, in my 1st year, ardently seeking to convert or influence others into seeing, what was best for them! Thus, we try to boost our own self-worth! (My parents, were both Communists). It seems intrusive to me now, and unnecessary, to thrust unsolicited opinions on others. They are generally full up with their own. That, has been baggage and conditioning enough, without adding to their load. Life, in many guises, showers us abundantly with teachings and teachers. We learn from, or resonate with different ways and beings, for a long or a short time, on our unique path. Best to listen to the Truth in one's own heart, and stay authentic in service of Life, following our Soul, or higher Self-guidance, which has ever guided me.

*

In one memorable inner Journey, I found myself rejecting all concepts taken from others, such as Love, Goodness, or any other ideas or states, I was meant to exemplify, or believe in. As I let myself relax, around my rejection of 2nd or 3rd hand ideas, I found myself coming down to deep-down safe, supporting ground, where I felt totally held, in a place of 'Unknowing,' embraced in unconditional acceptance. Here I need agree with no-one, nor be anything other than as I am. Strangely, a deeper knowing feels accessible here. I experience this space as solid, safe ground. (I acknowledge the teachings and blessings received too, via each religion, every spiritual way, and each group I embraced, for a while, from childhood, right up until now).

*

But back now, finally! to the Dec.17th process, shortly before my book-to-be dream, where I found myself choosing, to go deeper than I had ever previously been. Though the steps were very solid and safe, yet every step seemed to drop me easily, a long way down, through elemental layers of Earth, Water, Sunfire and Airspace.

My Mentor, seemed blue-skinned, maybe of Chinese or Malaysian heritage. He appeared very detached. If his eyes had beamed out love, I would have quickly felt more confidence in his support. Still, I trusted that all would become clear. I had not then realized that, when I had voiced out loud, my prayer, that I was ready, for whatever beings, were waiting to work with me, this was the invitation Lu Yin, as I later came to call him, had waited for.

We landed in my solar plexus, but I sensed my chest area, was involved too. My pelvis area was dark, & felt full of contained energy, fire, & power. However, my chest seemed weak, devoid of much life passion, the rib-cage white & fragile. A memory surfaced of me as a very young baby, feet flailing in the air. I had been contemplating too, the ways I had felt betrayed, rejected, at times abandoned, by close friends, parents, sisters, most boyfriends, & both legal husbands. What becomes very evident, is my abandonment of myself, such as neglecting to state clearly, what I would like. When I do this, with my Mentor, he responds immediately, in his capacity as a healer, & my whole chest area seems to become suffused with Blue. I had tended to think others incapable, of fulfilling my real requirements and, unlikely to offer support. What I now, learn instead is, that all possibilities are here, on our life drama stage, for the unconscious suffering we create, or not, for ourselves. We choose, our creations. My baby self, needed to feel loved & taken care of, more consistently.

As I go deeper in this process, I find myself in vast Darkness, but it is cold too. I have tended to resist cold, especially in the form of snow, covering the colours and scents of the land. I choose surrender now, though I cannot believe at first, that 'God,' or Love, could be even here. Yet still, I drop all resistance, to those aspects of life I do not prefer, such as cold. In this deeper letting go, I truly sense, even amid this dark coldness, there is after all, a Caring Core, a Heart, which I can nevertheless Trust, and sense, as a place, even here, of creative potential. The vastness of cosmos manifesting as me, is also ever-changing, diverse everything else.

While writing this, I have remembered a scene in my twenties when I was sitting by the 'Round Pond' in London, Kensington Gardens, on a freezing cold day. I had imbibed, some LSD, and instead of tensing against the cold, I kept internally repeating, "let go, let go, let go." As I did, a heat started to rise, up through my body, until I really felt warm. I imagine the Himalayan yogis must do something similar.

More recently, remembering an incident with my father, when I was angry with him! I was racing across the deeply snow-covered field, with him in pursuit. I do now wonder if, that was when my snow 'phobia' began, leading to often fainting, when surrounded by snow. He suddenly stopped chasing me, & turned back, so I reached my rabbit warren haven, with its' copse, of elm trees. I often climbed high into the branches. (My 1st fracture, as a 12yr.old, was a fall from one of these).

*

In another recent 'Journey' event in Cardiff, I had arrived to help others, as a 'trainer,' and my body had suddenly begun to feel strong discomfort. I asked to have a 'Journey' process promptly myself, and the Mentor who appeared as I went in, was the 'Haidakhan' Babaji, (my spiritual guide, in many incarnations I believe and, so very deep in my heart). He was so vast, I thought he is not going to fit in the awaiting chariot, for the journey into my body, and indeed, the vehicle was breaking apart even as I leaned back in trust into his body, yet still he was holding some guiding reins! As the process deepened, suddenly I lost all sensation of physical body, solid chair, or floor. With a start, I rapidly opened my eyes a moment, to check, then realized, the whole world of physical reality exists within, my inner being!" What relief, what gratitude I felt towards Babaji, for facilitating a direct experience of this.

I am brought (in the nr. Solstice process), to this same awareness, in an even deeper way, knowing my being to include, all the polarities. Cold & hot, comfort & discomfort, fullness & emptiness, safety & danger, Yes & No!

I had found myself at some point, foreseeing, moving into uncharted territory. I dreamt one night, I was travelling with companions, but when I checked the map, the area we were going to, was empty of landmarks or roads. I have felt some sense of disorientation, when leaving behind, my 'safe,' yet dis-empowering and limited image of myself, yet feel a constant and spacious sense of solidity and presence in my body, while also a more expansive awareness of myself as Cosmos, with its' vast depths & mystery, especially when I stop to really connect with me.

On the 21-12-2021 'Winter-Solstice', I have indeed been travelling deep, in 'unchartered' (in Earth human mind terms), territory, where my Quantum field self is home, yet who chose to incarnate into our many Earth lives so, has had never-ending adventures & experiences, & I delight in the daily deep meditations happening with the Global Stargate Community, recalling the multi-dimensional beings we are, with expanded visceral or visual experience, of this!

*

However, I was guessing back then, in the hologram world of perceived time, that letting go of attempts to control life, was important, while allowing the immense creativity, awaiting expression, enough structure for tangible, visible forms to emerge, our senses can easily access! Our souls are calling us, to come out from hiding, avoiding, ineffective powerlessness, or inertia, to follow our heart's calling. We will not find our gladness of heart and joy, through effort, struggle, pressure, nor by trying to make Life happen, in a particular way. It is as if avoiding Emptiness, is avoiding me.

*

I am going to tell of a strong episode in my life, which is very much part of my 'Forgiveness' story, from many angles. This happened in my fruit-picking years, which I will write more of in the next Chapter.

In my mid-thirties, I went through an emotional, mental breakdown. Interestingly, a new friend ' once met, in the foothills of the French Pyrenees, who had an in-depth understanding of Astrology, had made me a chart, showing four key points, when particularly momentous events, would intersect my life. The breakdown was at the bottom point, of the intersecting cross. In hindsight I realized, indeed sensed as it was happening, I needed to crack apart, the construct of normality, of false identity. I did not have the awareness and clarity I do now, but felt it imperative, I should <u>not</u> emerge at the other end, of whatever was happening to me, back to normal! A call from my Soul. My daughter was 9, nearly 10yrs. old. We had followed the grape harvest in the last weeks of October, from 'Raymat' in Spain, to the Charente region of France, near Cognac. We were living with the family in their farm-house, enjoying their farm produce, fresh vegetables, and the Charente butter and milk from their cows.

I was saddened, by one cow they kept in a narrow metal enclosure, no room to walk, nor enjoy daylight, plus its cow family. The dogs were fed hunks of French bread & dripping, & would search out, as we harvested the grapes, any which fell to earth, found under the vines. Earlier, in Spain, I had been eating just grapes for many weeks!

Near the end of the harvesting, I was very aware on All Souls' Day, November 2nd (my mother's birthday), that the veil seemed thinner, 'twixt different planes of reality. My malaise seemed somehow linked. That last morning, feeling particularly exhausted, I kept repeating like a Mantra, "I must sleep. I must sleep." That afternoon, a small group of us, were taken to pick carrots & other vegetables for the evening meal. As I walked up the first row of plants, I found myself moving into an altered reality, passing plants in the row, trance-like, incapable of picking anything. That was the last conscious memory I had that day, and for some time after. My Spanish friend Jose, working there with me, told me months later, that I came back to the car friendly and talkative, but back at the farm-house, went to lie down in a field, and was still there fast asleep in the dark, hours later. I only have occasional flashes from the following days and nights. I no longer knew how to take care of myself, how to dress, what to eat, nor how to use a toilet. I remember picking up a bar of soap, from the bed-side table, and like a baby, trying it out for food. I imagined too that somehow, I had an etheric connection with the cows, a sort of tube or artery, and was being nourished by them. Maybe it was so, with these cow 'Mother' representatives. Max, my boy-friend, arrived from England, summoned by telegram, and took over my care, feeding me only raw food, washing my sheets, and he had also contacted his cousin Gerald, to drive over with his big van, to take us back to London. Meanwhile a doctor came to see me, prescribing serum treatment. I have no memory of this, but am told, I did order him, to keep away from me and thankfully, Max was able to protect me, from what he knew, would be against my wishes. Back in his mother's flat in Earls Court, I still had not remembered, how to feed, nor dress myself. One day, Max told me, he was going to visit his friend Norma, in Fulham. After a while I started to panic, got up from my bed, wrapped a sheet around me, and slipped past my daughter Samantha, watching T.V. She had been asked to keep an eye on me, but was unaware of my movements, as I went outside. I asked the first approaching couple, for help to find Max. They hurried on, but the next couple simply asked me, which way he had gone. I pointed in the Fulham direction, so they suggested I walk with them. As we walked along the 'Old Brompton' road, my attention was drawn to a small Greengrocer's, and I told my companions I would stay there, so they took leave of me. The shop-keeper, an Indian man, came towards me, and asked me what I would like. I noticed the gold ring on his finger, I pointed to it and said, "That." He simply asked, if I would like to sit down, at the rear of his shop. I said "yes," and relaxed peacefully there. Maybe just 10mins. later, Max walked into the shop, so all was well. The scenes I am describing here, will illustrate the extent of my incapacity at that time, to take care not only of myself, but of my daughter too, throughout the two months of this experience. Another day Max took me to see an 'alternative' health professional. I was taken to his office, and at first hid under a table, then ventured out to examine the contents, of the sugar bowl on his desk. Not much direct interaction happened with him at all, other than his attempt to part me, from my comfort hot water bottle.

*

Then official local 'health' visitors began to come to the flat. I had been on Dr. Ollendorf 's register (whom I had originally chosen because he practised Reichian analysis and orgone therapy and, was the controversial Wilhelm Reich's brother-in-law, all of whose books had interested me.

Reich both scientist and psycho-analyst, died in a Federal Penitentiary in 1957, though if he had lived till the 1970's, his ideas and experiments would no longer have been rejected and ridiculed, as Science was catching up! Robert Ollendorf died in 1973, around when, I was going through this break-down. Max got to speak about me with, one of the original trio of doctors, & his response was to strike me off their register declaring, "She always was psychotic!" I have read in 'The Molecules of Emotion', how all available copies of Reich's life's work, were rounded up for an official book-burning in the U.S.A. As early on as the 1940's he was linking Cancer to the failure to express emotions. The masses often take about 50yrs.to catch up, with more progressive or enlightened ideas! On another occasion when I had become more mobile, though I still depended on Max, to prepare food, or show me where to pee, I was searching around the floor in the living room, for a suitable pee pot, when I became aware of, a 'Social services' lady, observing me. Not long after, a trio of them arrived. By this time, I had a better grasp of my situation. I was called into a room with one of them, a man. He proceeded to ask me questions in order to fill in his form, presumably to fit me into some standard, statistical analysis. Or so I guessed, when he asked me when, I had last had sex. Since by now, I could engage intelligibly enough, I challenged him, since this felt so useless and ridiculous to me. I suggested he had no real idea of how to help me. He promptly acknowledged this, and I thus avoided, I suspect, getting sectioned, for not fitting the norm. Max reading Krishnamurti's words, to me, was also not giving me the guidance or key, I so needed at that time, though I so appreciate his care and support. Only young children, could accept me just as I was, and those, like that Indian green-grocer, who maybe was able to simply recognize or accept, that I was going through some spiritual life crisis, without feeling threatened nor, reacting negatively, to this. I am thankful for all open-hearted beings!

Max & Samantha took me to visit my parents. My sister Cristina, had invited us to stay in her home. Before boarding the coach, I went down to the toilets, but could not navigate the coin-operated barriers. A kind attendant helped me, but my next memory, was of coming up to ground level, and running panic-stricken down the road. Then I blanked out, for the rest of the journey till arriving in my sister's home. I curled up, very tired, on the floor, till Max persuaded me to move, concerned I guess, not to upset anyone. Next day, he took me walking to my parents' home, about a mile away. At first, I was happy, enjoying walking in the sunshine, but as we drew nearer to their home, I again blanked out. When I next came back to, normal awareness, I soon registered, that my parents were busy trying, to classify me into some category, such as schizophrenia. Only Max could I wholly trust, to keep me safe, beyond the vast tentacles of the orthodox medical system. I am describing this flipping in and out of different planes of awareness, because my usual state is to be very conscious of every action, from waking to falling asleep.

The only other time, I can remember absenting myself in that way, is the first time I ingested fly-agaric, (those beautiful red, white pock-marked 'fairy tale' mushrooms found growing, near Birch trees). (In Siberia, reindeer and those who tend them, consume them -or the urine thereof, to enjoy altered states). As I drove, as I was not noticing any effect, I kept taking another bite of mushroom. I met my husband 'Berris,' in Berwick St. (Soho area), as pre-arranged, had a short conversation, set off back to my car, and knew no more, till I came to normal consciousness, near the Rajneesh 'Kalptaru,' meditation centre, in Chalk Farm, to which I had been heading, yet with no conscious knowing of how I had arrived there! I must have been somehow guided. When after 2months I was again able to take care of myself and Samantha, I came across 'The Primal Scream,' by Arthur Janov, and read that when someone is in, a so-called psychotic state, he/she is on the edge of a breakthrough. "I knew it!!! It was in fact, my growing it awareness, that I wanted more clarity and depth, in my relationships with Max, Samantha and everyone, that anyway, then propelled me into the start of my therapy journey.

*

In 1976, I joined Jenny James' primal therapy community, then housed in Villa Rd. Brixton. She had written 'People not Psychiatry.' 'Squatters,' had taken over the row of terraced houses, and the 2 or 3 houses we used, had doorways knocked through, interconnecting the dwellings into one home.

*The first time I lay down on a therapy couch, I could barely utter a sound, I was so shut-down. I certainly felt challenged on many levels. I would say my main learning, was the concept, which filtered in, for the 1st time in my life, that I **might somehow be responsible**, for the life I was experiencing. Up till then, I had really believed, I was suffering at the effect of a cruel world. A glorious martyr, or victim.* During this time, I hardly saw Samantha. She was with the younger people in the Community, including Jenny's daughter. I guessed, she was being encouraged to see, all the ways I, as, her parent, had adversely affected her life, the same as I was encouraged to tell my parents (by letter), everything I felt they had done wrong. A lot of focus on blaming, later to lead to distressing repercussions. I no longer, feel any investment these days, in blaming, particular people starring in, my human dramas, as I know how innocent we all are, when we come into, our Earth-Body experience. Focus on judgement or blame, is bound to bounce back, only making for a life of conflict and defensiveness, rather than ease, trust and, open-heartedness. We have decided as a soul, to experience ourselves as dense matter, with free will to 'err.'

A sequence of events led, to Samantha being taken to my parents' home, without my permission. They may have meant well, but the adults, (living communally in a neighbouring House) who took her, disapproved of "The Screamers," the label our 'Community,' had been given by them, which no doubt prejudiced their decisions. They made no attempt to hear my point of view. I had gone in the morning, as agreed with Samantha, to pick her up, fully intending to leave the Community, as I felt totally let down, by them and Jenny James. When I found out days later where she was, and learnt of measures, my parents had taken with local authorities, to deny my access to her, I felt totally betrayed, especially by my mother. No matter the conflicts which arose, our connection had always seemed strong. In the family battleground dynamic, I would be allied with 'Mummy,' versus my two sisters sympathising more with 'Daddy.' Not that my parents did not have, their own alliance, but all their emotional dramas, took place behind, their closed bedroom door, never voicing any conflicts openly, so we would hear my mother's tones of hysteria, though not the actual words.

I was in tears and heart-break, for many weeks, about our separation, my only support, coming from the Rajneesh 'Sannyasins.' I had been increasingly visiting, their Meditation Centre, very involved with practising the Meditations, receiving too, lots of massage at this time, which helped me release, some of my grief and, find healing. I felt embraced by this group, as a human being of equal worth, not someone untouchable, judged by my emotional baggage, as seemed to be the norm, in the Jenny James, set-up. After all attempts to find Samantha failed, (including feeling treated as a criminal, when I finally did track down her new school), I ended up engaging the help of 'Social' workers, to arrange meetings on neutral ground, to hopefully, re-nurture enough trust between us, that she might choose, to be with me again. I had been focussing on affirming for a long time, (from reading Louise Hays), that Samantha would be with me, by a certain date. When there was just one week to go, I almost lost heart, then instead intensified my focus. Two days before the end of that week, I got a letter saying that, she wanted to live with me and attend 'Académie Francaise,' in South Kensington, for her schooling. She indeed came back home, (and thus when Rammiel, my son was born, on Feb 14ᵗʰ 1983, I was blessed in having Samantha there, as my photographer!)

*

I was 37yrs.old when she went to my parents, and during our separation, I had met and married Berris. Previously I had turned down every offer of marriage, including with her father Bob, but felt I would have a better chance, of having Samantha back, presenting a more stable, respectable front. Interestingly, I really did start to feel safer, within the containment of, my marriage with Berris, and physically felt an inner shift happen, allowing my heart to open more to Love. Though Samantha was back, still some sort of more special closeness of Mother & Daughter, seemed to elude me, like there was an invisible, barrier between us. It was not till 2010, I was suddenly hit by, the realization that I was 69yrs. old, approaching my 70th birthday, the following year, & whatever defences I was keeping around my heart, it was time to let them go. I was at a 5day Journey Women's Retreat, and we had been looking more deeply, at our individual woman's story, doing a lot of process work. That evening, we were gathered close, by candlelight, in a relaxed way, on the floor, different women starting to share, their truths, such as having had pregnancies, or children, they did not initially want, or longing for a child, but unable to conceive, and so on. I had never regarded my 40th, 50th or 60th birthdays as being particularly significant, but had long felt, my coming 70th one, would be so. Something really opened in me, triggered by their vulnerable sharing. I felt deeply, if not now, when? No more time to waste. I must open my heart wide, to my closer family. I began to consciously, express my love out loud, to my sisters, and to my son.

*

One day, I suggested, to my daughter Samantha, we go walking with her dogs, and invited her to share, if she felt to, anything about the past, we had never talked about. I expected this would be, about that difficult time, in Jenny James' Community, instead a whole stream of dissatisfaction and judgements, spurted out, regarding the way I had been as a mother. I was able to acknowledge verbally, her courage, in voicing all this, though felt shocked, somewhat taken aback by, our widely differing perceptions, of those early years, yet I felt no anger. However, some nights later, in the still hours, I began to realize I was more deeply affected, than I had acknowledged. I wrote an 11page letter, but then, similarly to the past years, I stuffed it out of sight in a bag, and did not post it. I had written about those early years from my perspective. *When, soon after, I received a 'Journey' process, and was asked at the onset, what issues had been surfacing to be healed, I neither mentioned, nor even thought about, what had been happening, most recently, with Samantha. Big-time avoidance or what? As the chariot went first to my genitals, then up to both nipples, before stopping between both breasts, I assumed "Oh, it's going to be about sex." The red, wounded area, I saw in there brought, however, a sudden memory to do with my daughter. I had buried away the pain, of that time so deeply, I had no idea, it was in there. I had stuffed it away, out of sight and awareness, like the letter. During this process, I came to a measure of forgiveness, of both* myself and her, but knew it was not complete. I did however, reclaim a sense of my own worth, both as a woman and in my motherhood. I had felt rejected and found wanting, and I needed to let go of that, and any anger at being judged. I did later post that letter, giving my version of, those early years. The flow of Love still was not fully happening, but I realized, I did not need her to change, just that I could feel free, to express openly and honestly. I certainly felt closer. Then in June 2011, I received two significant processes at a Journey Intensive weekend. Days earlier, I had been re-arranging my 'photos, into 21yr. sections of my life. When I had come to the shots of Samantha, living at my parents' house, I had realized I still felt upset, even angry, at her choice.

In the first session, Babaji appeared as my Mentor, a silent supporter, a very upright, still, shining presence, staying this time to the side, leaving me to be centred in myself, on my stage, as it were. The body-entering vehicle awaiting us, was in a rocket or bullet shape, designed for great speed, & shot up to my left breast. The outer surface felt vulnerable, & the floor of the breast was red & raw-looking.

A memory surfaced, of me, in an empty room, I was finishing painting white, in Jenny James' Commune. I was feeling alone, unsupported, no sense of loving connection, with anyone, including my daughter, as I rarely saw her. The new revelation in this process came, when I realized, what had transpired, with me and Samantha, during my breakdown, deeply connected, with whatever she was feeling, living separately with the youngsters, while we stayed in the Villa Road Community. Her trust in me as a mother, had been deeply affected. As I looked into her eyes, at that earlier time, I saw her soft vulnerability, and my heart totally opened to her.

In effect, she had no capable, hands-on mother, at that time. No wonder she had lost her trust in me, both in the Communal set-up, leading such a separate life and, during my months of breakdown. She did have Max, as a father figure but, in relation to me, she had to be the adult, while I was the child! This later resulted, in her determined resolve, to never again, let anyone control her life, which has made her strong, but did build too, a protective armour, around her inner vulnerability & softness. Or so it appeared to me. I remember talking to her in the Commune one day, suggesting we leave, and I could enrol her in the school, off the 'Kensington Rd,' by the park. She agreed but events took a different course!

All the adults, including my parents, other than Max, were seeing me as wrong, or brain-washed, and trying to attach the appropriate 'not O.K.' label to me, such as psychotic, or schizophrenic. All unreal nonsense. So, between the 'blame culture' in the Commune and the prevalent belief, held very strongly by my parents and much of Society, in the orthodox medical system, with its pharmaceutical synthetic drugs, (still going on), my more 'secure' reality, somewhat fell apart. In truth, my Soul was calling & precipitating me, into deeper inner exploration, towards a doorway of freedom. It was time, for me to trust, my inner voice, which was speaking loud & clear. I felt myself now reclaiming, that *child part in me, in her intrinsic wholeness. Back now in the 'Journey process,' by the end, a huge fire and energy of creativity, had emblazoned in a stream of, golden & pink light up to my heart. I am being challenged, to speak my truth, from the Love in my Heart, and to stay true to my core of, immense Life force, that is waiting to flower through my unique expression, - "life's longing for itself" (Kahlil Gebran). I must learn or have the courage, to open to all I can be, as I let drop any view of myself as lesser, or deficient in some way. Amen!*

This indeed was happening, that I was connecting more heart-fully, with my sisters, my daughter and son, friends, clients, doing the work I love as a 'Journey' practitioner, feeling elated, on my adventures on the open road, - the delights of bathing in stream, river & sea in glorious sunlight. Finally, when I made time, not long after the session, to visit my daughter, the whole day with her felt magical. We sat in the sunshine, and shared from the heart, more openly than we had, for many years, no longer disconnected from myself, and the buried pain. Now, after this deeper forgiveness & healing, Love is flowing freely again. Only after I made that deep commitment to express love, and take down any barriers that kept my heart defended from real closeness, with present family, have the deeper, more hidden traumas, been surfacing. We were able to talk more, in those few hours, than we had been able to, for many, many years. I was telling Samantha how happy I was, to feel I have a daughter again. When I telephone her, she is so open to what I share, that my heart feels as if, it is glowing afterwards. Though there were perhaps 35 years of disconnection, allowing only more superficial relating, it took less than 2 years for the buried pain to show itself, once the intent was strong, to allow Love to flow, any impediment gone. It only took release of my anger, grief and, pain, for full forgiveness to be possible and, for the relationship to be wholly transformed on both sides. One consciousness, - everything and everyone always connected, without separation of time nor distance. Any healing in one place, affects the whole. It is liberating to free our bodies of stored pain and negativity, at the root of dis-ease.

Today, I was doing yet another 'final?' re-edit (!), on the last day of Christmas, (Jan.6th 2022, - a day of gift-giving, in Spain, when the 3 Kings arrived, bearing gifts, for the birth of 'Christ).

I would like to add here, I had slept in my car in the Manor house garden, throughout the time, I was attending the London Stargate Gathering, at the end of December 2021. James, 'Jungleyes' brother & Harriet's twin, has invited me to sleep in his mother's four-poster bed, any time I go to Kew. Maybe next time I am in London, though I did notice a 'for sale sign' as, he is in a process of change too, though hopes to create a new home for himself, with the garden area, even after the Manor House is hopefully sold! There are foxes living in the woodland area, and his mother used to feed the foxes, squirrels, birds & a rat. I loved that about her and did the same, when I looked after her home and garden, while she went for an occasional break to her land in Jersey, and I looked after Jungleyes, during his breakdown! It was Jungleyes, who originally showed me, the traders' fruit & veg market, which started in Covent Garden, then moved to sites, increasingly further afield from Central London. I became his driver to the market for many years, from the 1980's I believe.

After the two-day Stargate event, in the early morning, I enjoyed seeing a fox coming in, early the next morning, before I drove to the Traders Fruit Market, nr. Hayes, & bought a couple of £6 each, boxes, of medium sized Hass avocados, before visiting lovely daughter, Samantha, Dec.30th 2021, for a couple of hours, very relaxed, & friendly in her Bicester home office, safe from her 'barking-mad' Rottweilers, who are very big, unsure & unfriendly, towards people they do not know or trust. (Mick walks the strongest ones, & Samantha, the other two. Only one of them, the 'matriarch,' is friendly with me, but I could not get to meet her). I had a little daylight, to drive to a familiar lay-by, the far side of Oxford. Unfortunately, there was so much two-way traffic, throughout the night, as I lay in my car-bed, that from about 4.30p.m. darkness, to 1st light 6.30a.m. - I lay sleepless! Also, the whole road system has changed, from when I was last there, a year or two ago, diverting me for some miles, to the Motorway, so I got very lost, though in beautiful woodland scenery, in my attempt to avoid this. Thus, I gave up the idea of visiting my sister Carmen & Michael in Bath. Maybe for her February birthday, I will get to see them, though their visiting grandson Tor, has succumbed to the Covid discomfort. Since I had not slept, & spent so long in unknown territory, lost, as the road layout has been changed, I took a very different route home than usual, so, did not stop to eat. Not surprising then, having arrived back to Stroud, and emptied my car, I suddenly nearly fainted, so had to sit on a wall, while the blood came back to my head!

I am well used to fainting since I was a child, so recognize the signs quickly. I remember my father, being very judgemental of me, when I showed any weakness, if my legs got tired as a child, when he took me on bike rides. He never learned how to be emotionally loving, with a hug, for instance, or a kind word.

*

Sadly, my father & I, were unable or unwilling, throughout most of our life as father & daughter, to come to an accepting and loving way, of relating with each other. Only after his 'death,' after much time spent on, my inner healing of our early years together, have I come to true forgiveness, understanding, and unconditional love, accepting his vulnerability and humanity, in the face of his own life challenges. I no longer have any conscious investment, in blaming the particular people, who are part of my human drama. I would like to have loved, forgiven and, truly seen him, sooner.

In the final hours of his physical life, I deeply remember, sitting on one side, of my father's bed, where he lay in a coma, my two sisters on the other side. They had travelled to Spain earlier in the week. Once I had been told he was dying, I had asked him telepathically, if he would wait until I got there.

I travelled from London to San Sebastian, and reached the hospital at 10p.m. My sisters mentioned his fear, or resistance, during that week, of letting go to dying, - at least that is what I understood. Sitting there, my hand on his arm, I felt really saddened, by this rare, physical contact with him, only possible because he was in a coma. How judged & unloved I had felt by him, thus had aimed back similar attacks. Midnight approached. I was drawn to speak to him, again telepathically, afraid to speak aloud, in case my sisters, might be rather shocked or upset, by my words. I said, "It's O.K. You can go now, and you'll find you're not sick any more, and you'll be able to stand up and, feel strong and fine." As soon as I said that, I felt the pulse in his arm stop, followed a moment later by his breath. (I believe, while he was in that coma, he was no longer caught in his human judgements, rather he was one with his Soul being. He waited for me). And he was gone. Since it was midnight, we stayed up all night in the hospital, though I was the only one of us, fascinated, by visiting & revisiting my father's shroud-dressed body, in the basement mortuary. My sisters were shocked, that we were given that freedom. I even tried to take a photo. With his spirit gone, his face was like a vacated waxen mould. My father & I were not able, to come to a place of healing, forgiveness and, love, while he was in his physical body! Nobody's fault, but never-the-less, it has been imperative for me, to access and release any anger and pain still held & buried in my body, till I have known all was healed, and could feel only love for him.

My sister Cristina, had approached me, asking if I would translate folders full, of the War-time letters written from Dec.1937 to June 1946, between our parents, from Spanish to English. His letters were of course censored, before posting, from wherever the Army was based. Some almost indecipherable, from damp, so, difficult to decipher, plus different quality writing papers & so much handling. Now, in 2022, my **final** re-editing, and having completed the translation, of those letters too, I intend to get them into 5 folders, in a simple format of, each of the 5 Sections into which I have sorted them, & maybe self-publish. I deeply regret, not having shared a loving relationship, other than sporadically, with our father, before his death. I now feel certain, that however we may be related to each other, in our next life together, there will be love & harmony, between us.

The depth of my Journey Processes, have been such a gift and gateway for me, to find 'who' I am. I have been guided, in many other ways, to let go of so many internalized judgements and resentments, I had clung onto for so long. Proof that people are not to be trusted. "I'm right! I'm as good as, or better than you, & don't need **your** approval!" Such fleeting illusions of control and power over one's life and happiness. With judgement as my focus, it was myself I was feeding, so unloving & harmful a diet, & self-judgement lurked beneath, of course. We are all innocent, whatever role we play in life. We just told ourselves a story, from the womb onwards, about our world, who others are, who we are, plus what to expect, based on usually mistaken notions. By the time parents, teachers, religions & society have moulded us to fit in, by learning rules of behaviour & thought, we can end up with such a false picture of ourselves, - not as good as… not loveable enough… thus entering the dream of Separation, with a very distorted and limited view of 'Reality.' Our bodies can feel so vulnerable, our sense of identity, worth, or pride, so caught up with physical appearance and how we are seen. We become caricatures of ourselves, disconnected from the authentic aliveness we came in with. What a negative picture!

*

I was feeling ready, to let go all I could, of my anger towards men, still held in my body, as it was still very much an underground influence. I had been reading Lucia Renee's 'Unplugging the Patriarchy,' which both gave much information about the 'power rings' which have long-time been controlling the reins of power, & describes much active, spiritual focus on 'unplugging' (this was happening around 2003-4), to lessen that control. The outdated structures, no longer serving the evolutionary good of the planet, are already, with increasing acceleration breaking down. Increasingly there is a huge wave of women moving into empowerment & fulfilment of their full potential & expression, bringing equality & balance into the male/female dynamic. Around 2010, my 'Journey' swap partner, Judith, (who had been training with pioneers of this inspiring change, including Lucia Renee, Claire Zammit, Katherine Woodward Thomas, & Chameli Ardagh), had initiated our 'Women's group' of 4, later 6 of us. At some point, she also shared much with us, from her feminine empowerment training. Encouraging each other to align with our highest possibilities, our group became such a cradle of support for exploration of those aspects which had held us back, such as lack of self-worth, seeing ourselves as victims of our circumstances, blaming, rather than seeing the ways we are responsible for creating this.

'The Shopkeeper of Kabul,' spans life in Kabul/Afghanistan, before, during and after the Taliban, describing how men still attempt to subjugate and dominate, stay most powerful, their women bored, living lives of slavery, as lesser beings. Yet already a wave of women even in Arabic Muslim countries, and other male dominant cultures, are rebelling, so, much imminent change). Still though, much rape & imprisonment of women and girls, who wish for equality and, freedom to speak out. By 2022, the feminine energy is coming in with more power and strength, and by 2025 a big planetary shift in higher consciousness, is anticipated.

One powerful process for me in June 2011, again involved ways, I had felt neither appreciated, accepted, nor seen by my father with eyes of love. It seems my presence brings no joy to my father. I invite all the men of my life, to a camp-fire of unconditional love, and my young self tells my father how I really felt. After we had reached understanding and forgiveness, my father held me in his arms. For the first time that I recall, I felt a man truly here, for me! I opened myself to feeling, Male fatherly support and love, embodying this in myself. I opened to the idea too, that a partner could show up, in this way for me. No wonder I have brought up my children without much Male support, never expecting safety, nor support, from a partner.

That night I dreamt I was with a man, who felt like a best friend. I felt so safe, could share with total honesty, and I sensed we could become sexually intimate, but even in my dream, I knew I was still with my husband, Sam.

*

More recently, I have been able to connect to the deep love I felt, for my father and mother, before I shut myself down. Having to leave his new wife and me, his little baby, must have felt very distressing to my father, triggered his vulnerability, for sure, not knowing if he would ever see us again. After all, in 1918 when he was 3yrs.old, his own father was killed, in World War 1. Five years later, he had a new step-father, a Methodist minister, whom he seems to have accepted, even if not being so close to him. He approved of some of the rousing sermons, the latter delivered, especially in the ex-mining villages. So, for a while, our father-to-be, Kenneth Thompson 'Southerly,' (to avoid libel suits, surname changed!), did call himself a Christian Socialist, and did half-heartedly accept his new family situation. Kenneth organized a night's shelter, for the Jarrow Marchers, with 'Lady Cecilia's' help, in a disused Mill, & he liaised with the Police for a Rally for the Jarrow marchers, one of the many Hunger Marches, converging on London, in hope of a better outcome in their lives. With his team, he regularly sold, 'The Daily Worker'. His stepfather joined in giving speeches. in their place of shelter. Kenneth also gave much time and energy into mobilising support of, money and food, for the Spanish Republican government, driving with companions through the streets, addressing the public through loudspeakers. He organized too, a Conference of all the Left-wing and working-class movements, (such as political parties, Trade Unions, and Co-operative societies), in order to set up a Cumberland and Westmorland Spanish Aid Committee. These activities gave him a much greater sense of fulfilment, than the short-term, supply-teaching that only began to be, occasionally offered to him, as men began to be recruited for war. Though Kenneth had obtained a degree in Durham University, and completed his teachers' training, yet his first paid work, came about through increased involvement with the Brampton Basque children refugees' Hostel. By the time he met, our mother-to-be, he had bought Hugo's 'Spanish in Three Months' (as initially he knew no Spanish), and started teaching English to 'La Senorita Ezquerra Nunez,' (pronounced Nuniez – z like 'th' in think), or Lolita (short for Dolores). She was one of two Women teachers from Bilbao, who had brought 100 of the Basque refugee children, in their care, on their hazardous journey, up to Cumberland. They were given refuge, in the building Kenneth, had initially rejected, as unfit for the Jarrow Marchers. He had quickly felt drawn to her, and she helped him, become proficient enough in Spanish, in 5mths, to be offered a low-paid teaching job, with the boys in a 2nd Basque children's hostel in Keighley, Yorkshire. (When I, Sonelle, was growing up, there was still very much a class system, - those who spoke King's or Queen's English, a better class than those, like me, who spoke with Northern or midlands dialects - translator). As I mentioned above, Cristina had initially given me, 5 folders (the 1st of many), full of letters, I never knew existed, written between Kenneth & Lolita, with more folders following, containing all further letters, from 1937 right up until Summer 1946, giving me much information about what happened, with the Basque refugees, plus politics & events in Spain, & elsewhere; - (though they rarely ever mentioned Jews)! - (Lolita had left her belongings, in Cristina's home, where she lived, following our father's death in San Sebastian, until, her mental state, made it appropriate, for her to go to a local Care home.)

Reading Laurie Lee's 'A Moment of War,' which is set in this same time-frame, Spain's true horror is made clear. I have read too, 'Only for Three Months' by Adrian Bell plus, books by Paul Preston, who dives deeply into the true horror of Franco's Spain, including, 'The Spanish Holocaust,' given that Franco and Hitler created Concentration Camps, with the same harmful intent, to stamp out, freedom of speech and heart. He sets out a crazy record of the conflicts, bravery, manoeuvring, treachery & suffering, unleashed by Franco's bid for Fascist control, in Hitler & Mussolini style, in 'The Last Days of the Spanish Republic'. I finally read 'Franco' by Paul Preston, which had been on my book-shelf for months! (Today, almost Easter 2022, so many refugees, divided families, in Ukraine & wherever else, so many maimed, killed, losing their homes, livelihoods, Country, imprisoned & tortured). In the 2020ies, this is still very much held in the consciousness of the Basque people, who lived through the Spanish Wars. This I know, from staying in the Eco-village, Lakabe, (an hr's drive from Pamplona, in 2019 & 2020). (I am genetically ½ Basque).

On March 3rd 1939, Kenneth & Lolita married, starting their wedded life, with a ready-made family of Spanish adolescents, still not returned to Spain. She had little experience of cooking, yet it seems she took good care of everyone.

War was declared September 3rd.1939 of, that same year, and I was born in Huddersfield, October 25th 1940, in a time of World War 2 rationing, shortages, & separation from my father for long or shorter periods of time, bombs regularly falling nearby, from when I was a baby. We had left our Huddersfield home, to be nr. the Scarborough Barracks, where Kenneth was training, for 6mths. to become proficient as a driver, gunner, & signaller, and hating it. He had found rented accommodation, for Lolita & me, before being sent overseas. He was able often to join us, from the Barracks. My father did not permanently come back, until I was approaching my 6th birthday. I was named Maria El...., and my parents had just bought their first house, before the War, on the strength of, the teaching post, my father had finally, been offered in Huddersfield, - with a loan of £10 from a local bank, (£5 purchase deposit plus moving costs)!

When I was 1yr.old, he was sent to the Middle East, becoming one of the 'Desert Rats', (named after the jerboas in the African desert). Later, he was posted to Italy. Our Scarborough landlady, contrary to assurances given, to my father, had turned us out, Mummy being pregnant with Carmen by then, nor would his relations help. I had always mistakenly understood from Mummy, how much the hospital nurses, loved her babies, so, buoyed by their Care, she had found the strength and courage, to take her 15mths.old toddler (me), and Carmen Margaret, her new-born baby, in 1942, to go through the streets of Carlisle, knocking from door to door; - till a very caring family took us in. The truth is, the same place my father had rejected as unfit for the Jarrow Marchers, became the Hostel for the Basque refugee children, their teachers and, carers, in 1937. My mother, a teacher, was one of those refugees. Later, when Kenneth was overseas fighting, in the Middle East, then Italy, and Lolita needed a home, Lady Cecilia, gave Lolita, me & Carmen, her gardener's cottage, in Brampton, Cumberland, which though very damp, we had as a home for the rest of the War & demobilization. Lady Cecilia, very liberal, who had befriended Kenneth, when as a young Communist, he had been looking for fit shelter, for the Jarrow Marchers to rest; - 'Auntie' Sanderson & 'Uncle' Bob, with their grown daughters, Kathleen & Margaret, lived initially in the other half of the Cottage. They made us totally welcome, showering love on me and

Carmen. Kathleen was the last one still alive, 98yrs, old, when I last travelled to what is now labelled Cumbria. - (Cumberland and Westmorland became Cumbria in 1975). I drove 'up' June 10th 2015, to visit her, after first walking up to a part of Hadrian's wall, past the Lanercost Priory, along the very road, where we grew up in Brampton, Cumberland, in our early years - the woods still there, with stream and red squirrels, near Chris House. I then, spent a delightful time with her, in a nearby nursing home, - she gave a rather different picture of our past, so I wondered what really happened! She seemed in better health than I anticipated, with a clear mind as far as I could tell...yet, I got the impression, later as I was leaving, that the Carers knew better! I am sure my parent's letters, gave an accurate sequence of events.

As I drove through the Cumberland hills, I felt a strong sensation in my heart, 'I'm back in my motherland'! I would not enjoy snow & cold, in the Winter-time. I am happy though, to live in Stroud, in the 'Five Valleys' in the South West, much warmer, though prone too, to occasional flooding. Stroud has a very vibrant, alternative Community, yet though many of us live more freely, - fear, drug & mask free, still some feel safer with vaccines & masks!

So, by the time Carmen was born, we were living in a much safer area, without the bombs & sirens, I had grown up with in my first 14 to 15 months. Having translated my parents' letters, from those years, I now have the facts, as described above, that it was Lady Cecilia, (mother of Liberal MP, Wilfrid Roberts), who was compassionate enough, to give us a home with Kathleen, Margaret & family, in Chris House next to their Manor house. - Wilfrid had played an instrumental part in co-ordinating voluntary relief groups including a National Joint Committee for Spanish Relief, which was discussing possibly evacuating women and children, from Spain's worst danger zones, such as the Bilbao & Guernica regions. My & Carmen's mother, was one of the Bilbao teachers.

*

Later, letters had been posted to Kenneth, my father, advising him of my mother's fragile psychological & physical state, however, these usually took weeks to reach him. By the time he was given 'Compassionate leave,' Carmen was of course, already born. He managed, with the help yet again, of his influential good friends, Lady Cecilia Roberts & her family, to avoid being posted back overseas, so between then and, his release from the Army, by which time I was already 5yrs.old, there were periods when he was able to visit us regularly which led, later, to great distress for me, as I had become very attached, as a 5yr.old, to my 'Daddy,' during one period of a few weeks, experiencing great grief and loss, when he again left. In fact, one of the few memories imprinted indelibly in my memory, was one early, dark morning, black-out curtains too, I suppose, and me sitting at a table with both parents, 'crying my heart out', with my parents sitting in silence, unable to offer comfort or solace. *Recently I went back yet again, (in a 'Journey' process), to that scene. I'd resolutely decided, that week, I had really had enough of fear, around lack of money, food feeling rationed and, feeling restricted in, my life choices & possibilities.* Food had indeed been rationed throughout the first 7 or 8yrs. of my life. I could clearly see, the correlation between the life, I was creating at 71yrs.old, and the whole ambience or backdrop, to the physical life experience, I found myself in, as a baby onwards, with shortages of Food & Love, instead Wars, Rationing, Hunger Marches, Unemployment, no longer remembering, that I chose to come. This all permeates some memoirs my father wrote, covering the period up until I was 9yrs.old. One of my early Brampton memories, is of marching soldiers, one of them, pointing his rifle at me, in jest. Or, grenades throwing practice, in the road in front of our cottage, which would set me & Carmen, running inside screaming, to find some hiding place. I dreamt about soldiers, in pursuit of me, for many, many years. I did get pulled out of the birth canal, by forceps, before I felt ready! Second thoughts?

(I hope to get the completed the translations, from Spanish to English, of our parents' War-time letters, from December 1937 to June 1946, (1,163 A4 pages onto two sides of the page!) – The letters gave me a much more intimate understanding, of them, and their relationship, with each other and, us children.

*

*Anyway, I asked my friend Judith for a process, and received two more at a weekend, ('**Journey**' Event), so, three processes in the same week, staying totally focussed on the same issue! The key process went back to 2mths.old, & the other two went back to, my 5yr.old self, in two connected scenes. At both times, I made maybe my most life changing decisions, about family, the world, & my relationship with it all, such as, "The World is a dangerous place. People are powerless & incapable of giving me the support I need. My needs cannot be met, & no point in even asking for what I need." I basically separated at some deep level, from my blood family, & the human family, not trusting there was anyone, who really cared. I certainly decided "I don't matter." I see so clearly, the way I orchestrated the events, for much of my life, in my relationships, from those inner convictions. I expected to be left, to be betrayed, & created that lack of safety & trust in every intimate relationship, that particularly mattered to me. In the 1st process, (with Judith), I prayed, to open-up, to the flow of Love & Abundance, to feel greater ease in my body. I noticed more reluctance than usual, to go deep, but did so, anyway. My Mentor was Tara, for the 1st time. (I am told I was, unusually, a male priest of hers, in a former life, wandering the land, speaking of Love)! She offered me total compassion & protective support. I landed with her, under the ribs of my right breast, feeling a lot of pain, nausea, great grief & loss, with the memory of imminent separation from my father, yet again.*

It was constricted & dark in there, yet very quickly, I dropped into feeling safe, contained and, nurtured, which soon expanded into a huge spacious embrace, & interestingly, I was also experiencing both my parent's bodies, as vast presence, not dense, physical forms. I felt no need to blame them, for their being unable, to help me feel seen, heard, & reassured. Instead, I, (that 5yr.old), had a quarrel with Life, to have been landed in such a world of Terror, Fear, Horror & limited Food & Love. All this, since the womb onwards, had led to many of those Life-forming decisions, mentioned above. After conversing with Life, & reaching a sense of resolution & acceptance, I let go of such dis-empowering beliefs, such as "Others don't have the capacity to be a source of safety & support," I choose instead, "I am a totally precious part of the Whole. All of Life welcomes me & wants me to be here fully. I can never be destroyed. Life deeply loves & cares about me. Others are a great Source, of all the Support & Resources I need, to thrive." Though I felt a definite shift inside, I knew further uncovering, was needed for completion. Two days later, I received another process, & kept that same unswerving focus, to open to Abundance, Love, & Ease in my body, rather than stay in nervous anticipation, of future lack or loss. This time I was going through many layers of emotion, and Tara again turned up, at some point. My memory brought me, to my 2mths.old baby self, at my mother's breast. I had connected before, with myself as, that baby at the breast, plus my lack of feeling safe or, nurtured by my mother, due to the turbulence of her panic & distress. Already in my mother's womb, I was absorbing the feelings from her traumatic experiences in the Spanish Civil war, from which she & her colleagues, had fled, with the children; horrors such as bombs dropping, & nuns being burnt. (Earlier in her life, Lolita, had deeply contemplated whether to become a nun). Now, she was faced with, her fears about her ability, to survive, this fast-approaching World War, my father having just received his call-up papers. She would be separated from, her new husband, with no great command of the English language & customs, little income, now facing an immediate move to the Barracks, from our home, plus whatever life-threatening horrors might be faced inevitably, by the armed forces especially, in this War, but equally by whoever else's time is up! Only now, finally, at 71yrs.old, did I find the way to fully connect, to her Love, beneath that overlay of Terror and Fear. What an opening it was! Suddenly I felt the gateways had opened, to the Great Mama of the Universe, & a flow of Love & Abundance coming into my Life. Already I had come to total forgiveness, of my parents, for seeming wrongs, but still it is important, to bring to light, the choices made long ago, that set fixed patterns, running through our lives, unconsciously creating our experiences, however positive we try to be. It was important both to be aware how, the recurring events created in my life were reflecting exactly, my underlying unconscious earlier decisions, beliefs & vows, but also, to maintain a committed, unwavering intent to free myself from the past.

I was surprised one week in my 80th year, while very relaxed, hearing in my morning meditation from the Alcazar group of Masters, (channelled through Prageet & Jules), about abundance, to suddenly burst into tears, very unexpectedly, then felt a wave of love, embrace me &, calling me Sonelle! I felt so embraced in love. It seems, my feeling of 'being excluded, from Love & plenty,' had started as a baby, 'real' Love, eluding me, ever since more or less. Now, I feel connected to the Mama of the whole world, in an embodied and intimate way, and am totally included. Everything started to reflect that back to me in 'magic' ways ever since. Each example of this fills me with Gratitude, and a deeper Trust in Life. The Universe vibrates in synchronous resonance with, whatever is being broadcasted out, from my inner being.

There always was, a strong attachment, between me & my mother, yet it had felt often, like emotional entanglement, based on two-way neediness. I came across these lines in a novel, - "It was time she apologized to her daughter for holding on too tight, for making hoops of steel, out of bonds of love." (Catherine Dunne's, The Walled Garden.") That was how, I came to experience her embraces, however strong the emotional bond. As my inner connection with myself & Life, has become more intimate, so, a deepened connection is here with family, parents, daughter, son, sisters, husbands, friends, & all. Probably I have made clear, but will say it again, though in 2011, in my 71st year, my parents, having died in earlier years, were long gone from, their parental roles, in relation to me, still I know our present & future interactions are transformed, clear of past blame. All is forgiven! I have reconnected, I feel, with all of humanity in compassion and Love. What a blessing! Reconnecting with the Heart of all, to give and receive from here! It is absolutely, never ever, too late to let go & forgive. I received the 3rd process, *the day after, still focussed even more deeply, on staying in communion with Ease, Abundance, & open-hearted intimate connection, with inner-outer flow. I noticed the bannisters on the left, beautifully designed and structured, but a gap on the right, maybe reflecting my uncertainty, about stepping more visibly, into the world &, how. A huge door appears before me, a winged, seemingly angelic Mentor, standing before me, on the other side. She is visibly quite ephemeral, so I ask her, to appear more solidly. She does so, & I see she has brown eyes, pale skin, and delicate faery wings. She waits for my requests before acting, - my Guardian Angel? The chariot too, maybe is not very solid, so again, I ask for a more solid form. The silvery metallic nose of an aircraft appears and zooms, very fast, to the* **base of my throat**, *being too hard, to proceed further now! I sensed more of a spacious chamber at the bottom, while further up, there 'was quite a big constriction, quite painful, allowing only limited expression, to find a way through, around the central blockage. Even as I look, a sort of screen with textured tapestry-like inlaid panels, and upper curved arches, appears from the left, impeding access, - a sort of ring-pass-not. The accompanying emotion which arises is, "It's not safe to speak."*

I find myself once again, in a scene visited, not so long ago. An older 5yr.old me, had just recovered, from being very ill with, so-called 'whooping cough,' after her first taste of school. (Actually, it was clear, in the actual letters, that neither my parents nor the doctor, were certain whether that disease label would fit! My parents both totally believed in the medical system). Cristina, born January 17ᵗʰ 1946, my youngest sister, was only a few weeks old, & was now also, very ill herself, supposedly from contact with me. My father was home though still, going through the Army 'demob.' process. They feared she would not live. Carmen and I were supposed, to keep very quiet and, keep well away. My father came out of the house, cross with us, for being too noisy, and I concluded, he no longer loved me, which solidified, my feeling of separation. I decided that, he cared more about Cristina, his new baby. She mattered more, especially I suppose, because of his repeated absences, from my life, which had eroded my trust. At that point, I shut down more than before, deciding not to even ask, for what I needed. My neediness went underground, trying neither to be seen, nor even acknowledged. I would make do, with crumbs, no longer expecting much, from anyone, from 'Life.' If I could avoid asking, for help or support, such as studying maps, rather than ask someone, for directions, I would - thus my receiving of Life's abundance, was severely rationed. What sufferings, what 'hells' on earth, we do create for ourselves, imagining it, a good investment of energy & focus. Not only did I then cut off, from my father, but I separated at a deep level from family too, first my 'blood' family, but just as much from my human family. "I'll manage on my own," I would think, not believing that anyone, could truly care about me. No wonder I so often cried, whenever I saw examples, of people's selfless love and compassion, towards their fellow human beings. I see clearly, the way I orchestrated events, in my relationships, to reflect these inner convictions, broadcasting this out, with my expectations and vibration. Life of course, has generously responded, giving me plenty, of what I focussed on receiving. We blame those who fulfil, these expectations, by betraying us, etc. unable to fathom why so little Love seems to reach us! I created lack of safety & trust in my intimate, & every other relationship with human beings.

Going to that key scene again, I replayed it, after first focussing on breathing in extra resources, such as; **'I can clearly communicate lovingly', 'Self-Love', 'I feel connected to Mother & Father Love', 'Safety', 'Courage'.** *Bolstered by, these extra resources, I was able to respond very differently. When my father came out, to get cross with us, I was able to ask him, "Do you still love me?" He assured me he did, explaining carefully, why, we must be quieter, (even if given his own emotional state, he could not hug me lovingly). This time, my awareness could extend, to my sister Cristina & my mother, in the other room, & I felt able to understand, the needs of the situation, & so extend my love there. When my father went back inside, I ran to Carmen, flung my arms round her, as I could clearly see her fragility & vulnerability, & said, "I love you. Let's play a lovely quiet game." I had no longer cut myself off from my family, or my connection to others! My adult, aware self, had embraced that 5yr.old, in a process, weeks earlier, but I had not connected deeply to everyone else, in the scene.* I 'phoned both of my sisters soon after that experience, to share the healing, of that past, I had experienced, though Cristina and I, both insist on, laying claim to the 'black sheep of the family' title. I noticed, I was spontaneously relating much more openly since, with the people I was meeting, anywhere & everywhere. This was happening, without thought nor effort, just naturally. It feels good to be more connected in this way. By the end of this process, my throat was certainly happy, to have felt so much healing love and attention. I felt free to express authentically.

*

The Truth is, that who I am is, Life, or Source, (or whatever other name describes the Infinite Intelligence behind the Birth of Existence or Creation), seen in all its vast and infinite faces, embodied as human being, in this one, who is being experienced as me. 'I am!' Life holds everyone, every created form equally, in unconditional Love & Acceptance, which to the mind, could seem neutrally uncaring, but really, as one comes into a deeper connection, is found to be full of such Care & Compassion, judging nothing as ugly, worthless, separate, wrong, or unlovable. How arrogant & near-sighted it would be for me, who sees & knows so little, to hold anyone in judgement or, lack of forgiveness. I could say, my belief about being 'excluded, from Love,' was reflected, to me, by, my mother's lack of ability, to stay strong herself, in Trust or Love. Given that our auras were totally intertwined, was she responsible, by letting herself be in the grip of terror?

As I have been translating her war-time letters, which describe how she interacts with me, she does just see me, as a baby who knows nothing! Did her distress, stem from the Spanish Civil War, or did her reactions stem also, from her early traumas and conflict in her family, & back through the generations? Forgiveness here, is Forgiveness there. It is helpful to express clearly one's intent, when clearing, the past, or present, handed-down patterns.

Presently, there is much healing of both ancestral & present karmic conflict, though it is probably inseparable! Who to blame? No-one. Consider we've all opted to play the Game of Life, in a variety of ways, in many roles, over many aeons! We are Here. Inseparable from the Whole, having **chosen** to play! **Didn't we?** Me & my sisters have the Viking heritage, as part of our ancestry!

*

Of course, Forgiveness of Self is important, for all the ways we have seen ourselves as deficient, unworthy, less, or more than another, carrying such a burden of guilt & shame for never being good enough! I have done 19yrs. of healing of my inner child self, so was surprised a few days ago, when I was suddenly filled with a deep grief, which had me sobbing aloud, but which felt from further back, than this life!

During one very memorable 'Journey' session, weighed down with this idea of not being enough, the image had appeared of a child-size body with no arms nor legs. I said out loud without pause, "Throw her on the rubbish heap!" Yet looking into her eyes, at her wounded expression of pain, compassion arose realizing too, that she, was me! Deeply connecting with my knowing, that I am totally Loved just for Existing, I embraced that 'useless' me as being precious & perfect as she is! As we all are!

*

This chapter would not be complete without reference to 'Zero Limits', written by Joe Vitale & Ihaleakala Hew Len PHD, or Dr. Hew Len. Many have now been hearing of the Ho'oponopono prayer of Forgiveness and the fundamental teachings behind the simple words. Ho'oponopono means, so I have read, to rectify an error, or make right. I will quote first the following simple prayer from 'Zero Limits,' regarding this key perception:

"I am sorry

Please Forgive me

Thank you

I Love you"

If someone comes with a problem or conflict needing resolution, I'd take full responsibility for whatever's showing up within my own field of focus, thus I believe the following quotes will illustrate Dr. Hew Len's approach; "I am sorry for the erroneous thoughts within me that have caused the problem for me and my client; please forgive me." 'In response to the repentance and forgiveness appeal of the therapist, LOVE begins the mystical process of transmuting the erroneous thoughts. In this spiritual correction process, LOVE first neutralizes the erroneous emotions that have caused the problem, be they resentment, fear, anger, blame or confusion. In the next step, LOVE then releases the neutralized energies from the thoughts, leaving them in a state of void, of emptiness, of true freedom.

With the thoughts empty, free, LOVE then fills them with Itself. The result? The therapist is renewed, restored in LOVE. As the therapist is renewed so is the client, there is LOVE. Where there was darkness in her soul, there is now the healing light of LOVE.' And so, as follows:

'I operate my life and relationships according to the following insights:

1. The physical Universe is an actualisation of my thoughts.
2. If my thoughts are cancerous, they create a cancerous reality.
3. If my thoughts are perfect, they create a physical reality brimming with LOVE.
4. I am100% responsible for creating my physical universe the way it is.

5. I am 100% responsible for correcting the cancerous thoughts that create a diseased reality.
6. There is no such thing as out there. Everything exists as thoughts in my mind.

So, 'To be an effective problem solver, the therapist must be 100% responsible for having created the problem situation; that is, he must be willing to see that the source of the problem is erroneous thoughts within him, not within the client. Therapists never seem to notice that every time there is a problem, they are always present!'

When I first read the book, and heard, these sort of statements, some years ago, my heart sang in recognition of Truth!

Doctor. Hew Len, as he is called, worked as a clinical psychologist in a facility for the criminally insane. It was an Institution so fraught with violence and Fear, that staff did not stay long, or pleading sickness, had many days off. They all tended to walk with their backs to the wall, in anticipation of attack. Dr. Hew Len asked if he could work in a different way from usual, with his 'case load' of patients. He would read their files, note the crimes they had committed, and then, in the same way as he does with every person, who approaches him with a problem, he would assume, 100% responsibility for healing, in himself, whatever has been presented in his field of immediate awareness. He relates to this, as to any part of divine creation, neither condemning anyone nor anything. (He sees Source/God energy in everything everywhere, - in furniture, cigarettes, hamburgers, whatever is often disregarded or, disapproved of, by others). S/he does not need to know how or why, this specific circumstance, symptom, or violent crime, has been attracted. The words "I'm sorry," do not come from guilty self-flagellation. He is stating he is sorry, that he is not conscious of how he is creating this distress in his reality, and asks for forgiveness for his ignorance or unawareness. "Thank you" is his acceptance that it is now taken care of, as he offers his prayer. Within some months, of working in this way with these deeply troubled inmates,' a total transformation was taking place'.

The prisoners began themselves, to take responsibility, for their horrendous acts, expressing their regret. Where fear had palpably ruled, the staff relaxed, now enjoying working there. The heavily medicated, needed less of, the suppressant drugs, those who had been dangerous and therefore shackled, were allowed to move freely, and others expected never to be released, were freed. However, with less and less patients, the ward ended up being closed!

There is no separation in consciousness so, what I heal or let go, of in myself, heals everyone. Do not try to fix others, change nor judge them, rather realize that if I am working as a therapist, healer, or indeed, in any other relationship, my clients are reflecting me, back to myself. Maybe all that is needed, for any of us, is to realize, we are indeed Master Creators & Artists of our Lives, in every second, all creating this interconnected World. Thus, what we express with every thought and emotion, or broadcast with every flavour or nuance of our aware, or unaware vibration is, in every moment going to send out, attractive or repellent signals, to everyone & everything! It is important to catch ourselves when we suffer, so we maybe choose otherwise, rather than heed the Ego Mind's choices to stay in Fear, Doubt or Judgement. To un-create my Hell serves me & serves you. There is no difference. Separation is mind created Illusion, apparently solid.

*

In these concluding pages of this first chapter, titled "Forgiveness," I can say I seem, to have come to the end of, with any conviction anyway, laying blame on anyone, on Life, 'God,' Universe, or any seemingly inanimate thing, for any of what, I experience, or choose. Yet still, I sensed a part of me, still not wholly ready, to let go the reins, the fear of being 'rudderless,' rather than being fully LOVE, fully OPEN, ALIVE, able to fully embody & express from the huge, fiery, ever-evolving Potential, totally surrendering to Life's beautiful Embrace. I feel so much Gratitude in the depths of my being when I do fully say Yes! How unloved this body has been, by my, & others,' judgements & comparisons. How can I not feel immense compassion for the lack of love & forgiveness we pile on this body self? The rigid, stay-safe, mind/body part, is cracking apart. I believe I will be ending this chapter with, one last Journey episode, because it touches deeply, on some of my early unhappiness, about being in a human body, & is, it seems, a common theme around the world. At some point since 'menopause', I had started finding sex painful with my husband. Since I believe, any pain can be healed, no matter whether the pain resulted from, our emotionally painful relating, or, as many would believe, the need for HRT treatment, or other aids, (because of thinning of the vaginal wall, after child-bearing days are over), I decided the time had come to heal this, now I was no longer settling for short rations of Love.

I met with my swap partner on May 20th 2012, an auspicious day! My intention is, to go ever deeper into Love & Trust with Life &, for my sexuality, my vagina, to be healed of all pain. In the process, I made my descent down the stairs. This time the left side of the banister & the steps, were totally hidden beneath luxuriant, fresh, vibrant growth, of new leaves & thrusting stems. On the right side, the steps were bare, wooden, & totally safe and solid. I enjoyed moving, feeling so aware of being nurtured by Nature. I went very deep, and saw a tall curved door, reminding me of China, with its curves and pinnacles. Behind the door, I found two male Mentors. One of them, my same Chinese healer Mentor, this time not blue-skinned, (who appeared in an earlier process I described), sat very still and centred in himself, in the Lotus position, strong, pure colours of blue & yellow in his clothes, holding everything in equanimity, as before, yet this time, the connection felt much more friendly, & warm. Another Mentor was there too, much taller, less sturdy, with grey hair & beard, & a gentle, wise, strong presence. As the process evolves, I sense he is my divine Male counterpart. A very pink, lovely vehicle awaits us – lots of Love energy. I assumed it would go to my heart, but it goes down to the womb side of my cervix. My memory reveals a 12yr.old me, with legs that feel spindly, without strength nor, real connection to Earth. I am aware that is also a time when my pelvis got cracked. (Recently, in my late 70's, I have had more bone fractures. I have realized, when I was younger, I disliked the hard solidity of things, like walls and houses. This may be why I manifested, so many fractures. I was resisting being in a human body! - translator). *There seems, to be* murkiness around the cervix – *I feel it is not a cervix that joyfully welcomes new life with love, into the Birth canal – so many miscarriages, and a still-birth.* (In spite of my strong urge for Motherhood, before Samantha's conception, and joyfully anticipating Rammiel's birth, long before his conception, thus being emotionally very ready for him, yet the fact of never being, in deeply supportive, stable, loving relationships emotionally, with the fathers involved, I did not feel the most joyous response to Pregnancy).

In this Journey, Shame was the main emotion I felt, from my vagina to my throat, but was quite soon aware, it was not just my shame, but a collective shame. I never saw my parents naked, nor make any physical contact. Sex seemed to be embarrassing, shameful or, unclean. Banned by my parents, from being seen on T.V. That was the strong message from adults, parents, & teachers. So much sadness & compassion arose in me for everyone, that the whole process of conception & birth, the intimate connection, of nurture at the breast, is so imbued with shame & ugliness, instead of being seen as part of the beautiful, sacred, Miracle of Life. Nature 'mating,' tenderness, the powerful surge of Life and fertility, of freshness, flowering, fruitfulness, is all beautiful. My heart fully opened, readying me for the experience, both inside and outside -on my left side, of that rich & fertile creativity of Nature. On my right I am seeing rather, stars, planets, space, Cosmos, and beyond, a vast dark emptiness & mystery, from within which, creation happens. I see and sense too, the intricate order and sacred geometry, within it all, & feel to bow in awe, at this vast unknown Infinity. I have always seen inner mandalas. I have been integrating this since, and really feeling how little, my body has been loved, by me and others. I feel to truly honour my body in Love. I felt a strong connection throughout, to my two Mentors. They helped orchestrate, healing rituals, to cleanse & heal this huge infection of shame, carried by human beings. (Our ongoing Women's group of that time, focussed on the same theme, soon after). This shame, so emphasized by the patriarchal Catholic Church, also by the other patriarchal religions of, Islam & Judaism, mistakenly limited interpretations of Christian & other Scriptures, plus personal agendas around power & control! Good to see pictures of the Christ, or

'Yeshua' looking less Westernized, probably in his days with the Essenes. It sparked my interest in cleansing through enemas etc.

The Essenes honoured women & lived simply, honouring the sacredness of Creation, of life. It would be good for children, to learn of the sacredness of creating a human being, through sexual intimacy. Maybe men could learn more respect & restraint, so no woman (or man) feels used or forced sexually.

Before the Autumn equinox of 2013, I enjoyed hearing Allana Pratt, deeply encouraging women, to experience ourselves in delicious, sacred intimacy and fullness with Life, with our creative, sexual Nature in its widest sense, open to receiving Life deeply, intimately, in every movement and breath, living in orgasmic bliss and fullness, deep relaxation and ease. Like a flower, a leaf, bees, a butterfly, a lion, a beetle, dragonfly, stone or crystal, a root or tree, a red kite or eagle, every created form! It would take me another 10 to 11yrs., for me to live in this blissful joy. Pro Creation! Birthing of Universes! Birth, & re-Birth.

*

I felt very ready, whatever pain surfaced, to complete in the last months of 2012-13, my karmic challenges with Sam, which felt to have taken a big toll on my body. Much had been released, and the pair of us will, I trust, find what is right for the next stage of our journeys. I felt a physical pull, in that last Journey, to my tall Mentor. Who is he, where is he? I had a sense I had joined with my Divine male counterpart. What will this mean in my physical Life? I am committed to finding Joy in my Life, with neither effort, nor strategies. Life's orchestrating itself in resonance with, my inner Consciousness shifts. Time to let go, of every trace, of past suffering, of any old programme still playing out, to fully allow a vibrational shift. I choose to consciously open, to total embodiment of Unconditional Love, absolutely allowing full-hearted Forgiveness of myself, and all 'others'. So much to release and forgive, on the Path of Love, to become a fully blossoming radiant, vibrant Self.

In fact, in Spring 2013, something deep in relation to Sam, an underground rumbling, began to stir in me. I had still not always, been having the courage to speak my truth, after years of Sam's over-the-top dramas! And the time was come! However, I will include that relevant session, regarding this, in the last chapter, about responsibility. This chapter's heading is Forgiveness, and since my relationship with Sam lasted much longer than all my other partnerships, I will have plenty more to write. Every Journey process, necessarily includes Forgiveness, for resolution to be complete, but also the realization that our choices created our stories!

*

Already I feel light and grateful, excitement bubbling within, just to be experiencing Existence here! This release, has enabled me to receive more of my good, both in the love flow of relating, and in financial receiving. Without my knowing how, my money keeps expanding, in unexpected ways. Only with my husband has this been with-held. I suspect there is still plenty of buried anger to meet, a yet deeper forgiveness to find, for my own, his, and everyone else's good. An imminent certain end of the long-standing, old karmic story! I shall describe this completion in the coming chapters. In truth, there was but one person I had to forgive; - myself! I have been the judge, the jury, the prison and, the prisoner. Time to leave every self-created Jail.

*

Over 2yrs.later (2015), Sam had left his body July 18th the previous yr.!! - but not before I had completed, in Spring 2013 I believed, my old karmic story with him, & come, after 23yrs. marriage, to Forgiveness! That part of how, we took our different paths, will be described in detail in the last chapter.

I sat yesterday by his burial plot in sunshine & hill-side breezes, surrounded by wild-flowers, and buried his malas, also his last roll-up he never smoked!

*

Although I had been sleeping well, every night, I had been waking tired in the mornings. I realized it did not relate to, whether, I ate raw food or not, did a fruit cleanse or, occasionally ate some cooked food, though the latter can result in a heavy dulling effect on my energy. (Nor was I in grief, about Sam's passing.) I had been aware of a deepening inner shift for days, since immersing myself more deeply in Rikka's Money Mastery teachings. I realized I was going through an expansion period, yet again. Therefore, I have been dosing myself with Perelandra Rose essences this week, which always work to bring me back into balance. At the start of the week, *Mon. July 13th 2015 I received a welcome 'Journey' process, & voiced an initial prayer, to release whatever holds me back, from fully expressing, fully being, & fully trusting & knowing all that I am as my true, authentic self. I have inserted these last paragraphs here, rather than the last chapter, because I wrote more, in this 'Forgiveness' chapter, about my birth into a world of War and, finding healing and forgiveness for all involved in this and, throughout all time! My inner journey, took me down steps which were much steeper, with bigger drops than usual and dark, but still felt very safe, so*

I descend very willingly and speedily, into the unknown. Even the door is much deeper down plus, it is very dark and mysterious. Beyond are seemingly dozens of, tiny beings flitting & flying around and, as I go through, in front to the left, I see them as nature beings, sprites, fairies, all beings whose focus is to bring energy into physical form. They have the 'blueprints', 'codes' or intrinsic Nature Intelligence, to perfectly translate energy, into visible matter. The carriage for our journey into my body, has winged-insect, sunny butterfly wings, with reins to steer the attached chariot. I feel the fun and gladness of these small beings inviting me, to join the creative play of designing, the faery vehicle. We first land in the Birth canal, which also gives the impression, of never-ending forms, being birthed into the world, then move also, into the Womb. Yet the main emotions arising are being felt, from the belly to the throat plus, down the arms, sensed as what wants to be birthed through the tools of voice and heart-joy action. Yet there is a fear of expression too, in my belly, anguish in my heart at having failed, to stay true, not having been enough! Failed! I stayed with this, not making it wrong, simply accepting it as it is and, before long I felt a peaceful expansion spreading, though rising fear and excitement too, from all that is awaiting expression, simultaneously with feeling the rise of empowering energy, right up from my feet, to my throat and down, through my hands, ... my own power, the innate energy I am, filling my body and being, funnelled into Joy, Fun, also the Ease and Love of, Creative expression. Not just self-contained, but as an expansive flow out to others.

The memories from earlier in the session, I left on an inner video screen, (to attend to later), were of me at 2or3yrs.old. She is still so very alive, full of dynamic, joyous fun energy, still trusting herself, whereas the 5yr.old who also showed up is very self-contained, weak, shut down, given up & caved in, no longer trusting herself, nor anyone else. As I invited those young versions of me, my present me, & my nature spirit helpers, to gather around a camp-fire of unconditional love, I also invited my parents, plus those representing, the societal mentality, of that time, bureaucrats, politicians, manipulative seekers of power, prestige & wealth, committees, &, everyone, playing small in Illusion! My 5yr.old is angry at, being kept in the dark, not told anything &, not allowed, speak her truth or, be real. "It's a mad insane world you're trying to make me fit into!" War, killing, we are not told anything, yet can feel it all. Not OK having to fit in, behave & be nice. Time for change! Time to free each other & ourselves! My Nature guides invite everyone, to join in the fun, of trusting & believing in the Real world, rather than turn away in Mistrust, believing in Separation. I ask the nature beings, to start cutting the cords, between me &, all others holding me tied, in any version of this false world, of so much limitation, lack, & suffering, back through the generations, through all times & dimensions. When I ask them, to clean out all that story, from my, & everyone's, bodies, I get a vision of a huge fiery conflagration, such as I have never seen before, in a Session. A Huge, collective Clearing of Illusionary Debris. Will it make a difference on the planet? I expect so and certainly, I feel different. My 5yr.old breathed in resources, she could have done with, for the scene, she left on the screen: True Expression Child-like Lightness Play Total Silliness Laughter

Relaxed Being Joyful Expansiveness Fun, humour, Jokes

I feel like sharing a bigger story, with my sisters and others, as increasingly I have already been doing. "I am Enough! You are Enough!" The Mentors add "Enjoy fun & Love, in Being and Expression." My Heart feels very grateful, my throat more confident, in my belly there is a Richness and, Trust in my innate Being &, in my Womb, a feeling of ever-birthing, expressing inner passion and Love, into tangible, visible outer forms. The general message is, to just relax &, enjoy ourselves more & more. I feel a commitment in my heart, to stay true to me. Over time, increasing radiant happiness. I Am!

Since this session, I also opened an Abundance account, in a conscious, deliberate way, & changes are happening, to reflect all of this. Finally, I am receiving some of the compensation funds, into my bank account, from the car accident 11mths.ago, as if suddenly, they are hearing me & acting! Seven years later I still have my 10% of income, Abundance account, in the Credit Union.

I also went for an optician's check-up, (as I have regular yearly sight tests). I have been short-sighted, since about 11yrs.old, over 60yrs.ago, & started wearing glasses, later lenses, very occasionally glasses for night-time driving. I always wonder if my clear-seeing, may be restored, as happens to some through 'The Journey.'

To end this chapter, I want to say, the challenges you meet on your path, are highlighting new creative possibilities, evolving in perfect timing, that your Soul Being will gift, or birth into unique expression, in the world. Plenty of early programmes get discarded & forgiven, 'en' route. Helps when we surrender, (without judging, or resisting, how life is happening in every moment, so all can dissolve easily, into the ever-present Love). Many Higher dimension Beings on call for support.

*

I added a section to this book, (influenced by my book-to-be, 'Mama y Papa,' mainly a translation of, my parents' War-time (1937-1946) letters. I feel a dream plus, 2 further Journey processes I will describe, belong in this Forgiveness chapter. I completed the translating but, have not yet published, these letters.

I had been working 3 days, in the Birmingham Mind Body Spirit show, interpreting auras and, was ready to set off, Sunday, Nov.13th, 2016, for my Journey Practitioners' Mastery event in Holland. I had arrived 5.30am, Mon.14th, at Western International Trader's market, bought a box, of 'clementines', and set off, still in darkness, for the North Circular. By the evening, I was parked in Harwich, in a peaceful road for the night. I relaxed in my car, & explored Harwich on

Tuesday &, again slept in the car. That night, Wed.14th, I had a surprisingly powerful dream. I was sitting alone, in the middle of a 3-seater sofa, my whole body seeming almost shell-shocked & bruised all over. I sensed this was the effect, of years of belittling verbal attacks, from Sam's angry Self, needing someone to blame for his inner conflicts. Suddenly, though my whole body remains in a slumped sitting position, Babaji, is standing before me, (in his later larger physical body), yet I feel the whole of my body warmly clasped & held close, for long moments, in a comforting, healing embrace, as though I were standing, his arms around my back, rather than his kneeling over my legs, before my slumped body. This is my most welcome, favourite &, heart-warming dream of Babaji. I find myself in meditations, bowing so deeply at Babaji's feet, as I know myself so deeply loved, since that night. I appreciate Babaji so deeply, as a dearly loved friend, requiring from me, no spiritual protocol.

(I have had some good, friendly Sam dreams, occasional unfriendly ones)!

This dream, provoked in me, such deep Trust, & feeling of being Loved & supported, that the whole journey, from boarding the ferry, early the next morning, then driving 2hrs.in Holland that night, plus early the next morning, seemed magically easy, much more so, than previous journeys driving in Holland. As I drove, I would be laughing, in outbursts of gratitude, with sudden tears, or Joy of Life. I reached the Mennorode Hotel and Conference Centre, before 9a.m., checked in around midday, and was surprised to find, I had a perfect single room, so was able to charge my lap-top and, listen to the Sophia Tribe Initiations, or Julie Renee Regeneration meditations, & follow my own rhythms, with my car parked close by. Again, I was crying with gratitude at being so blessed.

When Babaji has been asked if he is the Mahavatar, described in Paramahansa Yogananda's 'Autobiography of a Yogi,' he has replied saying "Yes," and has said too, he is identical with the old Haidakhan Baba, living around the town of Haidakhan, in Uttarakhand, in the years 1860-1922. He could also be a mirror, for the Goddess Naina Devi and for Lord Shiva too.

Friday Nov.18th to Sunday Nov.20th, we had in depth 'Designer' Processes, (i.e., Physical Process, journeying into the body, combined with meeting the many emotional layers, as in an Emotional Journey), but without scripts or formulas, resulting in our inner journeys, feeling so much more deeply, freeing. My partner was a Turkish lady, Zelda. As I have said, I had been believing, the pains in my back, were some sort of Ancestral healing of the War, Hunger, Fear consciousness, that I should nobly surrender to, but during the session, I began to question this assumption, as maybe being a false belief. After all, I know instantaneous healing is possible. Approaching the stairway, to take me on my inner journey, into my body and inner Being, I found the steps safe, but black & a bit narrow. No door showed up in the darkness, just a tunnel, with the bright light and colours of my Soul body ahead, and on the left, a large, brown-skinned Guide. A large motorized vehicle awaits us, which speeds to my Universal Heart area, a spacious area, with some golden light, though I know my brain is connected, too. Moreover, when the first pains appear, first in my right lower chest, where male wounds, tend to show up for me, then in the left, I am hit by the knowing, not only that, the focus in this session, is unfinished stuff with Sam, i.e., not only the War & Scarcity story, but a deeply buried guilt, layer to do with Sam! These sudden pains, are to do with his lungs, & all the symptoms which have shown up & intensified in my body, from the time of his Cancer journey, such as restricted breathing, some back curvature, like him & his mother, I have taken on, out of guilt, for not having been, loving enough, and for missing the moment of his death! The changed rhythm of his breathing, had alerted me at 3a.m. after only 3hrs. sleep, yet after checking how he was, I had gone down to the toilet, & lingered at least another half hour with inessential tasks. I did not fully acknowledge, how near, his moment of transition was, though I could have guessed, from the change in his breathing and focus. Clearly, this was resulting, in my feeling undeserving, of an Abundant, Joyful life. With every miracle & love blessing coming to me, I had been bursting into tears. My attention was pulled to my dream of 3 nights earlier. I had had no awareness, that my body, had been so bruised, from my acceptance, of the onslaught of 24yrs. of seemingly inevitable, verbal attacks, anger & blame, until that Dream. Whether my strong belief, that I had to see my relationship with Sam through to the end, was Truth, or a false belief, who knows. All fine, if I decide it is! We learn from experience & we have Infinity, to experiment and create in. I have no problem with being the age I am & having had the experiences I did. Somehow, I had not acknowledged the pain still held, in unexpressed sorrow, at my allowing, of Sam's ongoing dishonouring actions. (Listening, once I was back home, to Jean Slatter, speaking in a Teleseminar, she says 'Truth is a moving Target,' which I suspected was so! Allow 'truth' to Evolve in accord with our own perception!) Though Sam did admit to Dinesh, that he would be devastated if I left, (as his main Human Carer, Support, & his wife too, - though I do not know, what my being his wife, really meant to him), still his pain, led to his shouting at me right to the end.

He did briefly, after I released those 22yrs. of anger, start to honour me with respect, up until the steroids for his Cancer, brought back, his usual, old ego patterns, - he just rarely felt at home in his body & 'Being", carrying so much Fear &, lack of Safety. *My 'Journey' partner & I, set up a camp-fire of Unconditional Acceptance & Love, in my body, & I communicate to Sam, my 'past' pain & distress. Though there had been Forgiveness when, I had let go of a volcano of anger in the Spring of 2013, at being shut up by Sam's dramas, I had not realized a further Completion, & deeper level of Forgiveness, was still called for. During the whole period of, his affair & chasing various other women, my emotional pain had been, at times so intense, my Soul seemed to be leaving. When I had finally let go of the need to control, or be concerned about, what Sam might choose, following my release of volcanic anger, and having come into greater Self-Love and trust of Life, yet still unbeknownst to me, some pain was being held at a more hidden level. What happened next in my 'Journey' process, is that I saw Sam, in his new reality, wherever that is, & for the first time since his passing, could see him as a beautiful, Energetic, higher-vibration, Light warrior self, and felt he could see who I am in Truth too. Real Heart-open, waves of Appreciation, Love & Forgiveness, passed between us. This, certainly for me, was a much deeper, truer completion. Following this, I stayed with closed eyes in my inner space, but my body urged me to stand up, move my back, the pain intensifying in the right side, then the left side, then down to my left sciatic nerve, & finally, as I continued contorting my body, all the pain became concentrated along my spine, & I could hear spine cracking & adjustments here and there. A huge lot of cord-cutting happened too, between me & Sam. Archangel Michael was appropriately called in, for both of us, with his sword of Truth, cutting so many cords to the brain too. When this is done, my whole upper Heart area is full of bright Light flooding in, & the Sun's golden rays flood my brain too. Early the next morning, before breakfast, our Yoga instructor intuitively felt, a trauma Release process, was appropriate for us all, after the depth of yesterday's sessions. Perfect, and my spinal adjustments continued. The in-depth afternoon process, was fascinating too. Specifically, my guide and the vehicle which showed up, focussed too, on deeper Self-forgiveness, for my having permitted dishonouring or disrespect towards my body, from myself and others, during the years and many lives, of playing the Victim scenarios. The stairs down into my inner story, are wider today, more friendly, wooden stairs. I can see light behind 2 glass barriers, but the first is just a window I can step around, then a glass door. My guide is a man size green Nature Being, maybe a leprechaun, very friendly and mischievous. Our vehicle turns out to be 'a big Honey bee,' whose soft furriness is nice to ride on. The bee's radar knows exactly, where to go; to my surprise, into my vaginal area, yet not the usual passage-way. There are some secret passageways off to the right, where there is a whole bee colony, whose larvae seem to represent potential new, creative possibilities. These bees, are also my guides, who will have a special healing role, to play in my life, especially with the whole left rib-cage area. Itis time for a much deeper letting go, of all sense of Guilt, so I can truly feel I deserve gifts of Abundance & Joy. I deeply Trust, since the Babaji healing, how supported & loved I am, and the* **bees bring Honey for rib-healing, while the Green Being does some special strengthening web-weaving.** *It is* **time for Sweetness** *in my Life. At some point the leprechaun draws me into a mad, twirling, crossed arm, spinning dance, until it is so fast, we become just One Speed-of-Light spinning form, dissolving into atoms, cells and, molecules. Gentler, sweeter, merging happens though it is, also Fun, and playful, with full forgiveness of Me, & of all disconnected younger selves, from childhood until my 70's, as I see my pristine Innocence & Purity. In this full merging completion, we come up through a beautiful, water pool, Hathor and White Buffalo Woman are present too in this ritual. I sensed feathers of American Indians around,* *yesterday. Hopefully Mary Magdalene is here too with my inner angels of Love, Peace, Faith, Trust, Clarity, Reconciliation, Alignment, Atonement, Anointing, Grace, & Completion, (the Sophia Dragon Tribe I have been exploring with). It is time to let pain and suffering drop away, to dissolve in the Love. All honouring is here of, Sacred Intimacy & <u>Safety</u>. Any lack of Safety, was showing up in my left side today. I have asked the bees, with the nurturing, sweetness of their Honey, & the Green Being with his web-weaving, to continue this deep Healing until complete, even after we finish the process, though it would be helpful for me, to come back to eating raw food I expect.*

(Interestingly, in 2021, I have embarked on a healing Journey, with Irene Stein, with her special Royal Jelly formula, plus a daily oxygen & mineral booster)!

Sunday 20th brought another unexpected kind of healing, described near the end, of the Purpose Chapter. Maybe because of the letting go, of scripts & formulas, or maybe an increase of sensitivity, has led to much more freeing, unexpected, kinds of inner healing. It has been fun to experience a different depth to the inner processes, where logic is taking a lesser role. I am so thankful, to have released this deeper layer of pain, guilt, and separation from Love, having had no idea, that this deeper completion & forgiveness with Sam, had been needed. I feel also, the influx of Light is increasingly, coming in so strongly, that a deep shift has been happening in our bodies, allowing us to drop easily into our Hearts. Whatever is not in alignment with these Higher frequencies, the deepest, hidden Fear, & discomfort, is surfacing to be dissolved, very fast. My fear-Mind seems though, to have taken more of a back seat, even as I, & many others, are still healing the ancestral, collective trauma, from wars, and other conflicts. This has brought increased, physical discomfort, for many of us, on this consciously awakening path, as our bodies adjust, to be able to carry & reflect, more inner Light & Peace. My commitment to <u>fulfil my Soul Purpose</u>, and for my will to be one with Divine Will, is anyway now strong, as this is who I Am.

When Patricia Cote Robles, offered her online 2016 Winter Solstice Activation, she declared that, as so many of us, committed to this inner journey, have released so much past pain and limited conclusions, already we've 'far exceeded Heaven's expectations, allowing us to withstand much higher levels of 5th dimensional Solar Crystalline Light.' The 3rd dimensional plane, I have heard said, is the lowest dimension, to start reflecting this higher octave. I have felt a much deeper connection with bees, ever since the Process, I just described. I have read 'Dancing with Bees,' a book by Brigit Strawbridge Howard, intend to have too, a bee friendly hive, if my life allows. I read too, 'A Sting in the Tail' by Dave Goulson. Will read too, 'Biodynamic Beekeeping' by Matthias Thun.

To end this chapter, I want to say, the challenges you meet on your path, are highlighting new creative possibilities, evolving in perfect timing, that your

Soul Being will gift, or birth into unique expression, in the world. Plenty of early programmes get discarded & forgiven, en route. Helps when we surrender to life, in each moment, without judging or resisting, how it is happening, so all can dissolve easily into the ever-present Love. Generally, it is part of much of our Human, Earth experiences, to have a very limited perspective, of the ever-changing & evolving Mystery of Source Creation. Many Divine Highly Evolved Beings are on call for support. Some more evolved children are being born too. Who knows, in how many lives we have achieved different levels of Mastery. As I wrote these words, it was New Year's Eve 2016, a Time like no other.

Now years later, 2022, I have come to a very deep place of Love with myself, and feel safe plus, deeply trusting of Life, occasionally rocked by fear of lack, with little income. Big changes happened, with my house sold in 2019, & I made decisions which have resulted in very reduced income, yet so much support came my way. How this will pan out, I know not! Wonderful times to be alive, to exist, as the Earth planet Duality contrast between dark & light, or compassion & uncaring cruelty seems greater. Forgiveness has not seemed what was most relevant, since though I may regret many of the actions, people engage in, I am judging no-one, recognizing that not only, do so many not remember, their multi-dimensional aspect, but most likely, they decided to play certain roles, before their incarnation.

Chapter 2

Purpose

I began writing this chapter, half-way through 2012. Since the Winter Solstice, much light had been pouring in. I remember reading one of Michael Road's books, describing the showers of light he saw, at that time, on his metaphysical journeys. Increasingly, years later, strong vibratory shifts happening on our planet, affecting us all, are stirring us world-wide. Choices out-of-harmony, with our precious environment, are decimating, our wondrous landscapes, through greed, unawareness & carelessness, - this our Earth with her oceans, permafrost, snow and, ice-lands, (now melting), our mountains, valleys, marshes &, forests, gifting us endlessly, so we can breathe, up until now, eat, drink, & be spiritually blessed, by wondrous landscapes & generous diversity.

In England, Nature is impoverished, because our Councils suffer from, what Benedict Macdonald labels in his book 'Rebirding,' as E.T.D. or - 'Ecological Tidiness Disorder,' on our road verges & our gardens. These actions are killing insects, voles, resulting in birds, hedgehogs, etc., having insufficient food, from our poisoned Earth. We are not separate from Nature, so of course many of us have been getting sick! It is time for accountability, no longer ignoring actions where, the aim is supposed profit, at the expense of other life forms. Fruits & plants nourish us, so long as we do not poison our earth, destroy our insects, our birds and, other creatures. If we must sacrifice animals and plants for our food, it should be done in a more sacred way, like the American Indians, with reverent gratitude, for the life taken. The same with eggs & dairy foods. As an infinite being, in the quantum field, we will have had so many Earth lives, & surely lives in many other dimensions too. Still, we are choosing to experiment with duality, here on this free-will planet. Hopefully the Corona Virus scare will have made us more aware, that whatever the skin colours, races, superficial differences, such as the shape of our eyes or noses, we are one People. Our challenges must result, in new choices, as wise elders &, dedicated, deeply purposeful & resourceful young, look how best to serve our Planet Earth, & each other. We are born open to life, as equal beings, yet divide up our planet to be controlled, for the benefit of the few. Frontiers, armies, policing, harming others, ourselves, plus everything which can be seen. Men become strong, more often not for the joy & love of their bodies, but for defence, or to be admired. Women too, enhancing their bodies, in order to be attractive, rather than to love & honour their being.

Years ago, I received a 'Life's Purpose' Journey process. It is a journey going back, through a series of memories, whatever shows up, of difficult times, (maybe more of them, if we have lived longer), from the present, right back to the womb and the time before conception, when we were readying ourselves to incarnate. We had a clear sense prior to incarnation, as part of Divine Creator Source, of what we intended to offer, in service to life, to contribute, to a rising planetary vibratory shift. *Before incarnation, I felt I knew myself as One, with the All, and felt great Reverence, Gratitude, and Joy. I felt my mission was, to be a Channel for Love, for Healing and, to learn how to express this on Earth. I wanted also to recognize 'God' everywhere, in every molecule & form, to trust and communicate this, plus also, ...learn to laugh, with both a full, but light, heart, despite, whatever challenges and painful scenarios I might experience! My Mentor's last advice was, "Don't hold back. It matters to others that you share."*

At the Winter Solstice, eleven years later, in 2021 my intent was strong, to fulfil my Soul Purpose, the priorities of why I am here, now, & clarify, what I would most prefer to contribute, while I live in this body, maybe at least another 10 to 20 years. Publication of this book this year 2022, and the War-time letters, I finished translating, is one firm intent. My 80th birthday came, a week after I fractured my left wrist, in Oct.2020, & still, 2 yrs. later, has not regained full strength. I have had fractured bones, at times, since I was 12 yrs. old, seven or eight times, & wonder if this relates, to how much I used to find house walls & corners, too hard & solid, preferring when they were crumbling, so Nature's roots & mosses could establish a hold.

My first six or seven years, food was rationed, especially fruits. Since my twenties, I have often done much inner cleansing, with water fasts, adding lemon or grapefruit juice before coming out of the fast; other times fruit or juice fasts, or fruit and salads. While my father fought as a soldier in World War 2, our mother Lolita & me & Carmen, had plenty of goats' & cow's milk, eggs too, living next door to Lady Cecilia & family, with their hens & 'livestock.' Carmen & I, sometimes would be given the job, of collecting the eggs, from the hens' nesting places. Nature was still richly abundant, in variety of flowers, insects & wildlife, even in Brampton, a half mile from Hadrian's Wall. Recently I have read 'The Running Hare' - the secret life of farmland, by John Lewis Stempel, attempting to restore his farmland, amidst the chemically blasted lands, of the farms surrounding his land. Also 'Rebirding' which seems a very good guide book, our Councils & Governments, would do well to be learn from, to restore our land. New possibilities have been asserting themselves, primarily to do with slowing down, & reversing, the rapid despoiling, of our Earth, that has reached daily criminal proportions! I have read too, 'Dancing with Bees,' 'Wilding,' 'Biodynamic Beekeeping, etc. & other similar cries, for us to hear, before it is too late. I will add more writer's names, in the 'Resources' list at the end of this book. The latest, 'Working with Nature,' Jeremy Purseglove, 'The Hidden Life of Trees' by, Peter Wohlleben. I read 'Irreplaceable' - the fight to save our wild places, by Julian Hoffman, & found it the most difficult one to read, in the sense of it bringing me to tears, at every death from deliberate human poisons &, lack of empathy, with so much of life. An example is 'the actions of Vedanta Aluminium, in India, - 'displacing the villagers of the Dongria Kondh in the Nayagiri hills, which host sloths, bears, leopards, elephants & tigers, in a mosaic of resounding diversity. They are a subsistence-based, 8,000 strong indigenous community, in a series of hamlets, tending the fertile slopes and, harvesting the wild bamboo, jackfruits, honey, mangoes & pineapples, along with cultivating orchard crops of sweet papaya, oranges, ginger and bananas, all of which are traded, or sold in the local markets. Hundreds of waterways percolate through the hills, providing water for drinking, bathing and, cultivation, for the tribe.

Their relationship to the entire hill range is, both sacred & symbiotic…their religion, forbidding the desecration & pollution of the local sustaining environment, allowing it & its wildlife to thrive. The bauxite rich & forested mountain-tops act as enormous sponges, during the monsoon season, preventing flash floods from destroying villages, then slowly releasing the water throughout the dry season. Without the mountains, there would be no way for the tribe to exist there. So sacred & essential is the mountain, to the members of the tribe that, the cutting of the trees, on its slope, is taboo, the customary laws of the Dongria Khond premised on the principles of restraint, known as 'nyam'. As these traditional rules revolve around respect for Nature & the limits of what can be taken from the environment, the proposal in 2003 by Vedanta Aluminium, (a subsidiary of a London-listed mining company, Vedanta Resources), to build an aluminium refinery & an open-cast mine in order to extract the bauxite from beneath the Nayamgiri hills, felt like a profound & visceral desecration. It amounted to the physical abuse of everything the Dongria Kondh hold sacred. The state government however, seeing the extraction of 70million tons of ore from the mountains, as an investment that would bolster economic development, formally signed a memorandum of understanding with the company. Thus, our rulers or Governments betray us, our lands & seas & survival, for 'their' dreams of riches, created before any of them existed. Assuming they would be granted the right to mine the hills, Vedanta went ahead & constructed a smelter & refinery on the plains below them, displacing a neighbouring tribe who now live primarily on handouts in a purpose-built colony. The toxic sludge from the processing of bauxite, commonly known as 'red mud' is pumped into storage ponds on the land where the tribe previously lived. The Dongria Khond, seeing what befell their neighbours, have resisted every move made by Vedanta since then, fearing that their land, livelihoods & the dwelling place of their god would be destroyed by the mine. 'We worship the rocks, the hills, our houses & our villages, said one member of the tribe in a Survival International documentary, which was made to raise awareness of the battle his people faced. 'The mountain is our temple & our God.' Further paragraph from his book: - 'Despite the tendency amongst major world religions to ascribe the role of creation to one or more godly beings, in global terms - culturally, economically and, philosophically - our relationship to the natural world of that creation and, all its interconnected communities & systems of complex organisms, lean towards damage & abuse. And yet we assign a lofty degree of custodianship, propriety & respect to the human constructs, intended to honour the divine. As though the churches, synagogues, mosques, chapels. monasteries & temples of our own creation were intrinsically more valuable than the world itself. Deserving greater veneration than the nature that many of those sacred systems uphold as, the works of the supreme creators.' Indeed, our clothes, beds, food, drinks, homes, lap-tops, heating, the air we breathe, 'All' – come from this Creation, we daily abuse or profit from & depend on, for survival!!!

In Bob Dylan's words, 'When will we ever learn?' indeed.

I loved what Julian H. wrote about Henry Bestons' year, living in a cabin he built for himself, in the dunes, by an extremely exposed shoreline, on the U.S.A. Cape Cod Eastern seaboard, in the 1920's. He lived observing & sharing intimately, how everything in the wildness, survived extreme conditions, & Ocean storms, thus, became - 'well acquainted,' with the endurance required & challenges faced - by humans too. This gave birth to what Julian Hoffman called 'Bestons' fully luminous book, 'The Outermost House.' I loved Julian's H's deep honouring of Bestons' empathy & his understanding that, our viewing wild animals as, somehow lesser than us, was a failure of the imagination, an inability to empathize with other creatures & see, with clarity, their own inimitable brilliance.' - 'We need another & a wiser and perhaps more mystical concept of animals… We patronize them for their incompleteness, for their tragic fate of having taken form, so far below ourselves. And therein we err, and greatly err. For the animal shall not be measured by man. They are not brethren, they are not underlings; they are other natives caught with ourselves, in the net of life and time, fellow prisoners of the splendour and the travail of the earth.' - (a very short segment from this very in-depth book)! I am finding Julian Hoffman's book, the most harrowing of all these books, warning us about our deeply destructive ways of relating to all of Nature, including us. He seems to be going world-wide to find out what is happening to our eco-system, in our waters, on our Earth, in our skies, wherever. 'Field Notes from a Catastrophe, a frontline report on Climate Change,' by Elizabeth Kolbert, is equally alarming.

Today, deep sorrow arose, in me, when meditating, about every act of cruelty, by less than 'human(e)' beings, decimating all other life forms as well as ourselves, periodically, on our 'wonder-full' Planet! I am very glad that 'Ecocide' may soon, get to be seen as, an offence, as punishable & accountable as 'Genocide,' the sooner, the better.

*

Before going further, I want to quote from 'Co-Creative Science,' by Machaelle Small Wright, as to the nature of **Purpose**, as relates to the Soul. 'Perelandra, her garden playground, is also a nature research centre, founded by her in 1977. This research is centred around 'learning about nature in new ways, from nature itself.' ...and further, --' As a result of her research with nature, at Perelandra, she developed a new science, she called "co-creative science." Traditional science has been man's study of reality and how it works, from a more mechanical & limited viewpoint. Co-creative science is the study of reality and, how it works from nature's perspective and, by human and nature working together in a peer, balanced partnership.' Since my trust of Nature is deep, I trust Nature's (and her), definitions in her book. The whole book is deeply fascinating, but I am just quoting from Chapter 1, (so have left the spelling as it was in the original book). (Nature's communication in italics), regarding Purpose, Soul, plus 'involution/evolution balance'. 'Because nature supplies all form, and because all form, has combined with its consciousness, all matter has inherent in it two dynamics: an *involution* dynamic (the matter, means and action) that is supplied by nature and an *evolution* dynamic (the definition, direction and purpose) that is supplied by consciousness.' Still quoting, '*Humans tend to think of the soul as being something, that is far away from them, because they are in form. This is an illusion. The core of any life **is** the soul. It cannot exist as apart from itself. Like the heart in a human body, it is an essential part of a life unit.... SOUL: It is most difficult to define soul, since - at its point of central essence---the soul is beyond form. Consequently, it is beyond words. .... Souls as individuated life forces, were created and fused with form, in the moment of, the Big Bang. Beyond form, souls are also beyond the notion of creation........*

When a soul chooses to move within the vast band of form, it communicates its intent and purpose to nature. It is from this, that nature derives the specifics that will be needed, for the soul to function in form. It is a perfect marriage of purpose with order, organization and, life vitality, that is needed for the fulfilment of that purpose. Nature therefore, does not define purpose and impose it on a human soul. It orders, organizes and, gives life vitality to purpose, for expression in form.'

'The glitch to our human 'i/e' balance - (i/e means here, (involution/evolution)), is free will. We can make our free will jump right in the middle of our i/e balance and use it to distort our intuitive understanding of the soul's definition, direction and, purpose.' Obviously if we override our Soul purpose, with our preferences and desires through will-power, there are then two sets, of directions and purpose, likely to result in health issues, imbalance, and inner conflict..... Because of free will, involution/evolution balance is a difficult dynamic to maintain.

We frequently jump into the middle of it. For us, i/e balance rests not only on our ability to trust in the movement of our own soul, but also in our ability to consciously translate and perceive our soul's definition, direction and purpose and not use our free will to try to manipulate our soul. This is one of the things we are here, on Earth to learn: the marrying of our conscious selves to our souls and the full fusion of this with our physical bodies. I am not implying that consciously achieving our i/e balance is easy. I am only using an example, that is familiar to us all, in order to make i/e balance more easily understood. Well, if it was just left up to our soul and, nature, we would experience perfect i/e balance easily. It is free will, that adds the elements of excitement, confusion and, challenge. As we develop and discipline our free will, we expand our understanding to include the wisdom to know when and how to appropriately apply free will, and our experience of i/e balance will be unencumbered and beyond words.'

I would happily add another 9 or 10 pages at least, of nature's information. (Since I am quoting, I have left the words, almost as written in Machaelle Small Wright's book). I will continue my story.

I am aware, my over-lighting Guide at this time is, Melchizedek, (see the book of Hebrews, presenting the order of Melchizedek as the order of the 'New covenant' established by Jesus, - very different from the Levitical priesthood), maybe even in all time, I do not know.

I originally learnt this name, **from a being I met in a meditation** &, I did not remember, hearing the name before, so, years later I asked a clairvoyant, (still alive I believe, in Glastonbury, in 2022) 'Who is my over-lighting guide in this life?' then, blanked my mind, while she went deeper. After 2 or 3 minutes, she said '**Melchizedek**'. I had not otherwise, consciously connected with him.

Even as this chapter is being written, I am putting out, strong prayers of intent, to my guides, to my Soul, to fully align with my Soul purpose. There will likely be much of my life story, in this chapter, so it will be longer, but hopefully both at times, I receive clear guidance &, while navigating a way, through scenarios of pain & suffering, more unconsciously, hidden gifts will be revealed.

I had found reading my father's memoirs helpful, in gaining clarity about my parents, & our early years. So often, I wished I had asked my mother more, before she died, about her earlier life in Spain, yet I never asked her questions. Of course, during my recent translating, of the hundreds of War-time letters, written from late 1937 till 1946, between Lolita and Kenneth, to each other, it has given me, more clarity, & a much more intimate, understanding now, of their relationship to each other &, their parenting of me, Carmen & later, Cristina. Blessings on us all. Since undertaking that task, I have read too, so much specific information, from Laurie Lee, George Orwell, Paul Preston & other writers who experienced the Spanish Civil War, followed by World War 2. These books are listed on the Resources page. I have certainly wondered aloud, recently, with my sisters why, a home, of family unity & happiness did not follow, once our parents finally were reunited, their overriding years-long, most longed for, aim. I believe our mother's health & happiness, was affected life-long thereafter, by War experiences plus, her long-time, unresolved childhood trauma.

At present, 2022, many of my books are in storage, bit by bit coming to light & either kept, given away or recycled. Among them is a small book by, I trust I recall, St. Hilarion, about 'The nature of Reality.' Why grass is being grass, cows being cows, the lessons being learned, from taking on, each chosen form. Everything is Consciousness! I am reminded that, for many years, lying in bed, when I was younger, periodically, I would start losing my sense of being in my warm body. I felt I was a stone, with some different coloured consistency vein, running through. I got used to knowing, when this change was taking over my body. I love stones & crystals, - have some of my favourite ones of many sizes, with me, wherever I live, in my room(s) or the pockets of clothes I wear.

April 2nd 2022, Samantha with her husband Mick, & eldest son Michael, came to Stroud, very willingly, to help empty one of my Storage units, if it is manageable! Many of my crystals & books were there. I find it easier to let go of books, than crystals! I have done quite a lot more clearing since &, I have let go of many things from my past, but many crystals & some books, have found a place in my room. Feels good to let go of much of my past, too. Their son Michael, is now a handsome young man. They offered to return, so now I/we, have cleared half a unit, I want to transfer the furniture, from the 2nd unit into the other half of the 1st one. I feel sure it is doable! Today, September 16th, friend Rob, picked up the last 2 remaining heavy items, & took them to Stroud Furniture collection point! Everyday magic! So, down to one storage unit! This has internally lifted some of the weight, of all those possessions from 25yrs. of family life or so, in Stroud, plus whatever came with me, from 30yrs. of London life, in my Wormwood Scrubs Council house, - made more inner space in me!

Since I traded in crystals for years, I have many favourites bought at trade prices. Books easier to let go of, than my favourite crystals, though I was glad to give Guy & Penny some specials too of the latter. I have also been donating some to a local crystal shop.

During online Stargate Academy meditations, I have been connecting for years, with Alcazar, (participating, via Stargate portals, in journeying in the Quantum field, with thousands of others, around the world), channelled through Julieanne & Prageet. Recently, while listening to replays a 2nd time, rather than finding myself flying off, to higher, lighter realms, - this inter-dimensional wisdom, the channelled messages shared, have been coming right into my Earth body, thus fuelling unexpected happenings, such as one day, a very direct energetic embrace of my child self, & calling me Sonelle. I burst into tears, enveloped by a big energy wave of Love, - Sonelle was my childhood name, & so I was called, until Osho gave me the name, Prem Sonelle. My breast/heart/throat area is full, of energized heat, as in earlier years when, I was directing healing energy, through 'Quantum touch' etc. filling my fingers & hands too. It is interesting to me, that this last June Solar Eclipse, which in the U.K. in the S.W., was on Thurs.10th, between 10a.m. to 12.30p.m. I found myself suddenly very focussed, and setting into motion, whatever I must, for this book, to be published. The heat in my heart area, suddenly felt just as strong, in my left side too, as though, there is a new strength, in feeling my innate gifts acknowledged, and being supported, in a wider way. Since then, the warmth has spread upwards, through my throat & into my head or pineal gland area. The heat has been spreading too down to my sacral area and, I had been focussing on grounding this deep into the Earth, walking barefoot in the park. Days ago, (about 18 years, after being given a pastel drawing, in a Mind Body Spirit show, of Ja Karook, with an attached message!), it had turned up from my storage facility, unexpectedly, so, I decided to follow instructions, & look into his eyes. 'Wow'! He really did connect with me, as, I felt a strong 'whoosh' of energy, shoot down through my body, deep into the Earth, the first time I tried, days ago. Ja Karook, my Mayan guide, known by me, in a previous Mayan life, I am told. I have been feeling much Joy, in my Being, for many weeks or months, now, from my Stargate meditations, especially from the most recent programme, 'Into the Void,' which is a new experience for me, with our Global, mainly online Community, of thousands of us world-wide! (In 70 countries, at the latest count)! Joy, eluded me for so long. We meet physically from time to time, in different venues, & Countries, though for me so far, only in England. How deeply blessed I feel. I trust Alcazar, (the name given to the group of Masters), lovingly assisting us, deepen our connection with our multi-dimensional Being. I feel a growing warm connection, as well as with, various other, high-dimensional guides. (I especially 'pranaam' (i.e., 'bow with reverence,' deeply, to Haidakhan Babaji – especially after that dream I mentioned in Chapter 1). I trust Alcazar, it feels good. We are truly grateful.

Diana Cooper's Unicorn books, have connected me too, with the world of Unicorns, existing in dimensions of more light, such as the 7th & 9th, & I would love to remain in this body until at least 2032, when her Angels have assured us, light & harmony will have prevailed in all Countries of the Earth.

I will continue writing about events in my life, (during nearly 82 yrs.), seemingly pertinent, in relation to the theme of this chapter, gaining clarity on, how my sense of purpose, has revealed itself. May I clearly mirror back, for some of you, twists & turns in your own lives, thus fostering compassion for yourselves as well as, all 'other.' **This** moment, always a perfect moment, here now, & now, life-giving, breath-taking, exquisite, wondrous 'IS-ness,' - an Existence whose magic, we've many times failed to love & acknowledge. We are one Being, choosing to experience free-will, via separate body selves. Each seemingly other story, is part of our story.

*

My name Prem Sonelle, given by Bhagwan Shree Rajneesh, (a.k.a. Osho), came with his message; "see the Path of Love as Music." Music has seemed to burble always, like a stream, through my body, enjoyed almost like magic sunshine sparkles, harmony, colour, flowing in & out, orgasmic vibrancy, wildness, emotion &, order, sound &, still Silence. Despite music being a key to my heart, and having experienced, various other lives as a musician, my motivation to focus on music, in a more disciplined way, was not this time strong. I played various instruments with no great skill, nor dedication, (other than a good ear for exact tone), such as my violin, and more recently, my accordion. It feels a heavy instrument to physically lift now. My favourite T.V. show has been 'The Voice,' with Tom Jones, Will-I-Am, Olly Murs and Anne-Marie. Today, in August 2022, I hear the programme is returning, next month! As it did!

Like my mother, I always enjoyed sewing; making, altering & mending clothes for myself and family. I usually have sewing jobs, on the go, some recently completed, for friend Sandra, others I am transforming or mending, for myself & others. I have a good sense of colour harmony. I choose to make my clothes strong, (using strong thread), rather than being fussy about attempting to match, my mother's skill & neatness. Sewing is quite relaxing. Knitting is not for me!

I was young, a child, when I began consciously, to try to fathom, why I did not feel happy. I remember my compulsion one day, to escape from home, feeling so alone & alienated. I must have been between 7 & 10yrs.old. I walked to my school neighbourhood, about 5 miles away. That evening, as I wandered the streets with, a stray kitten I had found, with no plan of where I would sleep, my father found me. He had alerted the police, but did not get angry nor, make any big fuss. I had not anticipated, their being concerned to find me, & did not object, to being taken back, other than having to let go of the kitten.

As I tell some of my stories, I am describing different influences, strands that have seemed to seed, my life choices or, sense of purpose.

*

My mother had me and my sisters, baptised as Catholics, in case it would serve in some way, such as being allowed into Spain. Reminds me of the book I just read, 'Always Remember Your Name, The Children of Auschwitz,' where getting baptised as Catholics might be, a protection against incineration, in the Gas chambers. My father called himself an atheist. He would sometimes praise the Russian revolution, of 1917, which reflected his ongoing idealistic stance, somewhat diluted I realize, after his years as a soldier. Our mother, a 'lapsed' Catholic was, a Communist, (though I was never aware of that), like my father. They saw Communism as the ideal, seemingly not aware of the parallels between Hitler, Mussolini, Franco &, - Stalin! We children, were left to navigate our own paths. Carmen & I tried out, once we were in the Midlands, the village Methodist chapel, later the Protestant church, the former more relaxed & friendly, though giving me, no sense of God, nor any deeper meaning nor purpose. I found Protestant churches cold, somewhat austere, without heart. From my mother, I did get a greater sense of mystery, of other unseen dimensions of life, both after 'death' &, within this perceived reality, thus confirming my sense, that there was more.

*

My love for the insect, wild plant, bird and, the animal kingdoms, started very young. My early life near Brampton, Cumberland, was rich, in time enjoying extensive gardens & fields, walks through nearby beautiful woodland, by a stream, with bluebells, many red squirrels & birds, as well as domestic animals aplenty, near to home. Most probably, most of the land around Chris Cottage & the Chris House many-roomed ancestral home, would have belonged to the Roberts family, with their farm Manager, keeping a check on the area. However much, Kenneth & Lolita with their Communist ideals, were uncomfortable, with being beholden to 'the Gentry,' the fact is, for me & Carmen, Lolita too, despite a predominantly wet climate, our environment was a haven for Nature. Life in the cottage, though so damp, was a blessing for us, safely away from falling bombs. My love for wild life and insects, fields and woods began here. Cristina born January 1946, lived here more briefly. On my 2015 visit, 70yrs. later, I still viscerally felt, this land of hills & valleys, to be my motherland. One unpleasant early vivid memory, maybe as a nearly 10yrs.old child, in1950 I guess, seems to be in Spain, when we three children first visited Santander.

I was crouched with other children, around a deep well, all except me, laughing, at a grasshopper's frantic thrashing about in the water, trying to save itself. I am inconsolably crying about its' plight. Over the years, I looked after caterpillars, silk-worms too, & one time a white mouse. I was taking good care of her, so I believed, but one day put my hand in her soft nest, to clean it, and she bit me. I did not realize, some of the cotton wool I had removed, was in fact, her baby mice, discovered days later, on my father's compost heap. I felt terrible!

An earlier related memory is later, in Huddersfield, in the sooty fields by our home, too near, the big ICI factory spewing out, its sooty clouds of polluting waste. I found a birds' nest, put in my hand, crushing by mistake one of the eggs. I felt so guilty, but felt soothed when I explored further, & came into a field full of sweet pea flowers, of delightful colours, & scent. I never lost this love of exploring Nature's diverse wonders, enjoying watching insects closely, snails laying their eggs, ant colonies, exploring woodland, hedgerows of nuts, fruits, hidden birds, hearing the frequent notes of, the cuckoo calls, enjoying my secret dens, (especially during thunder storms), gathering field mushrooms, feeling connected & at home, in a way I did not find so easy, with people. I loved gardening too, though I mostly planted wild flowers. In every home I have lived in, since living in the Midlands, I have painted murals, mainly of trees. I love trees & have read 'The Hidden Life of Trees' by Peter Wohlleben, a gift on my 81st birthday from my sister Cristina, which I think should be required reading for Foresters! I would say my love for Nature & all animal/bird/insect life, was deeper generally, than my love for the world of people, for at least 69yrs. It seems clear, that when deciding, my life direction or Purpose, when young, I did not follow the direction of what I most loved, i.e., painting, writing, or caring in a bigger way, to the needs of animals or, the Earth. I did start to sell pictures, I painted on hardboard, but though I have continued to paint tree murals, in every home I have lived in, (except where I live now, as I re-edit my book), I clearly knew, healing, was to be my path, without knowing how I knew this. I qualified in many massage modalities; hypnotherapy, 'skenar' therapy etc. etc, but I did not find a true direction, for over 40yrs. when 'The Journey', in Nov.2003, became a trusted path for self-healing, & holding the space for others to use the same tools. For the first time, from Nov.2003, I had real tools I trusted, which have been powerful in my own healing & for holding the space, for the hundreds of men & women, world-wide, to find their healing, for nearly 19yrs. so far.

Cats, have always, I recall, been my friends. I always smile at them half-closing my eyes in cat language, with accompanying heart smile, to which they respond. Our 1st cat as a child, was Bonita, in Brampton. I have shared so much time with many, many cats. (One day, strangely,

I felt a fleeting energy of a Tiger speed through my body). My first kitten in my teens, had tortoiseshell coloured fur. We were so close, that even when I went on bike-rides, she sat on my shoulder. Sadly, she only felt at home while I was living there, so every time I returned to London, for the University term, she would disappear. Back home one holiday, I was cycling, miles from home & saw her! I called "Kitty, Kitty!" &, she came running to me, & rode back home on my shoulder. One time I made friends with a wild cat, at the bottom of the garden, who had given birth to her kittens, in our pigsty. Misguidedly, I took Kitty to meet her, thinking they would be friends. Instead, I had the shock of a wild cat, attacking me in fury, feeling betrayed by me, and leaving a scar on my leg. She took her kittens away, that night. The first cat I had, after leaving my childhood home, was from the East End community where I had lived with Bob. They had decided to have him doctored. I wanted to save him from his fate, so with Bob, plus my friend Angela, and her partner John, (a friend from the Community where Bob, had first met me), we moved, still in the 60's, to North London, plus cat! (Angela later came to Formentera with me one year, met my friend Jose, & they too, became long-term good friends. She died some years ago of leukaemia, & I felt honoured to be at her funeral, as we had remained friends. She was a beautiful soul being, of Spanish, & Irish heritage).

Thomasina, (left abandoned I seem to recall, in the next-door house in Latimer Rd.?) - was an excellent hunter, especially when she had kittens. She used to go to the Ceres bakery (1/2 mile away), for her prey, rats! The cats devoured all the insides, not the tail. (Ceres based in Portobello Road, West London, was one of the first UK real community, organic food shops. I could be wrong, as Lampeter, Wales, was at the heart of the organic veg. growing revolution, and there's still often more sense of community, than in England. Stroud is an exception)! Thomasina came, after the bulldozing of our home, with me & Berris. After the Squatters' Amnesty, through the Greater London Council, our next long-term home was very near Wormwood Scrubs, and the Prison. Here the cats multiplied, the female cats had kittens. Some lived in the garden. Softy & Turtle, I was especially close with, and I was telling Softy I loved her, as she lay on my chest, an hour before she was killed on the road. One male cat left and, was away for years, yet came back home to die. I deeply regretted once, deciding to find homes for some of them, as a lady with cages, arrived, & the ungentle way, she put them in these cages, I suddenly felt deep misgiving, about what their fate would be. I wished I had said, 'I've changed my mind.' Another cat I bought off the Spanish gypsies, & smuggled through the Customs, to England, ended up run over. We had visitor hedgehogs too, who liked to share the cat food. Later, in the 1990's, living in Stroud, (in the South West of England), my cat Ember, I loved so deeply, was killed on the road, when only 18mths.old, as he had started to explore further afield, and Ember's sister, I had given to the next-door girls, suffered the same fate. I felt more affected by Ember's death, than the death of my parents, as, such deep unconditional love and healing is shared with our animal friends. I have said no since, to 'owning' more cats, while in Slad Road, enjoying instead, so much more contact, with the garden birds, who have really trusted me.

Though we had a couple of dogs at different times, my father took responsibility for them, so I missed becoming close. I still feel guilt, about every time, since I was a child, I was ever less than kind, to a dog. The worst, is remembering, when we were very young sisters, in my father's car, as he was taking our dog Tico to somewhere, where we feared he would be disposed of. We never saw him again. My parents had planned a visit to Spain, for I know not, how many weeks. I do not remember them ever, trying to relieve our distress, in such situations. The three of us children, were sobbing in sorrow. I have been told by mediums, there are dogs waiting to greet me, when I leave this physical body. Dogs are more unpredictable, as they take on, more so than cats, much of their 'owners' emotional reactions. I have never been interested in being a vet, given my deep mistrust of doctors & their pharmaceutical 'remedies.' I did consider in later childhood, being a farmer's wife!

The year 2019, when I was first contemplating, taking the appropriate steps to get this book printed, I had been living, in Penny & Guy's home, no.22 Slad Road, since September. This came about totally unexpectedly, during the process of selling my no.18 Slad Rd. Stroud home. Penny invited me to move to their home, the other side of Maurice & Jane, no.22 Slad Rd., on condition that, I paint a mural, in her bathroom. I have never been clear, whether the offer was made on the spur of the moment, without due thought. I burst into tears, as, though I had been very focussed, for a long time, on living in trust & surrender, I **had** wondered, if my car, was to become my main U.K. home! In my new home, my room overlooked the garden, and my joy in the twilight morning hrs., was to watch, all the different birds, including jackdaws, coming to feed, and their interactions, around the many bird feeders, in the quiet early mornings. The blackbirds know me, from my no.18 garden. Their cat is called Beatrice, and their dog, Boosh, and I have felt my heart, so warm & open, to Boosh, for many months, more so than with any other dog, in this life, though I love Beatrice too. Boosh, was a Saluki-sheepdog mix, & I was privileged to become chief dog walker. She has recently left her body for pastures new, as she was getting feeble, in her 13th year. It was such a privilege, to have enjoyed my time with her. I recently read 'Soul Dog' by Elena Mannes, though it seems to be written for those, who are not aware of the Conscious intelligence, in all of Life. I was given a stray dog, Patch, during my Portobello Market crystal stall years, by good friend Jeremy, who could no longer keep him; and he was indeed inclined to stray at times, usually ending up at the police station. He was also my travelling companion. Before he died, I slept every night next to him on the ground, stroking him to help him through his discomfort. He probably missed having more of a purpose plus, enough walking in his life, not having wildness around him, nor sheep to herd. I saw an inner image, of him racing through, a sunny long grass meadow, after his death, and felt he was happy. Yet my vision of my perfect home, in some future reality, would/will include an area, providing wild life, with protection. Dogs, cats, cows, horses, & so many other animals, serve humanity, in so many ways. I noticed when I went Christmas 2019, to my sister Cristina's home, I felt much closer to Barley, (more of a white sand colour than 'Golden' Retriever), than I had done, in previous years. A new 'rescue' dog has joined her, since Barley's 'death.' Recently, I have been setting up, an etheric 'Stargate' in her kitchen, for her dog, as his health is challenged, and for Cristina too. I will say more about 'Stargates,' later in this book.

(Since I wrote that, I have been with Sandra in Spain, from September 6th 2020, until November 3rd this time, back to Lakabe Ecovillage, relating closely to the animals, landscape & men, women & children, we visited briefly & unexpectedly last year, in the Navarra hills). I had been wanting to connect, especially with Basque people, of the Nth. West area, given my heritage, ever since translating, my parents' War-time letters. (Lolita, my mother was born in La Rioja & my genetic heritage is ½ Basque, from 3 of her grandparents).

On our return, we went for the requisite quarantine period, i.e., a fortnight, to Sandra's, Welsh mountain cottage &, since my return, I have been living in Ish & Daxa's home. It is somewhat noisier, as instead of garden, there is a road, noisy during the day, so my view is of houses, though one tree. I felt sad, at Boosh being less in my life than I anticipated. Penny had said, I could use their home as my U.K. base, but while we were in Spain, she & Guy decided they needed to reclaim the space. She had thought I would be living in Spain, & just visit the U.K. from time to time. They are having an extension built, for Penny's Dad, in his 90's, though while fit enough, he does prefer independence. I know the feeling. Thus, somewhat sadly, & unexpectedly, though with grateful relief, I was soon living in Ish & Daxa's home. Ish is a very long time, well-loved & appreciated friend. More ease is slowly developing with Daxa, whom I like, but English is not a language she has mastered & we've little in-depth conversation or 'common ground.' I am grateful to have a home &, be picking up the threads of my Stroud life, since the quarantine imposition. It has been a very turbulent time, in 2020 to 2022, on Planet Earth, so far, widespread sickness globally, according to the media, as well as, much fear, panicked & **unwelcome** legislation & control. There is little awareness, that fast foods, our domination of Nature, to the detriment everywhere of diversity, of other life-forms, plus the pharmaceutical industry, giving us synthetic imitations of plants' healing natural medicines, to suppress symptoms, will have weakened our immune systems. We are part of Nature and, have been destroying our eco-system, with indiscriminate use of pesticides, which is the same as killing ourselves!

I have been quite tested too, these last months, as I fractured my left wrist, in a very sudden accident, while climbing among the rocks and trees, nr. Lakabe in Navarra, thus making me more dependent on help, for many normally simple tasks. Sandra, my travel/adventure Welsh sister & I, were staying in Lakabe eco-community, when I had my accident, in October 2020. However, I am also aware, that higher vibrational energies, plus, huge influxes of, Light and Love, are coming in more strongly too, and everything which is not that, is showing itself too! Part of the shift happening for Planet Earth…

Communal living, can bring both richness, heart-warming interactions plus, extra, challenging dramas. Looking back on the 11 or 12 varied Communities, I have lived in, some more deliberate & contained, others more loose-knit, I find living with myself, gives me more daily choice and peace. Land has, this year 2021, been purchased near Glastonbury, for yet another U.K. Babaji Gathering place! I will say no more about that, except, I hope it becomes a haven for Nature & people, of Loving sharing, Joy & creativity. They have been planting trees there, I am happy about.

*

In my secondary Girls' High school, I had a best friend, Elaine. There was not all that sniggering about body changes, being an all-girls school, unlike the previous mix, of boys and girls. Being the only two in our class, who loved to draw and paint, we so loved colours, and each other's company too, we usually, would be given some project for, the two of us, to focus on, seated at the back of, some other class. We took 'O' level exams, when we were 16yrs.old, including Art, after which Elaine left for Art College, but I stayed on another 2yrs. preparing for 'A' level exams in Art & languages. Elaine & I loved gymnastics, especially handstands, rope climbing, outdoor adventures, plus swimming, climbing trees, and roaming in fields and gardens, but we loved too, to probe more deeply inwardly. Scientology became a focus for a while. Neither of us doubted the existence of inner and outer, unseen 'realities.' After she left, Claire became my main friend, together with a more loosely-knit group, who met outside school for cycling, swimming, tennis, walking & general social gathering. Claire & I, travelled whenever we could, throughout England, Scotland, Wales, & Ireland, also in Europe, walking, staying in Youth hostels, which ranged from wooden cabins, to grand mansions, some very remote, occasionally in cities, such as Vienna. We loved exploring, enjoyed too, the beauty of the landscapes, plus sharing adventures.

This love has stayed always with me, of adventures. Claire's body is more challenged by health concerns, these days. My friend Sandra & I, walked in 2006, from Stroud to the Carmarthen hills, via the old ways, the Severn way, Wye Valley walk, Offa's Dyke & onwards, 258 miles in 15 days. We wanted to keep walking! She is still my main adventure travel sister-friend! – &, I still love walking, in this, my 81st year. She is in her 60's, yet my frequent choice of raw, organic-grown food, & much walking, best supports my health. As a child, I had roamed the fields with my sisters, but enjoyed most time, on my own, delighting in wild flowers and birds, intimately connecting with plants, the world of insects, the rabbit warren, picking mushrooms, eating sorrel leaves & blackberries, loving to climb and sit high in the trees. In Stroud, in April, I gathered nettle tops & wild garlic, for my salads.

*

Claire was from an Irish Catholic family. I started to go to her church with her, especially enjoying the Christmas Midnight Mass, and at 17yrs.old, I decided to be a Catholic, enjoying devotional fervour, the greater sense of sacredness and communion, the incense too! A lovely young Irish Nun, taught me the 'catechism,' so I went through a Confirmation ritual, taking on the added name 'Teresa,' after Santa Teresa de Avila. That 'phase,' lasted 5yrs. before my doubts became too strong, to stay on this path. In fact, it was a Priest, the prison Catholic chaplain, with whom I shared most, regarding my rising doubts. Formerly, he had been a tramp, and was very open and caring. My interest, even renewed my mother's involvement, with the church. (Interestingly, some years later, when Samantha my daughter was 8yrs.old, and we were living in a tent, by orange groves, in wooded hills, I had read tales to her, in Spanish, about Jesus Christ, and encouraged her confirmation as a Catholic, in a local village church. She enjoyed being dressed in her white 'bridal' dress, receiving gifts afterwards, from the villagers)! Her Catholicism did not last. (In my room here in Stroud, in 2022, I have pictures of Babaji, of Christ, the Dalai Lama, Tara, the Buddha, Anastasia, (written about by Vladimir Megre), Ammaji, a carved Cobra, as I honour the truth at the Source of all the ways. Babaji is closest to my heart, and in my regular Stargate meditations, I also invite Lu Yin, Gezra, the dragons, Star families from the Pleiades, Lyra, Sirius & other star systems. I have no visual picture of the Alcazar group of Masters, who are channelled through Prageet & Julieanne. I do feel their love! Thousands of us, from every Country, connect daily, in Stargate meditations, (sometimes too with Kryon, or Asil Toksal plus other channels of the Elohim Council of Angels), or other beings, from higher realms in the Quantum energy field. Many miracles happen, of healing and other manifestations. In fact, since the last week of 'Becoming Superconscious' until now, in Summer 2020, since moving 'Into the Void', Alcazar's most recent gift to me, has been that I now experience my body, **permanently filled with the warmth of Love/Joy, from sacrum to pineal gland & beyond**. I feel the love from Alcazar. Since the boost from Ja Karuk, pronounced Ikarook, my Earth connection has deeper roots! I feel deeply blessed. Joy eluded me for so long! This heart-felt 'Joy/Warmth' now seems permanent, as it has been constantly with me now, for months. After hearing Julieanne & Barbara Blum, discussing the 'rise of kundalini energy,' I have understood that what I am experiencing from sacrum to heart & out through my head, may well be a different way of experiencing this. It does not have to rise, up the spine.

I have added a carved Unicorn from the Faery shop, in Stroud, to my treasures, as I was just starting to connect to the 7th dimensional Unicorns, since reading Diana Coopers Unicorn books); a female white & light grey flecked friendly one called Rebecca. The next morning, a more shining white male unicorn, was standing a little apart, whereas Rebecca is nudging me in a friendly way. I love the Faery lady's creations & have too, a faery in repose, plus a woman's body with toadstools or mushrooms, rooted into her 'dead' body, plus most recently, a dragon lying in repose.

Back to my early twenties: I chose to study in **London** University, after school was done, feeling I would be at the hub of everything! It took me months, to get accustomed to London's traffic noise. The first year, I found a home with a warm and friendly Catholic family. Though it seemed they treated me, warmly, as a welcome part of their family, months later I got thrown out. After Mass in Westminster Cathedral, I had met Hank, (an American student in the London School of Economics), and he had become my 'boy-friend,' who later wanted to marry me. I could not say yes! I had not yet opened to Love, was not even aware sexually, nor ever had deeply kissed, nor had sex, was not even connected enough with my body, to feel desire, with him anyway. I had some notion that, women were meant to lie passive, receive, and were used by men for sex. I probably got that idea from my mother! Anyway, I had little illusions about happy marriages, so had said 'No.' I had written in my diary, I had lain in his bed one night, (though having little idea, what was expected), so we both made no further moves! And no doubt, that would have been that! However, my Catholic landlady, took it upon herself, presumptuously assuming it to be her right, to read my diary so, though I was a young adult, she had seemingly decided, I might be a bad influence on her young daughter, with whom I so often enjoyed playing, (I cannot imagine how), - an ungodly being such as me! She never thought, to give me good advice, rather than condemn me without a trial. I led a virginal life for at least another 5yrs.

In the Summer holidays, I had worked as a petrol pump attendant, where I had made a new friend Paddy, a young Irishman. He was at home in pubs, took me to the one next to 'my' Petrol Station, where he introduced me to a 'whisky mac,' thus, for the 1st time, experiencing slight tipsiness, once or twice. (Quite liked the taste, though I have never enjoyed the taste of any alcohol, in the 60+ years since! Previously, I had been used, in Europe, of course, to taste wine with meals, but did not like it anyway. Paddy & I enjoyed walking in Epping Forest, & other very simple pleasures. Though he hoped for more, there was no pressure. My landlady contacted my parents, to inform them, they had to come & get me, so, I packed my suitcase, and bags & left forthwith! I left the heavy luggage for my parents, but did not return home till I felt ready, maybe 10 days later. I slept in Paddy's van for days, and focussed on painting lovely scenes on the inside of his van, while he was at work. I felt disillusioned and despondent about life and relationships, conflict too about Catholicism. Paddy had a wife in Ireland. Again, we never engaged in sex, and I encouraged him, as the good Catholic I was, to go back to his wife!

*

In my 2nd year of London University, my close friend Elaine, from school, and I had reconnected, as she was still in St. Martin's College of Art, near Soho, so we decided, to live together, first in Leytonstone, near my East End College, then the year after, moving to Bayswater, frequented, as it turned out, by many prostitutes. We were in in our early twenties, and while we were living there, met our downstairs neighbour Des., of Caribbean origin, leader of a Steel band, and through him, the rest of his band. One memorable evening, they introduced us to a ritual, where we all stood in a circle, somehow entering a state of semi-trance, the focus being to feel filled with spirit. Not very deeply. Soon after, we both independently decided, the same week, it was time to 'lose' our virginity. She chose Des, and I chose Miguel from Des' band. We had not given up our flat, but I was staying with Miguel. He was a gentle, kind companion, who liked to please me, but at that time, maybe because just feeling affection was not enough, I was not sure, why sex, was said to be so blissful. I did enjoy the sense of companionship & felt at ease with him &, his community of Caribbean friends. When he had a gig, he and I had more food, special treats, yet there was never any feeling of stress, nor lack. All was friendly and relaxed ease, for weeks, until he voiced his idea of me, as his potential good, Catholic, white wife-to-be. I just could not have borne, such a restricted life, so could not fit in the box. He was ashamed of his darker Father, as was his mother! He tried one day to stop me going, on an anti-nuclear protest. I went wild and scratched his face, as he did not want, to let me out of our room. I am unsure why, being locked in, or out, of 'home,' the 2 or 3 times I remember, once by Carmen, once by Berris, brought up such rage. When my father chased me, not a frequent occurrence, I would escape by a drain pipe! Feeling I would have to, contract my life, to fit into Miguel's idea of a future together, I had to move out.

At that time, I was going on many demonstrations, and periodically in and out, of Holloway Prison. After CND protests, I had involved myself in direct action led, by the Committee of 100, which had Bertrand Russell as a supporting Voice! The first time I was threatened with prison, for civil disobedience, if I did not pay a fine within 28 days, since I had no intention of paying, I gave up the flat, and decided on a 5 weeks holiday in Spain. I enjoyed the break, and connected also with Spanish political exiles in Carcassonne, France, making new friends. (Have read various Paul Preston books, in 2020, which give much detail of the total confusion and chaos, from July 1936, to the sad, fascist style events, leading to the end of the Republic of Spain, - most recently, the one detailing Franco's life, from a boy, onwards). Anyway, I came back, walked freely to a police station, delivered myself to my fate, and had my personal belongings confiscated immediately! A police car took me from London to Reading, that same afternoon, where a court procedure was set up just for me! Soon enough, off I was bundled, in a 'Black Maria' to Holloway, that same evening. There my clothes & remaining personal effects, were taken, and after a shower, plus an inspection for possible head-lice, I was given ill-fitting prison clothes, then escorted, with various stops, involving jangling keys, for the unlocking and locking of heavy doors, to my small cell. It is shocking, the way prisoners, are seen as scum, in the eyes of some of the warders, (whom we called screws), and society. In those days, I resisted or opposed, police, judges, doctors, teachers or, any authority, using their power to control my life, especially my father. (My parents were both teachers)! Our prison food was porridge, for breakfast, with a little sugar (from our couple of teaspoonful's daily ration), dinner, potatoes, maybe a bit of over-cooked veg., a small hunk of cheese for vegetarians, sliced bread & margarine for tea, plus an evening mug of cocoa, with added bromide for sedation so I was told, via the prison grape-vine, plus a dose of 'liquid paraffin'? for those who got too constipated? Sounds unlikely! A first prison sentence, qualified any of us for the 'Star wing,' whatever that first crime might be, whether murder, spying, prostitution, civil disobedience, or whatever. I met inmates, having committed all of these. Our work could be sewing prison clothes, shelling peas for factories, dismantling 'phones, etc. for which we were paid 2 shillings & 90 pence (2/90) weekly. Gardening, was for some of the lucky 'long-timers,' - or maybe a job, in the prison Jam factory. I was able to order & buy a lb of apples per week. Those wanting cigarettes or make-up, were more stretched to get their needs met! There was a prison library, (from which I borrowed Dostoevsky's 'Crime and Punishment')! I returned to prison 2 or 3 more times, until pregnancy decided me, prison was no longer an acceptable option. Nevertheless, I was involved from the 1st big sit-in at Trafalgar Square, till the last at Wethersfield American Air Base. I still remember, how taken aback I felt, to be treated with courtesy, in my first interactions outside prison. I continued work, as a volunteer for the World Peace Brigade, sending protest ships to Russia, continued too, the protest marches with the Campaign for Nuclear Disarmament, with my daughter sitting in, my own design baby carrier. At sit-ins at the American Embassy, American Bases, in Trafalgar and Parliament Square or, on marches, & so on, I enjoyed the camaraderie, the protest songs, the connections. The main leaders of the Committee of 100 direct-action group, had all been imprisoned for, longer periods, in fact while I was in Prison, I met the one woman among those, so penalised, and she joined me in our Peace efforts, once she was free. Two others of the freed leaders became closer friends too.

I also came to realize my fight was really with my father, however strong my revolt or outrage at insane, power tactics, threatening mass destruction. Governments after all, represent mass consciousness. My responsibility was not to fix the world nor, to divide people into good or bad, but to know myself. I have heard James O'Dea, speak in a very compassionate, and perceptive way, of a more evolved Peace Movement, where we now see our part in creating War. He, is the author of, 'The Essence of Cultivating Peace' 5 Keys to Spreading Peace in Your Life and Our World'.

*

I finished University with an undeserved BA degree in Spanish, as midway through the final exams, I suddenly felt, then wrote, 'this is meaningless,' and walked out of the exam. room. I was offered office work, I could have accepted, before I had even left University. I turned this down, having no interest in knowing more about the job, thinking I would feel closed in, unable to breathe. For a while, I took on work at home, for the Ministries of Health, - &, of Agriculture, Fisheries & Food too, translating their documents, to English. I soon enough decided it was too poorly paid for the hours it took. I have not easily fitted in to 9 to 5 type work, other than for 'the World Peace Brigade,' as my heart resonated, with the projects we were involved with, so have had very varied work experience.

*

A big part of this meeting of myself, has been my journey with sexual partners. After Miguel, whom I always considered a good man, my next significant relationship was with Bob. Though I never loved him, he fathered my daughter, so there must have presumably been, some life plan, decided between souls, that included, my spending that part of my life, with Bob. I was swayed by the intensity of his desire to be with me, making him tremble, almost shake. He carried much inner disturbance, from his early family life challenges, and would disappear without warning, for weeks, with no word as to why, nor where. I also felt disturbed, sensing something toxic & dark, around our sexual relating, though I would not have been able to give it words. Indeed, later, he very occasionally played out suppressed urges, in ways which shocked & repulsed me, designed mainly, seemingly, to involve attempts to humiliate me. The real severing of our bond, came when, alerted by others in our community, that he was in bed with a woman downstairs, I went to her room in the early hours, to check with my own eyes, returned to bed, fell straight asleep, & experienced in my dream, the snap of a cord! Samantha was still very young when I left Bob. I had thought, I could help 'fix' him, with me as the sacrificial martyr! Doubtless we were both armoured, with walls around our hearts, as must already be evident, both he and I, having in those days, low self-worth. He was a creative, frustrated man, who meant well, wanted to feel loved, and we remained casual friends till his death. I arranged, when Samantha was 8yrs.old, for her to resume, seeing him, with some regularity, until his death. She remains in regular friendly contact, with her step-brother & sister, & their mother Mary, whom I learnt to like too. More about Bob in the last chapter.

The 60's was the time of many experimental, alternative schools and communes. Samantha, conceived in the Central London Community, where I lived for a few months, took her 1st breath approx.1hr. after Winston Churchill expired his last. From the upper floor Maternity ward of Charing Cross hospital, near Trafalgar Square, I watched Churchill's Funeral procession proceeding down the Strand. It was a time of snow. We were living in South London, when she was born. Not an easy pregnancy. This was before, I had begun to learn in depth, about raw food diets and healing. I had difficulty facing food, bled a little, and felt, I needed to go to Spain. As soon as we got South, to Bordeaux, then across the frontier into Spain, my appetite &, well-being increased. It was not a time I believed in marriage, so I rejected Bob's offer. I will not focus here, on the more traumatising episodes, with Bob, including during early pregnancy. One morning, after I had left Bob, when Samantha was a 2yrs.old toddler, I had woken up with a strong impulse, to take her to point out, the house where she was conceived, near Central London. I talked to her about Bob, ending up hours later, going homewards, down Portobello Rd. market. She and I were living now, as part of yet another Community, off Portobello Road, nr. Notting Hill, West London. Suddenly I lost her, among the crowds. I felt extreme panic, fearing I might never again see her. I hurried home, in case she had found her way there, passing Bob busking, with his guitar. I came back to him, minutes later, saying I had lost her. He went immediately up in Notting Hill direction, while I took care of his guitar, and shortly after, felt profound relief when he returned carrying her. The whole day felt very synchronous.

It must have been around then, that I was introduced to LSD. That first time, I asked a friend, to be with me, as I had heard, one might commit suicide. That morning I had been reading, about women being tortured in Vietnam, by putting snakes in their vaginas. As my being expanded into multi-dimensional sensations, the woman I was with, became a Vietnamese woman, and I was looking into her eyes, with tears pouring down my face. All the walls had lost their solidity, becoming streaming energy and colours. I absolutely knew, I would never kill myself. Later I went walking outside on my own. I chose to be alone, most times I took LSD, especially outdoors in Nature, or Parks, opening deeply, to experiences outside usual reality limits. Hours passed in moments, escalators seemed to change direction, matter no longer dense, nor solid. I had recently read "Be Here Now," by Baba Ram Dass, and books by Timothy Leary, and Aldous Huxley, wanting always to see my deeper purpose.

*

Max lived in the same house, as me, with his 'girl'-friend and her 3, later 4 children, (two of them he had fathered). One day I was sitting in Holland Park with him, on a sunny day of many flowers, when I was suddenly hit by a wave, of knowing, we would be together. I truly had harboured no thoughts nor desires, in this direction, yet suddenly, unquestioned certainty was here. I said nothing but, so it came to be. This became a deeper partnership, fulfilling a mutual interest in spiritual & health matters. I was 28 years old, when this deepening exploration began, of inner purification, diet, & body health, though I did have a stillbirth, plus various miscarriages too! My initial inspiration came from Luis Kuhne's book 'The New Science of Healing' which I came across in Spain, in my friend Jose's home. Written in Spanish, I avidly devoured it. Finally, I could take full responsibility for keeping myself healthy. I need never go to a doctor again, - such liberation! The author had learnt, from close observation, of Nature, thus I learned, not only about the digestive process, and the movement of waste gases, through the body, but how to live in greater harmony with natural laws, so, reducing toxic density, in our being. I wrote to Max back in England, saying I would love him to make slatted benches, for steam baths. He co-operated fully with this, spending day after day too, in the British Museum, copying the English edition of Kuhne's book, by hand. We made many copies &, started distributing these. This concern with trusting my health to Nature, never again taking prescribed medication, nor antibiotics, (which I had never taken), from doctors and drug companies, aware I can depend on my own knowing and experience, has remained constant. On this level, Max & I had much, to share and explore.

We mainly lived, in co-operative harmony & freedom yet, with emotional commitment, plus deep physical intimacy, missing, - not a romantic love. I do not quite understand how, although Max & I lived together, & sometimes had sex, yet somehow, it was as if we were good friends & partners, in spiritual & health exploration, yet I felt no commitment in a romantic, nor married way. I never really felt him there for me, in that way, never talking of love, nor offering much financial support, even when I was miscarrying, or pregnant, seeming unconcerned, as if not involved. He was emotionally somewhat damaged, as his mother, who was quite rich, had been raised by a guardian, so there was an emotional bonding, somewhat lacking. His track record was, of abandoning his children & partners, so I suppose he may have felt anxiety, at new responsibilities! I would take myself off, to live in the woods, the New Forest, Epping Forest, or go on other adventures and travels alone, though on occasion, with him too. We were co-operative friends and companions. Occasionally a more intense, strong emotion, would erupt from him, but mostly, vulnerable feelings & much else was left unsaid. Looking at all my earlier relationships, this seems so! So many truths, feelings & thoughts, left unspoken between human beings, protecting ourselves from possible pain. Only now, have I become so much more transparent, outspoken, aware of common insecurities, deepest longings, fears, the same, no matter the Continent, religion, sex, race, whatever. We remained friends till his death.

In 1967, Natasha came to live with us. She was, about Samantha's age. Her mother Norma was Max's ex 'helpmeet,' (olde English), I like that word. Max was the father of Norma's 's two youngest, a daughter and son. Birth complications had affected Norma's bonding with Natasha, & I was in the do-gooder idealistic mind-set, where I wanted to rescue the abandoned, or less loved young, of the world, to prove to them, what I did not wholly believe myself, that others did love and care. Norma is a good mother, & I have never had less than respect & liking for her, still do. She, (Max's partner when I met him), was, and is, a lovely woman, who has never treated me any way, but well. I did not, in my emotional immaturity, consider that Samantha could be damaged by my decision. On the surface, all appeared well, but looking later at the photos of that time, there is such a sadness in her eyes, and she later told me, that Natasha was sneakily, not very nice to her. I saw none of this! Of course, they would both have had, major adjustments to make emotionally. I treated them both the same, as far as I was aware, with very occasional hiccups, when some less lovely emotion would surface in me. Yet it took most of my lifetime, till my 70th year, to even truly love myself. Now, in retrospect, my heart finally wide open, and a firm commitment in me, to stay that way, no matter what the challenge, I see that I did not do so great a 'job' with anyone, at that time, which brought up in me, much sorrow, for all the ways I had not truly opened my heart, to love. Only after years, of undoing all the ways, we become disconnected from Love, thus allowing the veils to thin between us and, our full embrace of All, can we truly see each other clearly, as well as our precious selves, with open hearts. I took so long to pour all the love I wished to express, into the world at all. Please forgive me Norma, Natasha, and all of you, with whom I interacted, with less than, the integrity & sensitivity, and love I would have preferred. Yet it does seem, my time with Max, was part of my Life plan, thus whatever karmic consequences I may have incurred, in my blind acceptance of Norma's & her children's, most likely distress, at Max's abandonment, this is how it is. I knew it was to be.

I was motivated, to travel with Samantha and Natasha, to Morocco, because I had learnt from Luis Kuhne's book, that whereas in cold countries, disease tends to linger, with long-term chronic symptoms, in hot countries, the body's attempt to cleanse itself, of toxicity & return to balance, tends to result in a more dramatic or fast eruption, like the measles and, other childhood illnesses.

The orthodox medical system, of this time, will try to suppress the symptoms, thus fighting against, the body's natural attempt, to restore itself to full health. My intention, was to provoke a 'healing crisis,' in myself. So off we went, with double push chair, and since both Samantha & Natasha had erupted in spots, days earlier, I had been using steam, and appropriate diet, to support their bodies in healing. By the time we arrived in Casablanca, in French Morocco, they were both restored to health. From there I walked, and at nightfall, made us a bed in some road-side woods. I had no specific plan. At some point next day, after walking a long time in the sun, I decided to board a bus, which took us to the coastal city of El Jadida. So many people approached us, as we sat on the beach, that evening that, after refusing various invitations, to go their homes, I decided at some point, to accept one of the offers made. We became guests of a family, & I communicated in French while learning Arabic. I enjoyed buying grain, taking it to the mill, to grind into flour, making the bread, taking the loaves to the public oven &, enjoying such fresh, wholesome, dark bread. I also wore the traditional 'djellaba,' integrating myself, into life as an Arab woman. (I have remembered two of my past lives. One where I was a girl, who loved my Turkish land, and religion, though I did not like the segregation, being kept out, of the Mosque, when the men were in there praying). My main objection, was to men's attitude, to women. They, did not suffer the restrictions, they imposed on 'their' women, and felt it acceptable, to have sex with women musicians, singers or, entertainers, whom they saw as, 'fair game,' probably seen as whores, and lesser beings. Their wives were strictly controlled, as to their movements, allowed out only with permission, and I voiced to him, my outrage at this. When I returned 15yrs. later, the wife and mother, of the household, where we were staying, had started to rebel! I loved our weekly visits to the local Turkish Baths, or 'Hammam', - I am not sure of the spelling. We would be seated, on the wet floor, with buckets of clean water, a huge space full of women and girls, sweating in the steam, scrubbing each other's backs with red 'pumice' stones/rocks, putting henna in our hair, getting so clean! My love of steam baths, began here.

I was disappointed on my return to El Jadida, 15yrs.later, to find Western busyness & stress, already encroaching; the simple ways I had so loved, disappearing. I returned a couple more times to Morocco, but to Spanish-speaking Tetouan, where again Samantha & I were warmly welcomed by a family, after my money was stolen. Said, had seen me upset in the street, and invited me to his home. I enjoyed sharing in the house work, washing floors, preparing food, enjoying couscous, (without the meat), salads, and plenty of sweet mint tea, (less sugar for me). Natasha was no longer with us by then. The wide padded 'benches' by the walls of the main room, were used by any of us unmarried people, for sleeping. I did have brief sexual involvement with Said, the eldest son, though I felt his uptight attitude, towards me & sex, probably despising me for being available, as he then became less friendly. At meal-times, we would sit on the floor around the circular table, sharing from, the same dish, using our fingers. I was considering moving, to live in Morocco, and teaching English, wishing I had not thrown away, my degree, seeming meaningless to me, at the time I got it. I also went travelling, thinking I would maybe, find work fruit-picking, but found none, enjoying instead the adventure of new places and friends, especially in one small fishing village, where the local police, let us sleep on their terrace, with the dog who, early each morning, made his way, to the harbour, looking for fish, as the fishing boats arrived. Everywhere, we were welcomed, by lovely families, learning their customs, sharing food such as sweet, fresh couscous, from the wheat newly harvested, growing next to the police house. None of the Spanish arrogance.

*

Years earlier, I had worked for years as an I.V.S. volunteer (International Voluntary Service), and a group of us, had gathered one Summer, in a small village, in the hills in the South of France, to build a road to connect, mainly older remaining villagers, with the valley's main road. While I rested a few days in a house, in the Pyrenean foothills, when the work was done, my Spanish uncle, Felix turned up, on a surprise visit. He was to travel further North to Germany, and would pick me up 3 days later. I told him I had contacted a Spaniard, I wished to meet. His was the only Spaniard's name, on our World Peace Brigade (for whom I also worked), mailing list, and he was at that time, enjoying a holiday in Formentera. My uncle forbade me to visit him, assuring me he would know, if I disobeyed him.

As soon as he left, my resolve propelled me to journey there fast, finding Jose living (on holiday), simply, in a tent, within a pine-tree grove, goats as his neighbours. I enjoyed two days of sun, vegetarian food and. goats' milk, in the company of this peace-loving being. During the Civil war, he had been brought up, in the Catalan anarchist camps, and he had given me a booklet to read, my first taste of Krishnamurti's writing. He became a friend for life. This was years before I related sexually with men, in my early twenties. I got back to where my uncle, (with hidden intent), expected to find me, (my parents must have given him my address), and we set off, on the journey to Madrid. Surprisingly he had a young German woman with him, named Sigrun. We stayed at an hotel in Pamplona, & as I sat reading Krishnamurti in the garden, early the next morning, my uncle found me &, asked what I was reading. As soon as he saw the Spanish booklet, he surmised I had been, to see my friend, declaring he, had had me followed and, that it was people like Jose, who were responsible for terrorist bombs and carnage. In fact, it was Franco, who thought it O.K. to unleash a Spanish holocaust, with Spanish Concentration Camps, using the full horror and killing power of Italy's or Germany's bombs, to test his might, against his supposed enemies, (i.e. Spanish civilians in areas of greater unrest, many hundreds of casualties being women, children, the old, the poor, who wanted the riches seemingly enjoyed by the privileged few, or the educated idealistic reformers, taken over - as young men are, by the age-old delusion, that war will create the possibility of a sane, fair system of peaceful government). My mother, his sister, had lived & worked in Bilbao, not far from Guernica, whereas Felix, (brother Jose Mari too), was fascist, in his work & sympathies. Anyway Felix, remained henceforth angry, barely speaking to me. Yet unbeknownst to me, I was serving his hidden agenda, which was to tell his wife Toni, that Sigrun was **my** friend, so she would not suspect, his infidelity. I was so innocent, it never occurred to me, that Felix & Sigrun, were actually 'lovers.' I only discovered many years later, he had conducted a campaign to discredit me, not allowing my name, to be mentioned in his presence, by my Spanish relations, thus I was later, (unbeknownst to me), blamed by his wife, for taking Sigrun to their home! He & my uncle Jose Mari, both held influential positions, related to Franco's government, Felix with the Ministry of Art, Culture and Education, (he was an accomplished artist himself), & Jose Mari as a Censor for Radio Madrid! To demonstrate the extent of their paranoia and, their arrogant patriarchal mentality, they had their sister, my aunt Maria Luisa, enclosed in a Convent, her whole life, till her death, for having a baby, while young (18yrs. old) and unmarried. They had the power to sign her in, to keep her locked away, much to my mother's distress. My parents secretly visited her, when they made journeys to Madrid. Another time, both uncles arrived, when I was staying with my grandmother & Aunt Carmina. They interrogated me in an empty room, asking what papers, I had secretly passed on to Jose!

Such paranoia! Jose & I remained friends, where I'd visit him in Caracagente, among the orange groves; - (where orange trees first introduced from China to Spain).

Max & I went to Gstaad, in 1968, to hear Krishnamurti speak & to the Barbican in London too. We visited Brockwood Park later also, a co-educational school inspired by Krishnamurti's vision, encouraging 'academic excellence,' also self-understanding, creativity, and integrity, in a non-competitive environment, for about 70 pupils.

*

I did not feel met, on a deep intimate level, living with Max, & felt too, financially unsupported. One day after going to, the main London fruit & veg. traders' market, (based in those days in Covent Garden), to fill a sack with free food, lifting the sack, had caused bleeding, the start of a possible miscarriage. Max knew this, yet still chose to leave me alone all day, while he went to visit the mother of his children. When the foetus was indeed expelled, that day, it had such a tiny, perfect form, maybe an inch or so long, I ended up swallowing this, to reabsorb it, as I did not want to get rid of it, in any way! Max was quite shocked when I later told him. Another time, I was about 7 to 8 months pregnant &, feeling so unsupported, I just left with my 8yr.old daughter, &

hitch-hiked first to my friends' farm in the South of France. It was Carmen, my sister, who had first introduced me, to this family farm, not so far from Bordeaux. The parents had been, refugees from Czechoslovakia. A large hanging

on their kitchen wall, proclaimed 'There is no Authority but God.' All four daughters were open-hearted, beautiful, strong and, resilient. They ate vegetarian food, practised yoga. Plum orchards, fields of green beans & tobacco plants, and the delight in sharing with this special family, is what I remember most. I was sad when they dug up, the plum orchards, since the blackly oozing tobacco plants, gave more profit. Not my favourite plant!

I did not realize the family imagined I was intending an abortion. Shocked, I decided to continue our travels to my chosen destination, in Spain, where I could sleep under the sky & trees, and enjoy sun & fruits. I had intended to have the baby on my own, cut the cord myself, and bond in a natural way. I had spent much time preparing before Samantha's birth, 1965, extensively studying Edna Wright's & other books on midwifery, & painless childbirth. She was one of the early pioneers of that time, both a writer and, teaching us women, how to breathe and be more self-responsible, during the birthing process. She was attached to Charing Cross hospital, by 'The Strand,' in London. Though I felt more empowered from her help, still I was left somewhat scared and alone, for long hours, though this was my first child. So, this time I had decided, to steer clear of hospitals and doctors. Things did not go according to plan. Approaching the Spanish border on our train journey, contractions began, so I wondered, if I could use an empty room, off the platform, but failed to escape notice! Instead, an ambulance was brought, subjecting my body to 30kms. of bumpy roads, to the nearest hospital in Figuerras.

The nuns were very censorious & rough with me, not realizing I spoke Spanish so, understood their less than compassionate judgements. The baby was painfully expelled, with their rough uncaring handling, & was still-born. Having refused the injection to stop my milk, I was threatened with force; then they became white sugary-sweet, when they thought they might get money out of me. (I never eat white sugar)! I escaped, with Samantha, as soon as I could, to my refuge under the pine trees, in the Lerida region. I relaxed & healed. I did not contact Max, but he found out from a mutual friend, that I was in Spain, and maybe the post-mark set him off in my direction. Relaxing in our glade one day, suddenly Max appeared! He seemed to have a radar, enabling him to find me, wherever I might be, when living in the wild. The same happened another time in the middle of Epping Forest! He had a very individual approach in his relationship with Life, which as a young man, had made him question the requirements, for gaining his qualification, to become an architect, thus he never completed. He would question always, the deeper assumptions he would be supporting, by doing any job, which meant usually he had to stop work! At that time, my call was, to follow, the fruit harvests & the sun. I started with strawberries in Kent, in the days when the gypsies, did much of this seasonal work. Samantha, my child would be among the rows, of strawberries, as I worked. Max started to sometimes join me, on these travels for harvesting.

Later it was grapes in Spain & France, cherries in the French Pyrenees, plums (for speciality 'prunes d'Agen'), plus green runner beans in Southern France, & potatoes in the New Forest. Much of the time in Spain, France too, we lived pretty much just eating fruit, such as blackberries, wild plums & pine nuts, almonds, cherries & also cultivated grapes, luscious ripe peaches, & apricots; - a strong time for body healing & soul. We slept out under the stars, swam in lakes, streams & water irrigation tanks. Sometimes, Max joined me, other times I lived on the hillsides, with Samantha too. One time I was on one of these hillsides, where I used to draw or paint, the local plants, then we wandered down to an open-fronted building, which had a fireplace in one back corner. Suddenly many men arrived & surrounded me & Samantha, with guns. I was questioning whether they were going to rape me, or what. It turned out, there was some bandit of local fame, who used to steal people's food or whatever, & they thought I was this bandit's woman! I told them I was a friend of Jose's, so they went to the village to find him, leaving a couple of men, with us. One of them was showing me his gun, asking if I wanted to hold it, but I felt repulsed & refused! At times, we slept in barns, sheds, even in, a concrete sort of barracks, with a shared cooking & water area, down the middle, with the Spanish gypsies, for the grape harvest. My friendship with Max spanned fifty years.

*

Before his death, I had still met him regularly, enjoying Kew Gardens, & Richmond Park, visiting too our friend Jungleyes, in a Kent neurological hospital, which combines Steiner inspired treatments with the more invasive orthodox approach. Max had been focussing a lot on transitioning from juices & fruits, to living on light, but though meditating daily & very connected with 'spacious Oneness,' he carried still, much of his early life emotional scars and deprivation. He died of pancreatic Cancer, which he did not know about, until the week he died. He had spent many, many years, still perfecting his book, 'NOW Life, NOW Architecture,' (in three parts). His frustration at not being able to realize his dreams as an architect, led to his ongoing focus, of creating building designs, created to interplay with the surrounding land, to best serve the needs of people &, the environment in a harmonious, sustainable way. He spent many, many years, perfecting his detailed skilful designs and drawings. I regretted death came to him, with his book unpublished. He was only 2 years older than me, so his death was unexpected. He used to work all day on his designs & writing, then eat a lot of raw food, late in the day, not the best time for digestion. Emotionally, he had not met all his unresolved stories from childhood, & though he asked me to do 'journey' sessions with him, he only scratched the surface! His intellect remained in charge!

I found myself more affected by his death, than I had with any previous death, of a human being related to me. He really did his best, to relate respectfully with everyone & love as unconditionally, as do cats, dogs & very young children. I honour him for this intent, no matter that other traits, it embarrasses me to admit, irritated me at times! Emma his daughter would love to publish his intricate drawings. I sent her a sum of money, but doubt she used it for the proposed intention, as I heard nothing since. He worked using the 'Golden Means' & I would have liked, to edit & publish his whole book, once I felt rich enough; though much will have changed, with architecture & environment!

Max's designs were drawn with great intricacy & very precise angles & curves. His heritage included Swiss genes, where clock mechanisms & precision reign!

*

In the Seventies, I got very involved with Circle dancing, initially only with Stefan's group, near my West London home. I would walk there & back, & started too, to collect the dances, from so many different countries, and as I became familiar with more and more of these, also created new dances at times. I have let go this month reluctantly, of the dozens of dance tapes! Though I still have cassette & tape player, my son & others younger than me, seem certain no-one would use these tapes any more. I spent so many years collecting dances & even creating new ones! Stefan & later his new wife Bethan, became good friends. I really enjoyed shared dance, ending up in later years, teaching some of these dances myself, in weekly classes, & even one time to, a large group of men & women in Columbia. My Polish friend Azucena became a close friend & dancing partner too. This remained a focus for many years, that I regretted finding less time for. Stefan was Jewish, so we learnt many Israeli dances, & it may have been Stefan, who told me about Subud, as he was very involved. I was initiated into Subud but, though their practice of the 'Latihan,' was interesting, where men and women (separately), opened themselves up, to receive divine energy in their bodies, being moved into, spontaneous physical or verbal expression, speaking in other 'tongues' maybe, or whatever else; - I was less open or ready for this. My mind would be questioning, all that was going on around me, so I did not persevere, finding different reasons to withdraw, such as not wholly resonating with the group. (I was never a hand-bag, stockings & high heels woman)! I did become, part of a Healing Circle, where we would direct colour healing & light to others, opening-up, our receptivity, & going to different locations such as Camelot & Glastonbury Abbey, to focus on Soul Rescue work. I felt in tune, with working in these ways. Many clairvoyants emphasized, over the years, that I could work, in any of these related fields. While I was with Max, I studied palmistry, in some depth, & used to take friends' hand-prints, then work out interpretations. I even played the role at one or two fairs, of mysteriously, revealing hidden aspects to those who entered, my tent. Max's finger tips with the spiral 'whorls,' for instance, revealed someone who would not easily, work with others, as he would need to find his unique niche. My finger-tip patterns, 'arches' though some 'loops,' show someone who's ' the salt of the Earth,' & can be relied on. Loops add some flexibility, but I could have difficulty expressing verbally, finding other ways easier, such as painting, or writing. (That used to be so, but nowadays, I talk a lot when I meet soul brothers & sisters, though love much alone time too). This needing to prove myself reliable, as if I need to show others, that Caring and Love does exist, has been very strong in me, since a young child. I want to see & be, the love, that would die for another to save them! Even now, I am near tears whenever I feel great Love in others, & my compassion is deep for others & myself. Conflict with people is rare now, though I am suddenly surprised on occasion,

Music and songs are keys to my heart too. I continued to paint. I drew & painted plants & trees on the hillsides in Spain, as mentioned, painted too, many other pictures which I either gave away or sold. I did not feel though, that this was, at that time, to be my primary focus in life. I did feel clearly, in my earlier life, that **Healing**, was to be more of a primary focus than painting or writing. Yet, from a child onwards, I have enjoyed painting murals on walls, sometimes on ceilings too, in my homes. In Penny & Guy's home, too, I painted trees, on their bathroom wall, though never quite completed the mushroom, a fly agaric. I painted scenery on a classroom door, in the Acorn School too, long ago. So, this is a creative thread which runs strongly through my life, a love of harmoniously blending colours, with the precision of harmonic musical tones. I hope this book's cover, will be as I have visualised it, more magic than serious.

I also love sewing, redesigning the clothes I buy, making new clothes & mending, which seems to be less done, these days. I love natural materials, colour & textures, thus always felt design of clothes and/or interior design, could have been expanded in my life. I did make myself couple of breathable bamboo face-masks, though rarely wore them. I made one for Guy too, with fly agaric design material, but gave only as little energy, to the whole fear drama, as needed, & carried an exemption card with me, on the London underground.

Now though, approaching 82yrs.old, in 2022, my focus is, to dwell always, in my heart being, radiating out Love & Joy, by simply being this, no matter if my present financial situation has been so challenging, for the last few months. I would love this book to encourage others, to love themselves deeply, no longer driven to direct unkind judgments against themselves, or any other sentient being, as no doubt everything is One Infinite metaphysical Being, simply appearing as the Many!! I hope my tree & angel pictures & my chosen photos, will grace this book, in the order, originally decided.

*

It was during the time that I had got involved with the 'sannyasins,' already briefly mentioned, that I had met and married Berris. I had had an inner fleeting image of his green eyes, from time to time, in earlier years and been told by a 'seer,' 6 months. earlier, that I was destined to meet with a partner, in November and, that <u>we were **meant to evolve** together, **beyond sex**, in this life!</u> We met at a work-shop, on November 5th. He too, had been told very recently, by a psychic, of an imminent significant meeting. We stayed together, from that evening onwards. He came to my home in Latimer Road, a row of vacated houses, being used as 'squats,' small gardens adjacent to the railway line, up on the nearby embankment. We were a lively and co-operative community, enjoying friendships, saunas too, (in a home-made beautiful wooden cabin). All the squatters were later, rehoused, by the GLC, who decided on a 'Squatters Amnesty'. We were offered a Council house to rent, in an area of our choice, so Berris and I, enjoyed the drama, of watching the bulldozers knocking down our squat, a sight which moved us (literally)! We lived mostly in London, but also on 'The Lizard,' very near Kennack Sands. We had sold the farm-house Berris & his former partner & children, had lived in, adding a clause, as I suggested, selling the Farmhouse plus a few acres ourselves, rather than via the Estate agent, for a higher price, £33,000 rather than £25,000, with a proviso, to keep the land free of harmful pesticides or chemicals. We sifted through all the would-be buyers, met with, and used our intuition too, in choosing our prospective buyers, or new neighbours to be. We kept 10 acres with the apple orchards and 'Apple hut,' (once probably used for apple harvesters), fields, an old railway carriage, (used formerly as a home), a stream, with all the land and path, gently sloping towards the sea, a 5minutes' walk away. Often, we would have with us, Berris's two children, Tala, and Thor. We would visit Happy Valley in Wales too, where Berris's mother, also sister, with her family, lived. Since I had initially married Berris, in order to more easily, get back my daughter, as I still at the time, did not believe in legal marriage, I suggested April 1st for our wedding day. We chose to marry in Oban. There were rainbows in the Sky, all the way there, which I saw as a blessing. I regret now that I did not initially, honour and celebrate this marriage, in a more sacred and special way. We went by boat to the island of Mull for our honeymoon, and I came to love Berris ever more deeply, maybe feeling safer as his wife. It is interesting to reflect, that troublesome signs, are there, right from the start of a relationship, but we dismiss these perceptions, hoping for, or living as, beggars for Love, while we have yet to experience, deeply loving ourselves and so, come to know the Love within. On that first evening I met Berris, I saw his, what I judged as 'play-boy' aspect in evidence, yet already wanted exclusivity with him! The relative safety was short-lived, even though on the practical level, we really enjoyed sexual intimacy, without inhibitions, co-operated well, had all the money we needed, land too, and were happy. Berris came with me to India, and decided to 'take sannyas' too. In those days we Rajneesh 'sannyasins,' wore clothes in many different shades of orange, pink or red, a mala too, with our guru's picture. For some time, I had resisted the idea of belonging to this group, wearing orange etc. then one day, resistances had dropped away, after hours of meditation. Osho, (a name later assumed, after some deep inner alchemy, rather than Bhagwan Shree Rajneesh), was certainly a charismatic being, with great Presence, an enlightened speaker, who gave regular daily discourses, & devised various Rajneesh therapies, particularly for the Westerners. Meditations, & discourses, were a big part of the daily programmes, plus Sufi and free style dance, music, occasional big gatherings too, generating more energy in an environment or room, than I had ever, experienced in any other room, in this life anyway.

*

I revelled in all this sharing & creative expression, & in becoming more embodied & real. In those years, (the late 1970's), I had been training & qualifying in many different healing & therapeutic skills, such as Aromatherapy and different kinds of Massage. These were early days, in the more holistic approach to health. It would be another 20yrs.before the book 'Molecules of Emotion' by Candace Pert was published, which became very popular in the more spiritually aware community, as more Scientists began tentatively moving towards glimmerings, of a less mechanistic view of the human body and Life. However, men's control of Research funds, plus reluctance, to recognize women's paradigm shifting discoveries, meant breakthrough remedies, which could have helped Cancer & Aids sufferers much sooner, stayed bogged down for years, swallowed up by, the patriarchal male competitive Old Boy's school mentality. Another 20yrs. again, before women were becoming more empowered, many now writing books like mine, & speaking from awareness of the inseparable relationship between metaphysical Being, Spirit, Body, Heart, Mind & all the Elements, in fact All of energy! It was when I was learning how to use my 'Skenar' machine back in the 90's, that I first heard of Candace Pert's book. As she tracks the intricacies of the body's information network, she is realizing that when the traumas are suppressed, and blocked, at the cellular level, there is an unprocessed information overload. 'When stress prevents the molecules of emotion from flowing freely where needed, the largely autonomic processes that are regulated by peptide flow, such as breathing, blood flow, immunity, digestion and elimination, collapse down to a few feedback loops and upset the normal healing response.' At that time Science was dragging behind what the alternative community already knew, as well as the Spiritual Wisdom of the Ages! Although Candace Pert 'came out' in 1985, going public on the East Coast, thus 'forcing her to bring her ideas out of the closet.' I was fascinated by her speculation about which emotional overtone, VIP, the '(vasoactive intestinal peptide), found in the frontal cortex of the brain, the thymus gland, the gut, the lungs, some immune cells, and part of the autonomic nervous system', might be associated with. When the receptors on the surface of brain and immune cells are lacking in enough VIP molecules, the HIV virus will attach to them, creating greater susceptibility to disease. 'Clinicians have the impression that increasing self-esteem seems to slow the progress of the disease'. She deduced that Self-Love, (my emphasis) - might well be the emotional overtone of VIP. As I am considering this, I realize that Homosexuals and 'Black/dark-skinned' people, Jews, Women, Gypsies too, have been seen as inferior, lesser beings, & we've certainly all known how deeply they/we (I add '<u>we</u>' as since we have lived many lives, we will have had different coloured skins, in different lives, which does make nonsense of such discrimination), have been, and still are, affected by any discrimination. Of course, their levels of Self-acceptance or Self-Love, are more likely to be affected, plus levels of immunity. I will have mentioned my first sexual partner, Miguel, whose father was seen as inferior, by both Miguel & his mother, for having darker skin. I am at present reading a Library book, the title, 'People like us' by Louise Fein, set at the start of Hitler's madness.' (Since I have had DNA genetic analysis of my heritage, I now know that though my father was 'English,' in fact his/my heritage from the North of England, was predominantly Viking, from Norway, Denmark & Sweden, even Finland, the Scottish border & Northern Ireland, a little bit from the N.E. coast of England (a little Yorkshire, though the Vikings also invaded York). The rest is from my mother, a little bit Spanish & the rest Basque, i.e., my ancestry is mainly Basque, a little Spanish, plenty of Viking! It would make a mockery of Racism, if everyone had their DNA tested)! Nomadic people, such as the gypsies or Romani, dark-skinned, & other less privileged peoples, are still having, to suffer discrimination, or have been taken from their countries & peoples, & been used as slaves. Maybe more so in the U.S.A. but England's Imperial Past, has an equally ugly story, which included much suffering & crime. Yet finally, there is an uprising, started in Bristol, where Slave trade was the foundation, of the levels of prosperity enjoyed. At least one key Slave trader statue, has been toppled, to the ground. Yet darker skinned people, with more enlightened spiritual awareness, such as Michael Beckwith, create, of course, a higher vibration experience. I believe it would be excellent idea, for all fascists to have their DNA genetically tested. They might well find they were less 'English' or 'German' or Russian etc., than believed. At least by 2020, homosexuals are more accepted.

'Today,' (which happened to be Dec.18th 2021), I repeated a favourite Stargate meditation, (in which Alcazar guides us, into the Void, of pure potential, encouraging awareness of, our multidimensionality, in the Void, the Blackness from which creative possibilities are birthed). I was fascinated this time, to find a black bearded, longer haired being, who I felt was a Viking, looking at me for a long moment, followed by an older bearded, hairy face, also looking into my eyes. It felt very real. I have no idea whether they were relations or, myself! I love such journeys into other possibilities! All energy's connected, in every moment of Earth time, yet birthed from beyond time, which is why, every moment it is important, where we focus our energies!

On the Planetary level, it is a time of much change and turbulence, including the 'Corona Virus' pandemic, with much engineered controlling hype. And still this story repeats, with different labels, taking slightly different forms, with effected by both beliefs & life-style choices. Covid 19 or, the Corona Virus is a more recent fear-enhancing 'baddy' or enemy. Though I feel this is not surprising, given that, the Pharmaceutic industry, has so weakened people's immune systems, with symptom-suppressing synthesized drugs! Also, a diet of much processed, generally cheap inferior food & drink choices, plus tobacco smoking, and/or drinking alcohol, more so in recent years, especially women, & with a big dose of self-judgement, does not lead to health. Healthy, organically-grown food, has never in my experience, been part of any Hospital diet. It does not take much intelligence to realize, that if our pesticides are killing so much of our eco-system, we too, as part of Nature, are similarly under 'threat'! My experience, is, that eating raw food, the enzymes therefore intact, especially if organically grown, leaves me replete, whereas when I choose cooked food, I feel ever dissatisfied. It is addictive plus, I get attracted to adding butter, or cream to cooked food, creating a build-up of mucus in my body, plus less lubrication & muscular elasticity. I do give myself permission, to change my mind in any moment. However, - each soul is born, I trust, with purposeful intent &, will also exit the body, in perfect timing, so all is good. It is common, that when a species, becomes over-populous & a threat to Earth's resources, there will be a solution, such as the plague of the 14th Century. Though there is so much panic & outcry, simply many have left, for different planes of existence, which seems a likely choice, for wise souls.

Since I live deeply in Trust & Surrender, since my 70th year, no longer judging any other Being, I am at ease in my Being too, in deep gratitude & Joy for Existence, feeling myself an Infinite Being, on a great adventure, though meeting challenges too. When the time comes, to fly off, from this body, I wish to have fulfilled whatever, my Soul's highest Purpose is, for being here. Yet just feeling this ever-present, heart-warming love & acceptance, Joy too, in my innermost being, feels sufficient, plus following my heart promptings. Thus, I am really taken aback, by a very occasional verbal attack. Only twice in the last 10 to a dozen years!

Anyway, back to my past exploration, of new therapies, which continued while with Berris, in my 30's to 40's. We both qualified in 'Postural Integration,' which is a deep tissue massage (like 'Rolfing'). We then decided to do the Rajneesh Therapist Training, and this is where the big challenges began! Bhagwan encouraged our meeting suppressed desires, & if we chose to play them out, to engage fully, rather than unconsciously. Sex became the 'biggie' here. There was considerable peer pressure, to engage in sex more freely, also much influenced, no doubt, by the sixties 'Sexual Revolution.' Berris voiced that since he had only related sexually, with two other women before me, he wanted to open, to more sexual experience, whereupon my jerk reaction, to this was, "If you do, I will!" so off I went, to have a 'coil' fitted. (My body quickly rejected every coil inserted). Nevertheless, I found it very painful, to occasionally witness this, during the training, & hard to handle Berris going off for a night, now & again, with some woman who fancied him. I would try to inure myself, against pain, by doing likewise, but it felt like attacks on my heart, & did nothing, to create ease, or safety in my life. I would react angrily at times, defensively at others. One time, TV cameras (Channel 4, I believe), zoomed in on our Encounter group, where I was declaring, I was going to take a man friend home, & Berris knelt before me, begging me not to. This after all his actions! I was not aware I wanted him to suffer, but neither was I really connecting with, nor seeing him, having had to shut down, to avoid, feeling too much pain. When I met with this other man, I did not even feel interest, and do not remember having sex. I think if I did, I was not present! That whole time period feels like, I was in some mad trance. Berris then suggested we should go separately, for a month each to India, though we agreed, not to really get involved, with anyone! As well, since my body kept rejecting the coil, I stopped using one. It was an intense time, when as well as my marriage unravelling, I also got pregnant and, Martello, not Berris, was the father! It was during my pregnancy, that I opted, to become celibate, which lasted 5years, rather than the three years predicted by the good clairvoyant, whom I had gone to consult. He said this celibate period was part of my Soul evolution. I was being drawn too, from Osho towards Babaji, & was feeling somewhat confused. (A clairvoyant said, my time with Osho, had been about working out, my more personal, emotional 'stuff' whereas Babaji was more about, service to Humanity, which helped me surrender, to the shift).

I had already decided I must learn to drive, rather than be dependent on Berris, for being transported. Thus, in my 40th year I passed my driving test 1st time, which led, during the next couple of years, since Berris & I had separated, to my jobs delivering parcels, in the London area mainly, plus working for a pet shop delivering special cats & dogs going to rich owners, often in Arab countries. I also became a taxi driver for a feminist company, which offered female drivers, for women needing that feeling of safety! My last delivery job, which must have been about July 1982, where I had a code name 'Ruby 1 2,' plus my car walkie talkie, I found myself on a longer journey, with plenty of heavy parcels to deliver. As I drove, I was thinking about my being 2mths. pregnant, feeling I must give up the job, but also remain solvent. On my return journey, I had an accident from which I emerged, shocked but unhurt, my van a 'write off'. I felt this was a quick response to my prayer! I continue to love driving, exploring new areas. Being on the road, I feel a great sense of adventure & freedom, knowing I can stop wherever I choose. To this day, I continue to enjoy my car-home. (As I was re-editing this, in February & March, 2021, I had a fractured wrist, so did not drive my car for about 7 or 8 months)! Now I do drive again, but my wrist has remained slightly wonky! Also, better to drive only when necessary. I am feeling conflicted now, as James wants me to go to the ceremony, for his partner Rosie's very recent death.

*

Before Berris had left for India, though I had decided, 'tit for tat,' to spend a night with Martello, Berris and I had agreed not to have serious involvements. However, the consequences are different for women, as we, are the ones who get pregnant. Martello had a gentle, light-hearted energy. I enjoyed a lot of humour and laughter with him, a welcome break from full-on intensity, like the moon after the Sun. It seemed he had a great need also, to unburden himself, so kept returning. It was not in my nature, to relate superficially, with another human being, so, though I still felt deeply heart-connected and, married with Berris, so not fully available, still I felt relaxed & open, enjoying Martello's light-hearted humour. Very soon after learning to drive, I had set off with Martello, Samantha & another friend, to Amsterdam, - my first experience of driving on the right. It was fine. We were on our way to a big Sannyas gathering, being held in a former Prison, with cells for our bedrooms. Meanwhile, I suddenly got a message, that Berris had arranged, for me to join him in Italy, - Sardinia, or Sicily. Unknown to me, he was planning a lovers' rendezvous, a honeymoon with me. I suppose, to put our marriage, back on track! There is a part of me, would have deeply enjoyed & welcomed that possibility, & I would have got on the train, had I known his intent. I went to the train, then felt too much inner resistance, to get on it.

I still feel, we will have to, meet again, next life, as we made a mess, yet again, of learning our soul lessons, together. Very occasionally, I still have dreams about him, with the love still strong, sometimes the pain too. I believe neither he nor I, were fully aware of, nor acknowledging, the escalating damage, so much emotional turbulence, had been having on our marriage. He came to the prison, & Martello was walking with his arm, round me, when we met. I returned with Berris to England, but he was very angry. I had no idea what he had been up to, in India, with other women! After all, - this sexual relating with others, though we were married, had all been set into motion by him!

Regardless of, my request & better judgement, Martello, had <u>not</u> removed his pile of clothes, from inside our home, (though I had asked him to), so Berris had deposited them in the dustbin. 'Dustbin day' the next morning, resulted in them all going to the land-fill site! I was feeling so conflicted, that unable to handle the tension, I decided on the spur of the moment, to go off to mountains near Grenoble, for a meditation retreat, (which Berris and I had formerly planned to attend). I 'should have' asked him to join me! I drove to the ferry, landed in France, panicked & thought, what have I done! I 'phoned Berris, telling him where I was, unsure, what was best to do. Getting no indication, he wanted me to return, or join me, I went on, to spend a week, in the sun & peaceful vibration of the environment. When I returned, Berris had got involved with yet another woman sexually, although she was married. I had a dream, where I was shown she was pregnant, so when Berris confessed this to me, I angrily burst out with, "You Stupid, I already knew," but before I had got out more than "you Stupid ...," he said "I know," consumed with guilt. It was O.K. for him to impregnate someone's wife, but not so, for me to get pregnant, after he had initiated sex with, partners outside our marriage. Somehow, we were not able to let each other hear, how much we loved each other, and regretted our choices, staying locked in resistant reactions &, habitual patterns, of relating. He was telling mutual friends, how much he did not want, to lose me, & I too knew the truth in my heart, yet we let the breakup of our marriage happen. Stubborn righteousness? Moreover, due to the pregnancy, though I hoped Berris, was the father, it was more likely Martello, which Berris found unacceptable, though Martello & I were simply friends, his only real commitment being, to his likely role as a father-to-be, to our coming child. Months before Berris was in my life, I had found the name 'Ammil,' in the book 'Tarka the Otter,' a Devon word meaning 'the glory of the Sun, bursting through the early morning mist.' Sometime after I was drawn to this name, I heard a voice tell me, to put Ra, (like Ra, The Sun God!) at the start, Rammil. I added the 'e' later, i.e., Rammiel, as so many angelic names end in 'el.' I had assumed Berris would be the father, but Life gave Martello as, my son's father, which was no doubt perfect, for **his** Soul plan.

It is interesting that this year, 2021, Martello, after his long-time partner died, to his deep sorrow, had decided to live in Rammiel's home, so I expected to meet him, once the crazy 'lock-down' was over. In fact, after 6 months, he went to live in Italy, a permanent move, he hoped. Doubtful. Already he is in Holland. He cannot seem to settle anywhere for long. I got on well with his mother, Nonna, as I called her ('Italian for Nan'), yet still loved Berris, not wanting to end our marriage, but Berris was keeping more distance between us. We were in contact, but no longer knowing how, to express our pain & heartache, nor how, to be together. We tried going on holiday together, to Rhodes, but mostly Berris stayed, unfriendly, & angry, unwilling to forgive, nor even to offer support at moments, heavily pregnant, that I needed physical assistance. My friend Mohammed, with whom I had run a small massage school, (teaching people to ITEC standard), eventually helped me, using Voice Dialogue, one of the various therapeutic techniques we had been exploring, to let go of Berris. I invited different aspects of myself, plus aspects I identified as Berris, to speak with each other, until they came to a sort of resolution, feeling I had done well at the time, to seemingly, let Berris go relatively painlessly. I still feel, (approaching my 81st Birthday), that, yet again, we made a 'cock up' of things so will need to meet again, in our next incarnation! There is a deep bond, whether acknowledged or not. Periodically I still have deeply emotional dreams about him.

I next made the decision to be celibate, feeling no man really loved me enough. I focussed on my pregnancy, listening to positive meditations, Louise Hays affirmations etc. & also visited, a good clairvoyant Peter Lee, I saw from time to time. Without any verbal input from me, he said, 'you have opted to be celibate & this is for your own evolution. It will probably last about 3 years.' Instead, it remained my choice for 5 years, until I read 'The Shared Heart,' by Barry and Joyce Vissell, &, let myself trust again, that there were men capable of commitment. I finally decided that I would open, to relationship again & actually planned, I would engage in sex, a 'ritual event,' on the Winter Solstice (of 1987 I suppose it must have been). I did not even tell Mohammed, he was to be part of my initiatory ritual, but my intent was so strong, all happened, without my saying a word, according to plan! He was/is a loved friend, but not, I sensed, someone for a long-term intimate commitment. As I wrote this, near the end of August 2012, I had hopefully navigated my way through, the last of the pain &, grief being released, in wave after wave, of 70ish years, of patterns of abandonment, loss, & betrayal. I was holding all in Love, looking to free myself, from old patterns, sure, that whatever it takes, I will create a very different Life experience, in coming years, of richness in Love and Intimacy, in financial well-being and plenty, & Joy, in my Being. I did feel, Gratitude & Appreciation, which seemed the nearest I knew, of Joy, for many years. Finally, in 2020 I live with this Joy in Life, yet no longer feel any pull, to having a physical partner.

*

Within that celibate time, two weeks before Rammiel, was born - (I was attending a rebirthing training, when one of the participants told me she had a message for me, from Babaji. It was mainly about my son-to-be, who was to be born, on St. Valentine's Day, exactly 1 year before Babaji, left the body he was then in. At the time, I assumed Babaji (of 'Haidakhan'), must be coming somehow, into my life, in relation to my son, rather than to me.

Throughout my pregnancy, I had mainly kept away from doctors, after one doctor had said "You go home and do some soul searching, Mrs. B…... You'll bleed like a pig," etc., (quoting Doctor!) I had to process out of my body, all that fear, he tried to instil in me. I had been very focussed, for my baby as much as me, on listening to Louise Hays affirmations &, inspiring meditations throughout the pregnancy. Rammiel was born at home. Martello of course, was with me, plus I invited Samantha to take photos, plus my dear friend & co-inner explorer Mohammed to attend. As the hours went by during which, an extra heater was bought, & those I had asked to be with me had arrived, it got to 4pm, & I was asking myself; will it indeed happen on this auspicious 'Love' day? (i.e., St. Valentine's Day)!

Deciding to relax in a bath of warm water, the planned **Water birth**! forgotten, I spoke to my unborn baby, saying 'it's a good day to be born!' Just after climbing out of the bath, my waters broke, 5pm approx. &, Martello hurriedly alerted the midwives, who had insisted on being present. I was in my bed-room, with dim lights, on my knees, so much energy & heat in my body, that I pulled all my clothes off. The baby was pressing, against my spine, it seemed, which was not comfortable. I did not have that closer bonding, with my partner Martello, for him to help me in physical ways, even if he had known how to help. (Obviously being fully engaged in the birthing process, it was no time to share my birthing knowledge & preferences). As the rhythm changed, as birth approached, the 3! Midwives, insisted on, my moving into the other bedroom, a more brightly lit space, **not** what I would have chosen, having immersed myself in books by Leboyer & other proponents, of natural pain-free Birth, with least stress for, the emerging child. Sadly, I had neither communicated my wishes & preferences, with my daughter Samantha, nor with Martello, or friend Mohammed. I had never met the three midwives before, sent no doubt, because it had been assumed, probably by that male doctor! - that at 42yrs.of age, I would suffer complications. In fact, the birth process was much faster & easier than Samantha's birth, where, though I had learned about breathing, to help prepare they had had me on my back, working against gravity! - thus, for Rammiel, it took only a couple of hours. Rammiel was easily born at 7pm, & as I took him in my arms, I was saying, "Isn't he beautiful! He's beautiful!"

The hours which followed were very precious, just lying with my baby. Emotionally, I was much more relaxed this time, as a mother. With Samantha I had felt emotionally insufficient, so had stopped breastfeeding her after a year, whereas Rammiel stopped when he chose, so was 6yrs.old, before he totally stopped. Samantha never again tried to feed from me. Sadly, she had telepathically picked up my unwillingness, it seems. As a result, I felt, of my choice, she sucked her thumb, till she was 10yrs.old. Martello stayed with me, until he began to have other 'girl-friends,' which I sort of accepted, but was not the highest possibility in my life! I even had the first of these, living in my home, & was friendly with her, as I did not feel Martello as my life partner, much though I cared about & liked him. We had a good friendship, but I was anyway still in my celibate phase. And, married, both legally & in my heart!! I saw much of 'Nonna,' his Italian mother & family, enjoying how they loved to feed us, with Italian cooking! Martello has been & is, a good father, yet a troubled being, looking always for his place or home, in the World, in country after country! He speaks neither to me, nor his brothers. Now 2022, after returning to Italy, having intended to retire there, in Nonna's part of Italy, around Bari, already he is in Holland. I wonder if he ever can settle! I think he has a friend there. I hope he one day, finds true peace & heart-opening in his being.

Graeme was one of my close friends at the time, & there is a deep soul connection with him, which became clear, by the deeply insightful dreams, we would both have. We also shared spiritual insights & explored rebirthing more deeply. He suggested my accompanying him, to Wales, to some Babaji gathering, to visit a close friend of his, but I decided at the last moment, to go to a Shamanic happening, with Azucena, (and of course Rammiel), instead. It was at that very gathering, in Wales that Graeme met & became close with Monika, who later became his wife, & the mother of his children. She too is a Soul sister about whom, I have had equally deep, significant dreams. Monika & Graeme, were becoming deeply involved with Babaji, (later took the names Durgadas and Hari Sudha) & through them, particularly nr. the end of my pregnancy with Rammiel, despite my layers of resistance, Babaji (of Haidakhan), came more fully into my life. I had gone through a period of confusion, in 1979 to 1980, until clarifying, via a good clairvoyant, that while with Osho, I had been working out my personal, emotional & sexual issues, whereas now, I was moving into greater service, to humanity, with Babaji; it rang true & so I relaxed. (Much to my surprise, I had a deeply involved dream about Durgadas, & Babaji too, while in Lakabe, very recently in 2020. Babaji was acting in a very playful Krishna-like way, like a lover-to-be. I did not understand the dream's message).

Celebration, was a strong aspect, of the Osho Sannyas Community, with dance, music, dynamic meditations, & Intense therapy groups. At that point Aids, was entering the Mass awareness, & there was pressure in the Sannyas community to get check-ups in order to get Aids-free certificates. I chose rather to continue my celibacy, than be involved in that whole story, withdrawing already from my Sannyas involvement, yet I have always, seen Osho as a True Friend on my path. My life path, has still taken me in recent years, to the Osho Leela Community, for Bhakti Gatherings. I enjoy that sporadic re-connection.

*

Babaji emphasised Service to Humanity through Karma Yoga, to see the Truth at the Source of all the religions, & follow the light in our own Hearts & not be sheep, - encouraging too 'Truth, Simplicity and Love.' Hindu type rituals are part of the practices, such as Aarti or Puja &, Fire Ceremonies - making offerings to the 'Mother.' Again, I had resisted becoming part of a group. What happened was, one evening I lay reading 'One hundred and eight Encounters with Babaji', then fell asleep. (I have never since, been able, to find that book again, which so deeply spoke to me). Around Dawn the following day, I was suddenly awakened by, an immense rushing wind-like Energy swirling, in the room, next to my bed, then heard the words *"I am the Lord of the Universe."*

I **knew** it was Babaji. Sometime later, I was reading a book about Christ called, "I AM WITH YOU ALWAYS – True stories of Encounters with Jesus." I read the words, "I awakened around 2:00 am. Knowing that this sound (i.e., that *'rushing wind sound'* - author*)* often, foreshadows a dramatic shift in consciousness, I remained very still, staying open." (&, in the book's footnote below), - 'usually precedes a lucid dream or out-of-body experience, or the presence of higher beings – especially Jesus. In Buddhism, it is referred to as "the gift waves" of a master. It is called "the conferring of power," and constitutes the "true spiritual initiation." In Mahayana Buddhism, the source is considered, to be higher beings - masters who are either incarnate or existing on higher planes of consciousness - who telepathically confer upon the recipient a gift of higher energy that will stimulate spiritual development.' So, began my deeper conscious journey in this life-time with Babaji, who has been with me through many lives, including, in India, so I am told, when I was an 'untouchable'. I now entered the world of Mantras, temple rituals & devotional singing. In fact, as well as receiving messages from other devotees, purportedly from Babaji, it was very much my spending time with Gopal Hari & Ambika, in temple & social gatherings - known more widely as Goma, whose music drew me deeper, (which includes of course, their sons Shambo & Veda), & later were joined usually, by 'Tabla Tom,' & Asha. Shambo, Veda, & Asha, all have new partners & young families now). A Joy. I would like to add, that one time when I had ingested some fly agaric mushroom, & I exclaimed 'Christ,' everything glowed so much brighter, I felt, 'God!' so, **that is** what the Christ is about. I did remember a couple of lives I had, when Christ was on Earth. One as a shepherd boy, & curiosity brought me to see him. Another life as a priest, in Egypt, & I was drawn to go & find out who this Jesus Christ was. I do not remember more. (I have mentioned elsewhere that we are supposedly playing out 12 different aspects in different realities, at any one time).

At the 'Harmonic Convergence,' in 1987, a time of greater influx of higher vibration energies, I was with Azucena at a Sun Dance gathering, a Camp, near Glastonbury. (There I met Martin, Kushuma & family, later a part of my widespread Babaji Family). Certainly, by Spring 1988, Gopal Hari & family were already a big part of my life, & friends Azucena & Verity joined me in those days. Azucena left her body in recent yrs. Verity, a close friend from my Sannyasin days, still is so. Her blood family is from the 'Calcutta Jewish lineage, (in this life). We have been friends over 40 years & I deeply love & honour her. We still meet for deeper sharing, Journey sessions occasionally, steam, sauna, swimming & we talk often, during this 'lock-down' period. Ambika & Gopal Hari, stayed heart-felt friends, though Gopal Hari, left his body, 3 months before Sam.

Babaji spoke little, relating through visions, individually calling people to him, & could & did, appear in many locations at once, interacting with each person in, unexpectedly perfect ways for each. He appears and reappears down through the Ages. My close involvement with the English Babaji Temple activities, lasted at least 25yrs. in which time I was part of the main decision-making committees, for different periods of time, mainly harmonious, while we agreed on coming to, consensus agreement, but quickly, uglier, conflicted & divisive, once the cliquey power pressure dynamics took over. I realized this was no longer part of my authentic path home to myself. More about that later. I drew away from ashrams, yet have found Babaji even closer, an ongoing support in, my being my true self. I still participate in 'Bhakti' gatherings (I enjoyed another one, at the start of June 2022), where, there is more of a meeting of people on various devotional paths, who love Kirtan, including my dearest Babaji friends, which is what Babaji is about, honouring the Source at the root of all the ways, not in creating religious difference.

*

Here I will add other threads and patterns, weaving through vividly, from childhood, onwards, - yet hardly mentioned. I had met Jungleyes, while I was with Berris. I was already sometimes, eating just raw food. He had been eating only fruit for many years, neither did he believe in cutting his hair, so had very long matted hair. Though I resonated with much he loved to explore, & some of his life-choices, I insist on my freedom, to change my mind at any moment, thus I draw away from, rigidity & imposition of one's beliefs on others. He was very persuasive, (to the point of being overly controlling with his girlfriends!) but, with a very active imagination, researching in depth, with intelligence, the truth behind his beliefs, & lived with integrity, focus, honesty, & compassion. He & his mother were very supportive & heartfelt friends, throughout the rest of their lives. I drove him on regular visits, to the Traders' Fruit market, which is still, about 45yrs. later, a regular part of my life, - well, until the orthodox pharma. medical giant, managed to gain so much restrictive control over so many of us, who do not share such beliefs! (Though often, I have chosen to eat just fruit, fast, or cleanse inwardly in other ways, I include herbs, leaves, & sea-weeds in my diet, get caught up too, every so often, in eating cooked food, which is initially very addictive, as the tastes can, be very stimulating, without over-eating, but quickly less satisfying. Yet the palate gets quickly jaded, after the first hits of strong tastes, such as salty, oily, spicy, mixes of many ingredients, etc. I studied extensively, exploring the effect of different foods on my body, & know how to cleanse myself & heal. Diet is only one aspect affecting health, yet I know what my body is happiest with, drink & food-wise. I did a year's training too, with Barbara Wren, ('College of Natural Nutrition'), author of 'Cellular Awakening,' & 'Return to the Light.' I felt in tune with her teachings, about living in greater harmony with

Nature, & the way in which the cells in our bodies, relate with light). Our Alcazar meditations deepen our awareness too, of the light of stargates in every one of our millions of cells, & in the pineal & pituitary glands too. The love from, the Quantum Field of all potential!

*

Fascinated too, by exploration of inner consciousness, Jungleyes & I, would visit Wimbledon Common, to pick fly agarics, or psilocybin mushrooms in Richmond Park, & other places.

When I really needed to find work, he had just bought a shop in Kew, to sell his crystals, so offered me his site by, St. Martin-in-the-Fields, (by Trafalgar Square), to continue crystal selling, on a stall. So, began my 7 or 8 yrs. of having my own stall, & really connecting with crystals. My Columbian boy-friend, (a brief & somewhat conflicted relationship), Jose, had got me interested in his emeralds, from his home capital city, Bogota. Rammiel & I joined him there in 1988, but I let go easily of that relationship. (I was shown & felt the signs, back in England, that the cord between us had snapped, - my cat had dead kittens on my bed, - the only time that happened, then a crystal heart, broke in half, on the same day). Since I had already organized, (thanks to friend Anthea), a journey to Bogota, with Rammiel, who was then 5yrs. of age, in 1988, I chose to travel anyway, around Columbia, using small internal flights. We enjoyed visiting Leticia, in Amazonia, where we bought huge, delicious juicy pineapples. We went in a boat down the Amazon River too, visiting an indigenous village, where we saw a sloth. Rammiel & I would set up our tent wherever needed, made a brief detour too, into Venezuela). A very special & powerful journey, with much sharing too, of circle dance from me, & deeper spiritual messages, with the more alternative spiritual communities in Medellin; - (Jose aside!).

I still, so deeply love crystals, especially the inner rainbow sparkles. Now in my 82nd year, when I am letting go of many of my possessions, many of my special crystals are finding special places in my present room, in Stroud. Others I am giving to a local Crystal shop. My years of visiting crystal fairs, plus many years of buying, & selling crystals, were a delight. I gained much knowledge, from Gurudas books ('Gem Elixirs and Vibrational Healing' Vols. 1&2), & other channelled information. I also made gem remedies. I did attend various trainings & courses, & offered crystal workshops for a while, but handling and enjoying, their beauty, shapes and, crystalline rainbow sparkles, is what I love.

Since Nov.18th 2020, I have a much smaller physical space to live in now, yet through my meditations, with the global Stargate Community, hearing the Alcazar Masters, channelled through Prageet & Julieanne, guiding our community of thousands, helped via the Stargates, we are guided into vast, expanded realms. My heart has opened so wide, with a perpetual warmth Joy/Love in both my physical & my Soul being.

An aspect important to me, in setting up my stall, 30yrs, previously, back in 1990, in Portobello Market, had been, to create a regular structure for years, where I was available & visible, not hiding, which felt important for me, at that time. In Winter, this involved getting up early, pretty much whatever the weather, in the dark early hours, to claim my spot. One gets to know all the stall holders, including all the long-time family fruit & veg. traders. I felt at home, after years working in Portobello market, & worked for quite a while too, in both the Spitalfields & Camden Lock markets. I am anyway, now at home, just as much in London, as in rural places. London is like many towns & villages all together, & I love Holland Park, Richmond Park, Kew Gardens, Osterley Park, Hampstead Heath, Regents Park, Syon Park, & so many more, of London's plant & wildlife havens.

*

It was at that time, of being a market trader, having decided to open once more, to sexual relating, that I had made a list of qualities I was inviting in my new partner-to-be. In hindsight I would have added much more! - but for that, no doubt I would have, to have made, the inner shifts too, or, released more of the past! I then surrendered this to 'God.' One day at the market, a man introduced himself to me, as Cedric. He told me he was a medium, guided to be together with me! I thought, well maybe this is what 'God' wants. Yet after knowing each other for some weeks, & with no sex, I just felt my energy did not resonate with his. Before this, I had a strong dream, on 3 repeating nights, which I believed were from Babaji, showing me, I was to be with Sam and, that we were meant to learn to walk in tandem, like two wild-pack dogs, two beings walking with synchronous, same end purpose! We still had not come, nearly 22yrs. later, to this degree of harmony! Yet appearances are deceptive, as here we still were, attempting, to find out, what our souls' intention was, in the situation, & navigating our way together, even if this did not always seem so. At the time, of the 3 dreams, my immediate response was, "Sam? He's not the sort of man I should be with!" Yet once again, trusting the guidance, I decided to communicate the truth I was being shown. Since at that time Sam was with a partner, I thought I would find ways whereby, I could simply honour & support him, so, shared on paper, what was being shown to me, in my life. I sent an open letter, that could be read by others, in the 'Edge Community,' describing the 3 dreams, & the decisions I had made, given the circumstances. Yet there came a day when his partner, was having an 'affair' with another man, & for whatever reason, Sam was no longer living in her family home, but in a caravan, on her land. He invited me one day, to visit him there, & I appreciated the welcome, yet my impression while in the caravan, was, he did not much love, or care for himself. Involved as I already was, in studying Machaelle Small Wright's co-operative way, of working with the Devas or Nature kingdoms, I began to share, this enlightened way of gardening, with Sam. The months went by, Cedric had come & gone, & I could feel my soul calling, in relation to Sam! Graeme & Monika, (their new names, Durgadas & Hari Sudha), had chosen to live in, my London home, for several months, then had later moved to the same land as Sam, & I sometimes went to visit them. Then shortly before Christmas 1990, I received a letter from Sam, inviting me to North Aston at Christmas, (Goma's home), to find out what the truth was between us, suggesting I meet him in Ambika & Gopal Hari's home. I accepted the invitation, arrived on Christmas Eve, but drove off first, to visit my daughter, who lived about 6 miles away in Bicester. When I returned, it turned out that Ambika, knowing well, why we were both there, had urged Sam to act. When Sam made a move, to engage in closer contact, with me, I resisted at first, wanting to be sure, he had made a definite break, from his previous partner. After a while, half-reassured, we moved into a warmer, more comfortable room, & lay down on our backs, on the carpet, next to each other. At his first touch, I flipped straight into a previous life, with Sam, where I lay with him, as his young wife, in a tipi. I knew in that moment, I had been with him, in many, many other lives, so, relaxed straightaway, knowing this was meant to be. Gopal Hari was ill, then Ambika succumbed too, so Sam & I ended up, looking after the entire household! Sam joined me in my London home, & within two months, had asked me to marry him. Two weeks later, he said, 'I'm wondering about the age difference.' I said, without pause, 'I'll be looking after you, at your death, not the other way round.' We went initially through our own ritual, in front of our Babaji altar, then chose a registry office marriage in Stroud, on Feb.14th 1991, with Durgadas & Hari Sudha as witnesses, plus Rammiel, my sister Carmen, & other friends. Afterwards, we gathered at Edge, & I taught them a marriage Circle Dance. I was 50yrs. of age, at the time, Sam, being 18yrs. younger, (same as Martello). I became pregnant soon after we met, but was miscarrying, even as we were getting married, which I later, was glad of. She would have been in her thirties by now. I did wonder if Sam, would have become more mature, & responsible, emotionally, had she chosen birth. Even as I wrote this, our marriage, at least, in the way we had been engaging, was fast unravelling.

I had been sleeping no more than an hour or two, most nights during the previous month, at the same time as, my whole energy frequency had shifted. My healing capacities & awareness, had increased & sensitized, and I was much more aligned with my Soul self, more aware of my heart & energy body. I had emphasized right from the start with Sam, that I was at that time, only interested in a deeply committed relationship. Sam replied that, he had never left his girl-friends, they always left him! A cautionary statement!? From my experience in the Sixties & Seventies, up to the end of my marriage with Berris, & my time with Martello, during Rammiel's early childhood, I was clear, I did <u>not</u> want a partner who, would be chasing other women, while we were together.

Sam turned out not, to be the easiest, of bed-fellows. Whatever traumas he was carrying, he would start up in terror, if I came to bed, in the dark, or, shout & swear in his sleep, at unknown assailants. If my opinion differed from his, about anything, it triggered his sense of rejection, to the point of huge emotional reactions, exhausting for me, which I had never experienced before, especially in the bedroom, always before, a place of rest, and safety! - (other than sirens bomb alerts). (Looking at 2 old passport photos of mine, before & after Sam, I appear in the later one, as if I aged considerably more than 10 yrs.)!

*

In 1993, Sam & I were still regularly at our Crystal (plus Essential Oils & Incense) stall, Fridays & Saturdays. I had traded there since 1990. When Sam could no longer handle (after 2 months) living in my London Council house, I carried on driving there weekly. I preferred to get to my London home, the previous evening, for the early a.m. Portobello Market Friday lottery, for a chance of being in the better part of the market. Once I had the permanent stall, I had to start from the poor end, & set up my stall, among the many Irish rag-traders, less trade.

*

At some point, I had set things in motion, to buy our own home, in Stroud, - grateful thanks to the Greater London Council, after an earlier 'Squatters' Amnesty, giving me a grant, for the right to buy a home, anywhere in the Country! (Very different from political attitudes, in the 2020's). My Council House, was close to Wormwood Scrubs & the prison too. Though we continued to sell crystals, in the Stroud market, once I let my Portobello stall go, my motivation for carrying on as a trader, no longer held much charge for me, much less of a buzz, so this gradually dwindled, resulting in less predictable income. I had got too exhausted, after some months of driving weekly, between Stroud & London. We were living too, in a tipi on Vibha's land, with Rammiel too, of course. So, we were beholden to her, as it were! I did feel the damp from the wet grass beneath the tipi, entering my bones! Vibha was Sam's former partner! Rammiel & Samantha, were both born in London, the cause I believe, of them being a little asthmatic, though I brought them up in the early years, on organically grown, natural foods. Rammiel never took to meat nor even to milk, once he was older & made his own choices. I would sometimes prepare 3 different meals for him, me & Sam. Rammiel, 'a casualty of his not so normal mother,' does like to fit in more, in work situations, with cups of tea etc. not his preferred choice.

*

A Bengali 'Guru,' was invited to Vibha's land & home & the loose-knit 'Community,' in Edge, & thereabouts, would gather, to hear his teachings, & were split mainly between, those drawn to take 'Guru Diksha,' an initiation with Gurudeva, on a devotional path more focussed on Krishna, & those on the Haidakhan Baba Shiva path. I was quite taken aback, when Sam took 'guru diksha,' & a new spiritual name, Shyam Sundar, rather than Vyasan. I was very resistant, to the practices in which Vyasan wanted me to participate, especially at 3a.m. in the morning, very clear, **my** closest, overseeing guide, is Babaji. Melchizedek's overseeing Presence in, the unfolding, of my life/lives, seems more remote. l continued anyway, to enjoy Kirtan & communal sharing. Eventually, Sam's ex-partner Vibha, put pressure on **me**, to leave her land, unless I was on **her** path, whereas Sam was allowed to stay! We both left, to go over the hill, to where we had first stayed, after we married, back to our dear friend Vijaya (formerly Elaine Twilley - or Laino of 'Prana' chants), with her partner Fred (gifted tree author & painter), plus her children. The Acorn (Steiner type) school, (now well-established, in Nailsworth), in its earliest days was based in Vijaya's home & had started initially with just Rammiel &, one other boy!

Around that time also, I had my 1st aura picture done, at a Mind Body Spirit Festival. It showed my asking the Universe for guidance, as to my deeper Direction, or purpose, as my heart was not wholly in alignment, with what I was doing. Sam was working at the Kirlian stand. I decided to try selling Crystals in the next MBS show, but it was a lot of work & profit-wise, no better than working at my Portobello Market stall. I asked if I could train to work at the Aura-reading stand &, have been working there annually, once, sometimes twice a year, for the last 40 years, excepting 2020 & 2021. We had an MBS show in mid-April 2022, in Olympia, & I am booked, if, the controlling powers-that-be, do not interfere, for one in Birmingham, in the last days of October! I enjoy giving these Aura photo interpretations, finding my insights & perceptions, increasingly deepening over the years. There has been increased light and expansion, in the recent photos, I have been reading, - an upgrade, which is heartening. In earlier years, we served in this way for hours, up to 10 days in a row. Exhausting, with very short rest & food breaks, but much joy in sharing, with so many focussed on spiritual search, including our work colleagues, whom we meet year after year, so, good friendships have developed between us.

I had introduced Sam, as already mentioned, to Machaelle Small Wright's books. Her first book, 'Behaving as if the God in all Life Mattered,' her autobiography, relates how she entered a co-creative partnership with Nature. She created a garden, Perelandra, in Virginia, where most of her learning, exploration, plus deepening co-operation, with Nature beings began & has taken place, resulting in a great harmony, balance & communication, between all the diverse life forms in the area, with everything flourishing & receiving care and nurture. Sam & I valued this way of relating to plants, soil, insects & the whole 'deva' & Nature kingdom. I so honour insects, for their role in the over-all scheme on Earth, so essential for all of Life. It distresses me to see the war waged on Nature, especially on insects, & birds by unaware or seemingly heartless, greedy human beings, such as the Bayer/Monsanto merger, controlling many of the world's seeds, 60% I read, with their 'pharma' poisons & pesticides. Attacking any one part affects the whole. (I confess I have found meat maggots challenging, less so fruit-fly maggots, on rotting fruit; also, mosquito and horse-fly bites unwelcome, something in me that drew their attention! I would never use poisons). I was pleased recently, to find an organization, called 'Buglife' which I now support in a small way.

Sam's paid work was gardening. He also learnt to make flower essences. I chose to make gem essences, once I got deeply drawn to the world of crystals &, have always loved stones too.

We lived first with friends, 15mths. in our tipi, later in a caravan, all on the same land in Edge, outside Stroud. When one day I found all my plants, trees & shrubs cut down, to the bare earth, & the beautiful ivy pulled off the walls of my London home, I was so upset, I decided no longer to live in a Council house, controlled by others in this way. Council tenants in London, at that time, as I mentioned, had the right to buy their own home, anywhere in the U.K. with the help of a grant, so I set this in motion, with help too, from my mother & a good friend. I was intent on finding our own home for me, Rammiel, & Sam; - however, once I let go of the market stall, our income became rather more precarious. We started with a small mortgage, yet since the value of our home, kept increasing over the years, we ended up borrowing & increasing the mortgage, to fund our joint lifestyle!

Inspired by Milton Erikson's approach, & good tutors, I qualified in hypnotherapy, in the 1970's - (learning about the enneagram was part of the Course), then I took this in a direction which fascinated me, and trained in Past Life regression. (Milton Erikson was unique in his approach to Hypnotherapy, teaching through anecdotes, stories, in unexpected, spontaneous and, intuitive ways, geared to the moment, and the person involved). Though I practised with many people, I did not feel this was a Life calling. For a while I got excited with the Skenar bio-feedback machine, developed for Russian spacemen, for healing support during space travel. I trained as a Skenar therapist, impressed, after my throat chakra was unblocked enough, after one session, that I became relaxed, about speaking on the 'phone! I ignored the channel who said to me, "You don't need that 'gizmo', you're a hands-on healer, get on with it." She 'inner-saw' with wonder, some beautiful dimension I have previously lived in. I wonder whether it was Unicorn or Dragon worlds! Months later, an ailing friend I lent it to, lost my Skenar device, a costly loss! I guess that must still have been, in my thirties.

Sam & I (in my 50's or 60's), continued to be very involved in the whole puja, temple, fire ceremony, mantras, devotional & 'Kirtan' practices, meeting our closest like-minded friends at each other's homes or larger venues. For years too, some of us went to different gatherings, such as the big Glastonbury festival, (before it became mainstream!), the smaller Healing Field Gathering, the Sunrise & Green Gatherings, Gaunt's House Summer festivals, etc. taking the Babaji Marquee, also camping, with tents, which allowed Temple activities, & a deeper connection with Nature & each other, as well as sharing much with, so many new friends. I loved those times.

*

Like most women, I carried the romantic dream, of true love, deep intimate sharing, my best friend, all in one! What I manifested with Sam, was the most challenging relationship of my life. In Bob I had met, someone deeply disturbed, but my heart was not open, which allowed me to snap the cords, very immediately, as I have in other relationships too. By this time, since my marriage with Berris, my heart had opened wider, leaving me more vulnerable to possible pain. I had become fearful of betrayal or, abandonment, as the original experience & pain of this, is easily triggered, when one opens to love from another. (As a young child I remember declaring out loud, - "l love everybody. Even John Gretorix," whose shortcoming was to be fat! Such conditional 'love'). I had not come to deep acceptance or, love of myself. Sam & I blamed & judged each other for years, reactions stemming as always, from deep self-abandonment! How cruel we have been with ourselves, not loving, forgiving, or tender, with this person, within whom our being is incarnated, likewise, those who reflect us back to ourselves, with whom, we share life's lessons, joys and, experience. Feeling so often unloved, & unloving.

*

Sam & I tried channelling for a few months, but both felt uncertain, about how real the connection w to our guides or the wisdom which got spoken. In (2011 or 12?) we decided to try again. I connected with a very loving being named Gezra. He seemed to be in some higher dimensional reality, & though I have no name, for where this is, his presence felt very real to me, & has continued to feel so, thus I've connected with him, in meditations, ever since. The message I keep getting, when I connect with Soul, & Source energy, is to keep bringing everything to Love, - Pain, Grief, darkness, everything, including disease & every shade & flavour of life, however dense. In 2022, I regularly connect with Babaji, Alcazar, Gezra, Lu Yin & St. Germaine, plus other higher beings & ALL! which includes of course, feminine wise, awakened beings.

*

After approx. the first 10yrs. of relating with Sam, I felt very exhausted. He seemed to need to explode, every three or so days, from frustration, or other volcanic emotions, throughout our shared life. Since my lack of safety was easily triggered, I was living in a state of alert, much of the time, as soon as Sam raised his voice, or even looked as if, the next storm or drama, was brewing. I felt dominated by Sam's moods, & welcomed his visits to his mother, etc. as relief & relaxation. I felt, much as I 'honoured' Sam, I was in a living Hell, & no longer knew if, I was being abusive to myself, to stay together. I felt myself a victim of these dramas, not fully aware. at that time, of **my co-creation** of our reality. Also, as our financial stress increased, I had got embroiled in juggling money from one account to another, getting deeper into debt. In 1995 my mother had contributed to helping us fund rewiring, damp-proofing, & wood-worm treatment, as required by the mortgage company, when we managed to buy our home, which created more safety & stability for me & Rammiel. She died 3 yrs. later, on October 28th 1998, the **<u>exact</u>** day I had been told she would, a month earlier, by a female voice in a dream. On the 1st anniversary of her death, I stood on Hampstead Heath, & got a visual sense of my mother, - as a young woman with long black hair, standing happily with loving friends around her. Two yrs. later, also in October, my beloved cat Ember, 18mths.old only, was squashed by a car. Such was the unconditional love flow between me, & Ember, that I was filled with grief. His sister I had given to Jane & 'Mauricio' next door, got killed likewise. I chose to have no more cats after Ember.

*

I had put the house in my & Sam's names, as I always shared the abundance in my life. Sam had his ideas about our future, but we never looked deeply at what we both most wanted, dealing the best we could, with underlying conflicts. Later in this chapter, I will describe a key letting-go, just before my 72nd birthday, of the sacrificial suffering, & painful 'rescue the World' pattern, I carried so long, in this and many previous lives.

*

Not long after, Sam and I decided on, *an energy clearing process for our home & the surrounding area. This is a process from Machaelle Small Wrights Gardening Work book 2, which involves co-operation with one's higher self, the Nature kingdom, Christ light, & other light beings, to lift up & out, any inappropriate, ungrounded, stagnant, scattered or, darkened energies from the area, ready to be cleansed. I visualized the area, surrounding home, garden, plus some feet further out in every direction. We drew a diagram to show the exact extent of this area. Sam read the instructions, while I focussed on the visualizing. On Hallowe'en, the last night of the same month, while I was on my night duty at the 'Supported Lodgings,' our home was flooded. The exact area I had visualized, was under water!* (I was working 10 or 11 yrs. on night duty, as a Carer, responsible for the welfare of up to a dozen, men and, women, in residential 'Supported Lodgings', 3 to 5 nights a week; - relief too, from Sam's emotional outbursts)! It seemed a good idea, for Sam take a holiday, as he wanted, as Rammiel & I were relaxed, about living with downstairs chaos, dealing with the flood aftermath; so, he went to India for several months, while our ground floor things, were either put on a skip, or cleaned from river silt, with friends' helping hands too, shifting much of the old out, & the new in, including industrial size dehumidifiers & fans. I dealt with the different contractors, sent in by the Insurers, choosing new lino, electrical items, wall & tile colours, furniture, & so on. *Rather than believe we caused a flood, I would say, we were in tune with, what was needed at the time, to bring those most responsible for flood defence & care of the wider environment, to more awareness of what was being neglected.* This did not in fact change for years, until more severe floods arrived, & we formed a Slad Valley Flood Action group! Sam and I had been together 11yrs.

(Over 10yrs. later, 'The Gloucestershire Wildlife Trust' - Roger Mortlock, Chief Exec., has finally secured funding from the governments 'Green Recovery Challenge Fund', so good things are starting to happen, for our local environment's plants & creatures).

*

Before I write more of the story of our time together in the 10 years since, I would say, I felt at that point, in 2012, I was reaching the last major hurdles in the way, of total letting go, of whatever I no longer wish to carry, into the life I was now birthing. *By July 2012, I really wanted a 'Journey' process, as I felt myself very ready, to release all the past suffering & pain, still held in my body, from old ways of relating, with the men I had loved, more deeply, this being so, especially in my two legal marriages. So, Judith & I met. (Release, not in the sense of, pushing away, but a loving meeting, & welcoming of the old pain, which is thus freed &, dissolved). I went very deep down in my process. The banisters were more ornate & wider, than usual, but very safe. My intent is to connect with ever-deepening unconditional love, to express from my heart, feeling too, trust & increasing safety, with human beings. The doors were big & curvy, suggesting my Chinese guide, but I opened to the unexpected, yet there he was, blue & yellow clothes, & turban as usual, but this time, he was on a higher platform, sitting in lotus position, & radiating increasing friendship & loving warmth, every time we meet, a fellow co-conspirator, in my coming to realize, who I/We are. We land in the Heart chakra, in the right side, where it feels very unsafe, as there is a steep, narrow precipice, with no visible bottom. A memory arises of me in the sea, with Max & Samantha. We are near the shore, but strong undercurrents pull us quickly out to sea. Max, intent on reaching the safety of the shore, swims back, but I swim after Samantha, who is fast being swept out to sea. I grab her, & manage to steer us sideways, towards some rocks, & get out. My belief is confirmed that I cannot trust, others will help me, in life & death scenarios. As I go back to my mother's womb, where I first felt unsafe, two emotions surface, both abandonment &, betrayal.*

The betrayal seems removed, up on a platform, so I intuit, I am trying to avoid that, by dropping into the more familiar abandonment below. When I connect to, feeling betrayed, over & over again, I connect first with anger, then a strong ferocity that I will, stand up for me, & take no more shit! Soon my whole body, experiences being filled with power, my own real support, without needy weakness, nor self-pity. I find so much Safety too, here inside me. I do not have to source this outside of me! I then experienced, my whole base chakra opening wide, which has been happening often, since. Though I experience vulnerability, connection & openness, I still feel resourceful. Judith was feeling the decisions I made about men, before my celibate phase, needed to be reviewed in the light of what I have now experienced. I brought to the camp-fire, all the men I have related with, but women too, as we are all in this relationship dance, plus, different ages of a younger me. I have of course, had plenty of lives, as a man too. Berris is the one to whom I needed to speak, voicing the pain I really felt, about his having sex with, the various women. He knew how that made him feel, when threatened likewise! He is a good business man, not so good at taking responsibility, for the stresses generated, in his relationships with women, including the mother of his children. It seems he is unwilling to deal with healing the past. (Later I received divorce papers, citing me with Martello, as the cause. I replied to the solicitor, stating that Berris was being dishonest, in blaming me, & told him, the truth of the situation. He tried to blame group pressure, too, but no-one forced us do anything, that we did not choose to do. So, our divorce did not then happen).

I was not willing to forgive as quickly as usual, but eventually did, & was so glad, this had finally surfaced to be healed, forgiven & released, allowing greater freedom from past pain. I did not even know, I was holding, so much lack of forgiveness, for Berris, for initiating 'adultery', then rejecting me & my unborn child, when faced with, the consequences of, his initial choice. Especially given, that he impregnated another woman! I felt compassion easily for Max, in his fear, but still it fed my earlier beliefs that, "Men are not safe, they can never truly love me." I have a terrifying memory, when I put my life totally in Max's hands & survived to tell the tale! We had arrived at friend Jose's flat in Carcagente, a village near the orange groves, in the Valencia region. Jose, was either away, or out. Not the age of mobile phones nor even, land-line phones. We climbed the stairs, to the flat roof above his flat &, could see a bedroom window open. We were above the 5th floor, so were looking down the deep, shadowed, inner well, probably over 40 feet deep, windows open, so, rising echoes of human chatter. We found some rope, & I do not know, how I dared, to trust both Max's strength &, the strength of the rope, to allow him to lower me, to the open window, my whole body-weight, my life, in his hands! I did manage to manoeuvre myself, into the room, where I lay in shock, shaking, on the floor. After more moments, I was able to summon enough strength, and presence of mind, to open the door to let him in!

My new amendment is "I commit myself, in this life or the next, to drawing to me, when or if, the time is right, the male partner who best, can really meet me, as true friend, intimate lover, who enjoys honest, wholehearted sharing, trust & commitment, as well as healthy autonomy." (I was open to the possibility of this with Sam, my then husband, yet felt too, it did not serve us, to stay together if, we continued unable to deeply open to, & trust the other. (10 yrs. later, I seem to have little interest in a new male partner in this life! **Enough already**)! *My heart, looks & feels much safer now, & asks me to stay connected, my Mentor suggesting, I stay both in my true power, & vulnerable.* Sam & I were not having an easy time, & when he left, to stay with friends, the following morning, we were both not happy, with each other.

In my Women's group, we were focussing on meeting shadow selves. I felt myself as a snarling wolf, with bared teeth & later, snake fangs, full of venom, felt too some nausea, as if I had a belly full of poison to spew out. I had hardly slept for 2 nights, then on the Tuesday morning I woke up, full of so much anger, that I could not attend to my usual tasks, before I had sawn loads of wood, funnelling my anger in non-destructive ways. I reclaimed my right to make changes in the garden, clearing what felt like stagnant, neglected or 'care-less' energies, & staying strong & focussed. I was clear too, that I wanted to vomit out, a lot of self-disgust, at everything I have allowed to happen for so long. Having experienced betrayal often enough, & when younger, hurt others without due thought or care, enough, to be very sensitive, to the pain triggered by the threat of infidelity, I have been very careful for many, many years, to live with integrity, never leading any man, to think I was sexually available, while married to Sam. He felt easily threatened, by my friendliness, with any man. One rule for him, another for me! Yet having opened to love, in my marriage, since I was carrying this fear, of infidelity, one day I was giving a healing session to a friend, & later as we chattered, mentioned to him, that because my greatest fear was, that Sam would, sexually relate to another woman, I would therefore attract this, to me! That very night, Sam spent the night with another woman. The next weeks seemed the most painful in my life. At the time I was still working as a 'Carer', in Supported Lodgings, a place where we 'carers,' physically took care of adults, who were neither mentally nor emotionally able, to physically, care adequately, for themselves. (Often, they were neglectful with personal hygiene, unable to manage finances, nor work, dysfunctional often in relationships, argumentative, some coping better than others. I was told from the start, that overqualified though I was, it was <u>not</u> my job to use my extra skills. We handed medication out, to keep people sedated, but they got no real help. I did eventually realize, that most of them, did not really, want to make change anyway). Though night after night, my emotional pain was too much, to allow sleep, I carried on working, so, developed too, extreme sciatica. I could feel my spirit on its way out. After weeks of this excruciating torment, feeling I was at the darkest point in my life, one day I was sitting, on the floor, crying out to 'God,' yet again, for help. Somehow, I found myself in that moment, drawn to get up, find the text of 'A Course in Miracles,' read some, every day, & though not able to make sense of it, yet I persisted. One day, I finally 'got' the message loud & clear, from what had previously been, gobbledygook! This, was a true life-line back, to the light. There was a way my ego identity, could not at all accept, that I was a wife, whose husband, was an adulterer, & trust being one of, my most shaky areas, it was almost like, I could in no way, allow to be true what was! Though I tried to let this go, & forgive, yet as no deep regret was ever expressed, I felt unmet & unloved, wronged not only by Sam, justifying his choice, once he returned; but Berris too, as though **I** were to blame, for their opting, for adultery! That moment Sam told me of his adultery, I did feel rage but held back from physical attack! This big shake up, in my life, drove me to whatever healing would ensure, I would never again attract such levels of pain, neither in my relationship with Sam, nor with any man. I did acknowledge already, while still feeling a victim, of his and others' apparent lack of, enough love for me, that my expectations, were creating my reality.

*

From the time of my **heart-felt prayer**, voiced aloud, on my 70th birthday, **to fall totally fall in love with myself**, I was led into a deeper and deeper opening, into my heart, uncovering &

healing, during a 2yr.process, my deepest, most hidden Heart wounds. I had already forgiven my childhood wounds, & come to Peace, & Love without condition, for my parents. Finally, I have really known what it is, to have a heart free, I feel, of deep wounds, radiating with such a blaze of light, warmth, ever-expanding compassion and, warm flames of Love. Such deep gratitude and relief, is with me daily. **But this was later!**

*

One mile-stone had been, my decision, to attend Anthony Robbins' work-shops. Before then, I had thought of myself merely, having similar problems to millions of others; mediocre, 'no big deal!' Now my **horizons** suddenly **widened**, with a feeling of **no limits**, to the possibilities in my life. I went to his Wealth creation workshop too, but could not take steps, at that time, into a more high-powered way, of bringing money into my life! It has never been my strength! Especially as, <u>even doing</u> these workshops, involved using more credit, thus creating more debt. I felt though, my priority was, to make whatever investment, would empower me, or give me clarity, as to who I am, with a clear new sense of Purpose, believing I would be capable of a good relationship with Sam, & others, only if I first came, to that relationship with myself! Thus, **commitment** to my spiritual journey, became my **deepest priority**. Sam, found this threatening, as if he believed, this meant my abandonment of him!

I had been told in 2002, about Patricia Sterry's, 'Block Clearance therapy. She is, I believe, a medium, and there is more information about various of her qualifications, on Google. She had created what to me, felt like a fun insightful journey, for seeing more clearly, how I was creating my life. She is the owner & director of the 'Tree of Life Centre,' still, I believe, in Cheltenham. I told her at the start, that I never again wished, to attract, nor feel, the level of pain & betrayal in my life, I had experienced with Sam, so I wanted to heal, whatever was necessary, for this to change. Though Berris had been 'unfaithful,' he was open, rather than sneaky like Sam, about his intentions. The Block clearance inner journeys, turned out to magically open many doors of perception. I also started to train with her, for the next couple or so years. However, though I wrote earlier, in this book, about Brandon Bays, & have described, a few of key processes I have received, of course none of them happened, before **Nov.2003,** when I attended my 1st **'Journey Intensive'** weekend, after I read Brandon's book, 'The Journey.' I made a choice anyway, to focus on these inner journeys, rather than continue with the Block clearance training. Thus, any of the hundreds of processes, I've both received & given, & my ever-deepening opening, to the Source of my being, only happened between 2003, & now. I released too, ever deeper layers, of my unwillingness to even be here, in such a world, plus my mistrust of life. Lack of trust, was my deepest underlying issue, when I first engaged with 'The Journey! I had not yet, fully recognized, **my** potent co-creation of, the reality I was experiencing. Such Masters in creation, neither aware of what we do, nor who we are!

For many, many years, the Babaji 'Samaj,' had been searching for land and buildings for a U.K. Ashram. Eventually, a place was bought with 13 acres of land in West Wales, between Lampeter and Aberaeron, near a small village. There was much division among members of the 'Samaj' (the name of the Babaji charity), regarding whether it should have been bought, or not, so, Sam & I had gone in March of 2002 to the initial A.G.M. not expecting to stay. However, with Pete, who arrived with gentle, playful dog Bessie, plus his daughter Minna, we dived in to work, the same evening, everyone else having gone home! Most of those who made various commitments to the Ashram, were never seen again! I offered no commitment, as I was not yet certain. 'Sanatan Dharma' - (seeing the truth at the Source of all the ways), was the name of our Ashram, & though Temple rituals, mantras, devotional songs, Aarti, Karma Yoga, all usual Babaji ashram activities, happened daily, we really welcomed & honoured any visitor, from different religious persuasions, allowing deep friendships & heartfelt sharing. Babaji did not encourage, creating another dogmatic religion. He encouraged following the truth in one's own heart, not being sheep, rather serving all humanity. '**Sanatan Dharma**' (Sanskrit), means just that, - **honouring the truth at the Source of all the ways**. We got deeply involved for the next 4 or 5 years or so. I regularly wrote in the Samaj newsletters, to update members about the Ashram activities & progress.

A Pilgrimage had been planned, from London to the Ashram. One day I visited a friend Sandra in her then Stroud home. She was in the middle of her garden, sun & flowers all around, when I asked her, would she like to walk to the Ashram in Wales, with me, - approx. a 258 miles journey! She simply said 'Yes' & for me, that is the moment when she became my beloved friend. And, so it has been, for all the years since, that she is, my 'Adventure friend' & there is a deep trust between us. We decided to start walking, September 9th 2006, from Stroud, though Widdy, Sam & held a little Ceremony, beforehand, at Kemble, a source of the Thames. We sat there, around a tiny trickle of water, directing love & healing, back along the River Thames to London. Others, were walking the London to Kemble section, in short stretches. The length of our chosen, route was about 258 miles, which took us 15 days. However, after 3 days, finding I could not breathe properly, due to carrying too much weight, I 'phoned Sam, asking if our good neighbour & friend Widdy, would deliver my car, thinking I could drive ahead daily, hitch a lift back, then walk unburdened, free of weight. Widdy joined us &, turned out to be, an even greater blessing, as he declared, he would be happy, to do the whole journey with us. At around 5.30pm every day, Sandra would switch on her mobile phone, contact Widdy, so giving him, an idea, of where we would reach, within the hour. It worked well. We walked on the ancient rights-of-way, cross country, sleeping out, or in a tent & the occasional Youth hostel. Widdy had often sorted out wonderful possibilities, such as the night we stayed in Saint Meilig's church, with its great ancient stone Cross & baptismal font, in Llowes, in the Wye valley. We were warmly welcomed, & since this church had been used down the generations for passing pilgrims, they gave us the big church key, & we were able to make beds on the stone floor, around the old stone font. We felt very blessed. Later I wrote a contribution for their newsletter. **We shared a wonderful sense, of freedom, adventure and joy, me & my adventure friend**! Sandra & I, felt like keeping on walking! Enjoyed Widdy's company too. This love, of being 'on the road', in fact, more often, going along old pathways, through woods, fields, many changing vistas, swimming in rivers, & loving every moment, has stayed with us, ever since. I lived mostly on fruits & nuts, found along the way, a perfect time to travel, with good weather most of the time. Sam, Verity, & other friends, joined us, for occasional days walking. We were met at the ashram, by a welcoming group of people, but already, there were growing conflicts arising, among committee members, as well as the larger Babaji family. For me, this came to a head, after my year as chairperson was done, having to my surprise, in an AGM designed to oust 'the old,' & change the power structure, been re-elected onto the next committee. A repetition happened in effect, of the sort of actions which, had originally created division. However, I felt optimistic that maybe healing could happen, & went off to work in the MBS festival for a week. When I returned, I checked my emails, & there found one that, I believed, was not meant to have come to me! It read, 'for us six only,' (belatedly, now, I wonder if in fact **I,** was meant to be one of the six, yet decided at that time, that I was being excluded!), - a meeting of six Samaj members, to discuss my written offering for the Samaj newsletter. I had written the truth, from my being & heart, about what 'Sadhana' meant for me. Yet I had been sensing for a while, that however deep my connection to Babaji, the daily Temple rituals, did not bring me, to as deep a connection with my authentic essence, as I was yearning for. I could see, how underlying deeper conflicts, were not being acknowledged, nor brought to light, in many of my brothers & sisters on this path, but rather, being projected onto others, so divisions, misunderstanding & mistrust went unresolved, sometimes for years. When I read that email, my immediate 'jerk' reaction was, "God, it's like being in the witch trials of the Middle Ages," (in King James' time). This was the **turning point** at which I drew away, **very clear**, that my direction was henceforth different.

*

By now, I was attending many 'Journey' weekend events, partly to support all the new people arriving, but also connecting with, those we would meet many, many times over years. I felt very inspired by, everyone's commitment to finding, our own authentic truth &, our willingness to embrace every aspect of ourselves, & so, bring every emotion, including every shadow aspect, we had judged as too ugly, such as anger or hate, into an embrace of love. So much healing was happening for us all, & it was wonderful, to see everyone freeing themselves, from past patterns of behaviour, from all we had rejected in others & ourselves. There was a strong feeling of connection & family over the years, as we shared that commitment, to support ourselves & everyone, in coming to love ourselves/others as we are, & come to inner freedom. The contrast between coming away from these gatherings, & coming away from Samaj Committee meetings, felt so opposite, like light versus heavy, & I had already, got a strong sense of my path diverging. I was resonating less & less with the whole Samaj group energy. Though I withdrew, from interest in being part of, a Babaji ashram, my ensuing clear symbolic dreams about Hari Sudha in particular, Durgadas too, revealed, that my deep love connection with them, remained unaffected, by surface dramas, likewise too with, other close Babaji family, regardless of, whether I would see as much of them, or not. In truth, in the years since, I have realized that Kirtan & honouring of the Divine with these, my close friends, does not change, I just am no longer aligned with the Samaj group objectives, yet very clear too, that **Babaji, is even more strongly close, in my heart**, as I connect more & more deeply, with the Source of my being. He did tell us, not to be sheep. The karmic play goes on! All is perfectly 'imperfect'. It must have been 2007 or so, when all this was happening. Many of us who had been so strongly involved, drew away at that time. The Ashram got sold, yet so many wonderful vibrations, had been implanted in the land & buildings, at 'Blaengors,' so many blessings, mantras & good intentions from all those who put our love, time & energy, into doing what we felt was Babaji's work, so much focus too, on energy clearing by me & Sam, of the land, that I felt certain, good people would follow, as they did! I have visited the lovely family now living there, several times. Much of what we envisaged, continues to flourish. The hundreds of trees we planted are loved, plus much heart-felt, beautiful vision, & much work, is going into the land, house & other buildings, - (we had been successful in getting planning permission, years before). The whole environment is continuing to be well blessed.

*

Near the end of June 2007, while I was again on night duty, as a Carer, our home was once more flooded. Just over 3 weeks later, with our walls stripped back to the brick, & the ground floor filled with dehumidifiers & industrial size fans, the house had just about dried out, when the big flood arrived on July 20th. Our car was ready-packed for us to leave that day, to The Healing Field Gathering, a few miles from Glastonbury. The rain was falling, persistently; thus, we began to feel uneasy about leaving. We continued to monitor the situation, noting the stream's level steadily rising, blocked drains here & there. I 'phoned the Environment Agency, who said, they would send us sandbags. When these arrived, I had to drive off miles, to get them filled with sand, so by the time I got back, the water was already beginning to come in the house. Again I 'phoned the Environment Agency to inform them of the situation. Their response, "Can you take photos?" felt somewhat inadequate, at a time when we were having to focus on, 'what do we need to do first, immediately? - such as, what to move upstairs! However, I said to Sam, "my camera is in the car so, I might as well get it. We went out, then I realized I needed, to go back for my car keys. Sam lingered to have a smoke. The water was already rising so rapidly, that I could not decide, what to do first, shut the kitchen window, to hold back the rising waters from the Conservatory, move the pan of food I had cooked, to a higher level, (I wish I had), go upstairs to reassure Sam, as he was shouting from outside, or rescue what I could! I tried to rescue stuff, from the living room, which was difficult, as already things were floating. I managed to get one of the fans upstairs, yet not much else. When the water reached breast level, it became time to escape upstairs. Everyone else had left their homes, in that stretch of road, except me. The road had become a fast-moving river, people were congregating in the park opposite. I had taken off all my wet clothes, put on dry clothes & got into bed to get warm. At some point when I looked out, someone shouted, pointing at me, "There's somebody there!" so not long after, firemen came along in a boat, offering to rescue me, but I told them, I was staying where I was. Sam slept in our friend Ish's house. About 3a.m. I heard a lot of banging, & shouted out of the window, "Hey what're you doing, are you trying to steal, or something?" A moment later, an Irishman appeared, stood below my window, and called, "I am so sorry to disturb you Madam. I'll stop now," & off he went up the road. He had probably hoped, to access alcohol unseen, from the Co-op (next door). I was a bit nervous, he might realize I was alone, so crept down in the dark, (no electricity of course), through the silt, to the back door, found it locked, & realized Sam must have returned, once the waters subsided, to make sure I was safe. We had to move to another cottage for 1yr., while we worked on restoring our home, to an optimum living space. So many people helped us, with cleaning whatever was to be salvaged from silt. So much got thrown out. With everything, we were deciding what should stay, in our home, what do we now let go of. Sam was totally traumatized, by the whole experience, whereas I was feeling the blessing within it. I felt it as a big cleansing, letting go, expansion, making way for much good. Our home physically expanded too, as when walls were knocked down, new extra hidden space emerged. We had a solar panel put on the roof for heating our water, & a very efficient 'Clearview' wood stove installed, (a superior model, with 'secondary burning,' so less fuel), to keep our home warm, making us less dependent on gas and electricity, & had the water-heating controls, installed upstairs &, switched off about 6 months, as the solar panel created plenty of hot water. The house was much improved.

*

I continued going occasionally to Journey weekends. I had completed the Practitioners Course in 2005 & now, had 45 case studies to complete, ready for certification. Plenty of resistance had surfaced, & I kept declaring I felt completely blocked. With the daily journey, from our temporary accommodation, to the work in progress, other concerns were put aside, except keeping my spiritual life a priority, continuing to swap journey processes, to support others & myself, by staying in the Journey energy, & attending events. At that time, Sam felt abandoned & challenged by my priorities, believing too, that he should be in charge, of the work team, whereas I found the whole process, happening organically, with close friend Pete, from Wales, supervising the restoration, so, felt it all unfolding harmoniously, with our chosen team of workers, who mostly knew well, what they were doing, so all was going perfectly. Feeling the assurances, we had been given, by the Stroud District Council, Environment Agency etc. about gutters, underground culverts, etc. being regularly checked & kept free of debris, had been empty words, we formed a 'Stroud Valleys Action group.' We finally did get a response, by threatening to go into the culvert ourselves, if they did not get it cleared, of the years of built-up blockages of rubbish, caused by years of neglect. Instead, we organized for local cavers, to go down, take colour photos, then made front page news with the results, in local newspapers, with the reports & photos. The Environment Agency **finally,** not only got the culvert cleared, but after more pressure from our Action group, after a 3month delay, had a grill placed strategically, to stop a fresh build-up of debris! Finally! Though we continued to insist on them engaging with, the bigger picture, to slow down run-off from surrounding hills, rather than spending thousands of pounds of government grants, on Environment Agency surveys, we have had no floods since. It is interesting, that we had briefly advertised our house, as being on the market, Sam's wish, rather than mine. No better land nor home, had materialized, & the day Sam's inheritance, went into our bank account, was the same day the flood came! Life had other plans. I was very happy with the more spacious, newly designed, decorated, and much improved home.

My determination was strong, once we were back in our 'new' home, to focus on, getting all my completed case studies sent in, which I did in the Autumn of 2009, so was glad, to finally be given, my Journey Practitioner's certification, in the Spring of 2010.

(Since my being in Ish's home, since Nov. 2020, so far, there has been one flood, in the same part of Slad Road, due to someone blocking the flow, by throwing a mattress into the stream. Such unawareness & carelessness! '**Care- more-ness**,' (my invented word), would be preferable! Guy & Penny's cellar in no.22, suffered, but the flood barriers I had left in no.18, kept the new owners protected). We are now in 2022! My umpteenth re-edit & the last, I believe!

*

My 1st Journey 'Women's Retreat', in 2008, had been a turning point in my life, when I simply, started to give myself permission, to really listen to myself, & not act, from guilt nor, any other dis-empowered stand. I had acted so much trying to fulfil, what I believed was expected from me. I had been feeling increasingly tense, around 'having sex.' I believed Sam was desperate for sex, not in order to connect with me, but to release his inner tension, & because, he feared physical consequences to his body, without this release. Not much feeling of love around this, & it had become important to me, to live neither from the harsh pressure, of expectations, from myself, nor others. Not long after, I manifested a bladder & vaginal discomfort, to the point where it felt totally painful to have any penetration of anything. Usually, I would have quickly purified my body with a juice or fruit fast, & sorted this out quickly, but I felt instead, to uncover the deeper consciousness behind what was happening. *'Journey' processes began to reveal various scenes, where I had let myself be used for sex, trying to fulfil what the man wanted, & leaving what would please me, out of the equation, as well as the deeper traumas of near rapes, or other demeaning, unloving demands. In one process, the 'magic shuttle' built for speed, went into my mouth, then zoomed fast to the mouth of my vagina, bringing up the various related memories, plus nausea & disgust. By the end of the process, I could let go of any feelings of being a victim, & came to a more empowered sense of myself, able to lovingly accept & honour, my sexual woman self.* I then eventually, months later, did my first gall bladder & liver flush, which sorted out any bladder issues, but I was still carrying some tension & discomfort in my vagina. I already described in the last chapter, my clearing, of sexual shame, & connecting more deeply with my own male aspect. Since that process, nearly 4 months ago, so much more energy had been coursing through my entire body, that even though my whole sleep pattern, had become very unpredictable & erratic, during the previous 2 months, I had felt able to handle, even the days, following sleepless nights, in a much more capable & surrendered way. Somehow, I had been unable to invite the Loving Intimacy, loyal Commitment, honest friendship, plus Sacredness, into my Love life, I would most like. Since I cleared the Shame, (plus other emotions trapped in my whole genital/base chakra area, using too 'The Emotion Code,' plus 'Quantum Touch),' I have felt a real opening & connection with the Earth & her creativity. *In that process back in Chapter One, May 20th 2012, where I felt I had connected with my divine male counterpart, I had felt drawn to kiss him on the lips, however, my mind protested, is that allowed? Not so long after that, when I was meditating & connecting with high frequency energies, in the Quantum Field, I had a sudden urge to direct my energy upwards, intimately, with my divine male energy, & with no physical nor visual touch involved, experienced the most blissful, spontaneous, orgasmic release, with clouds or waves of light around me, that I had ever experienced in my life, a total surrender &, merging in love. When I described this to Sam, he felt it threatening, which I found strange. To me, it suggests the possibility, or likelihood, if I should want it, of attracting the outer physical manifestation, of this inner vibration. It seems however simpler, to be free of these jealous insecurities. more freeing. I used to feel, I would welcome being so loved & honoured by another human being, that I would experience sex as both earthy, sacred, & beautiful with a partner. My heart has opened wide & my body feels more alive, sexual, & energy-filled, than 20 or even 40 years ago.* In February 2013, I attended Anaiya Sophia's 'Womb Wisdom' group, in Brighton, a deeper exploration of the sacredness of Woman plus, total honouring of one's Sexual Being where, in a room of about 35 women & half a dozen men, I was the only 'older' woman. Since I now feel so at home in my own body, in relation to both men & women, I was very happy to be greeted, in the first break, by a nearby man, who declared his gladness, to see me there, moreover comparing my smile to that of Ram Dass! I told him I really welcomed, such lovely reflections coming my way, & found myself moreover, partnered with a man in the afternoon. How lovely to be with men, who truly wish, to honour divine femininity & sexuality, as sacred! I knew this was because, I have cleared so much sexual shame, plus anger with men, (unless there is anything left still to release with Sam)! Who am I kidding? Maybe no surprise that a month later, I finally let go of 22yrs. build-up of anger with Sam, a volcanic eruption no longer to be stoppered, (described fully later). I am fully honouring my vagina as mine, in a new tenderly accepting, & loving way, as if I was only allowed before, to touch me, with the say-so of others, such as priests, society or parents! How insidious, this imposed conditioning, has been on women. Only in my seventies, having learnt self-love, could I, if I so chose, tenderly & truly, love my Body, reclaiming my sexuality, from the media, religions & all other conditioning, to experience my vagina, as a sacred Portal, a gateway to creativity, born from the Heart of Love!!

I've rarely if ever, been overly gripped by sexual wants, but when the idea is attractive, it arises from the joy & innocence we are. The shame we, as women, have carried, has been fed by the media, which thrives financially by attacks on 'others,' 'voyeurism,' through disparaging judgements, to maintain the status quo, upholding the old patriarchal paradigm of control, or manipulation. I felt confirmed & supported in the Womb Wisdom teachings, opening me to honouring Creation. Even by 2022, much has changed & women have greater equality, than in past years. The daily meditations I was doing, had anyway increased my energy frequency. I had been feeling myself aligning, in a very real way with my Soul, or Higher self, as if I was letting go of, a whole lot of, the deep traumas in my body, & feeling very ready to let go what remained of pain or grief from unloved & unloving relating in my past.

*

I was finally starting to practice hands on healing, as clairvoyants had been telling me to do for over 30 years. One of them mentioned, a Chinese man being involved in this, & in 3 recent Journey processes, he had turned up as my Mentor. I call him Lu Yin, (see Chapter 1), and the feeling between me and him, has been increasingly warm. Since this is synchronous with increased energy, strongly felt in my hands whenever I focus on healing, I have started to consciously call him in, each time I am laying hands on anyone, to create the possibility, for an even deeper healing, to happen. During the previous 3mths, I was flying off daily beyond Earth gravity, (guided by Maureen Moss), to her Golden Temple, in daily meditations, which felt as freeing, as our Stargate journeying, into the Void. I enjoyed these for a long time, & was seeing Lu Yin, also Gezra, my channelled guide, turning up together, within the Temple, feeling a close, bond with both. It does seem to have been primarily Male guides, who have appeared in the forefront, of my consciousness. Meg Benedicte's ongoing Vortex meditations, from Mount Shasta, in 2011 onwards, drew me too, & still do, to this day, every 6weeks approximately, since they began. They strengthen connection with 'her' Global Community, plus seeing, what is happening in my life, from a Soul perspective, helping me make a stronger commitment, to live from Love, knowing without doubt, that all is well, & is only getting even better.

*

In a 'Journey' process at the end of January 2011, I had met one aspect in me, I had always totally rejected, when seen in my father. The stairs down, were only solid for, the first 2 or 3 steps, so I just let myself drop after that. I had to give extra help too, to create a door, since not much solidity around, but they appeared as, great double gates of wood which, seemed alive, with a green glow, & beautiful flames, of shining green & magenta coloured, light behind. My Mentor had shining black eyes, & almost black skin, but again, only his face solid, yet a great presence of love, totally there for me. The winged chariot was so ethereal, I created doors, seat belts & a shining 'go' button. First it landed in my head, then settled in my chest &, both shoulders, which felt powerless &, very defeated, especially the right one. The surprising hidden energy beneath, was a critical cynicism, which turns to dust, (as not to be trusted), all Enthusiasm, Faith, Love, Light, & Good, - seen as based on illusion. I realized it was very powerful, with dark tentacles throughout my body, realized too, that this energy is so prevalent, in our human society, that this is fed to the point, where it feels like demonic energy, dampening life force, open-hearted being & joy. I also met a very uncared for, boring, dead, space, everything there dying, (like, for me, the U.K. ducks on the walls), from lack of loving care. I soon saw there, this useless, armless, legless being, I just wanted to throw on a trash heap, until I looked into her eyes, full of pain, and felt such compassion. I realized how loveable she is, just for existing, with nothing to prove, no special appearance, success, nor actions, needed, to totally matter and be loved! She, was Me! By the end of the process, I felt I had been exorcised of a life-long dark, dampening presence that had seemed, almost impossible to extricate, from my sense of identity.

Because so many remain caught, in the illusion of separation, we have fed this energy, so it's indeed become a demoniacal, dark, numbing energy, creating such horrors as, careless scientific animal experiments, racialism, (not just with different colour skin, but any different life-style or religion), 'top cats' & minions, & long-term destruction of our planet, our beautiful Earth, with all its' plants, all its' creatures, including the insects, & magnificent lions, tigers, bears, elephants, etc. often enclosed in barred cages, for quick profit. (Doubt, judgement, fear, greed plus, cold-hearted research, to physically prove chosen theories, are its relations).

Afterwards, I feel more able to laugh for no reason, more here for me, delighting in Life-energy bubbling inside, & determined not to dampen this down. At the start of another process, about 5 months later, I had been feeling how much, I had expected what I offer, <u>not</u> to be of real value, to others, yet I experienced the whole process, from a very open, expansive, trusting place. There was no banister on the way down, yet I felt I did not need one. Each step was a panoramic aspect of Nature, deep Earth, plant kingdom, water, or Sun glow. Even the offered balloons, (representing different quality resourceful gifts) had beautiful colours, in tune with the energy they held. I feel no fear about the depth of the process. I experience myself as a warrior being, my Mentor also a Warrior seated on a horse. We both carry swords of Truth, but I feel too, his love & compassion. He seems to represent the Dark, (the potential in the blackness of the Quantum field?) - & me, the Light, this time. The horse places himself in front of the carriage & lands very fast, almost jammed into my 'Universal Heart' area, *or upper Heart. There's turquoise colour patchily around, but a general feeling of dustiness, cobwebs, neglect, as if seldom visited. The connection to my voice, is impeded by an almost solid blockage in my throat above. The anger & frustration I feel, is turned inwards until, I give up the fight! I then find myself & everything, being pulled down into a black hole, yet I feel no fear, rather, that all possibilities are here. (I realize now, in my 81ˢᵗ year, that this is the same Quantum Field Blackness, or the Void, we regularly connect with, in daily Stargate meditations, with which I engage with such deep trust, love & joy, these days)! It seemed my father saw no value in whatever I could offer. After I had expressed, any pain in my heart, about this, with much more energy & presence than usual, & come to deeper forgiveness & love with my father, pink glowing energy was travelling from my heart into the neglected area, so now there is a feeling of connection, rather than neglect, & my throat's opening to express more, from a higher universal Love.*

I have mentioned releasing one big barrier to abundance, once I connected fully with Mother Love, which created openings in me that started to attract more clients, & people relating lovingly with me, who had not previously done so, yet still there was not any huge change, in my ongoing deep-rooted issue, regarding mastery of ongoing financial ease

At **that** time though, during the last yr. or two, (2013-14), once Sam's strength, was failing, I experienced bigger extremes, of feeling more squeezed than ever, financially, until the last weeks, as death approached, he was able to receive 'Personal Independence payments. My marriage was seemingly, coming to a speedier end too, than anticipated. Yet initially, I was not feeling fearful nor contracted around this.

Another day I did a meditation with Emmanuel Dagher, where I really connected deeply with money, knowing it purely as energy, as Love. Again, there was a new influx of clients, just at the perfect time, but still not any feeling, of really moving out of a reality, restricted by what I can spend, plus continuing debts. A lot of pain & grief, started to come up, in relation to Sam maybe, leaving my life, even as I know, I will create a joyful life of love & plenty, in my fast arriving, new reality. I made it a daily meditation to soften my belly, surrounding arising feelings with Love, inviting all Pain to show itself &, be released.

*

One day I had again woken up, with emotional pain present, & twice that day I had asked, "How come I trust & recognize Love in the eyes of my Guides & Mentors, or any higher beings, but cannot trust I will find Love, in the eyes of my human friends? (I know now, years later, that I too, am Love)!

I went that afternoon to my dear friend Sole's home, she, her husband and, child, have just moved into. Our intention was, to do an energy clearing, of her house, garden, & 5 feet further in every direction. When I first arrived, I was somewhat falling apart, & being herself, strongly on a spiritual path of awakening, she was able to compassionately hold me to truth, so I could quickly come to deeper calm. *As soon as we started the clearing process, calling on our helpers, Pan, Devic beings, Christ light, Higher selves & other Beings of Light, I felt totally aligned with, my expansive & focussed self. We drew a sheet of Light up, through the whole space, collecting ungrounded, scattered, dark, & inappropriate energies, gathering them in a large bundle, & sending them on to, the next higher evolutionary level. When we had completed this part of the process, we thanked all those who assisted. This included, blessing, & thanking, this Dark Void. I was struck forcibly by the appropriateness of this, & deeply felt "I really Love you, Darkness!" Something deeply shifted in me, & I knew that living, from this unconditional Love towards all that appears in my reality, is a way of then recognizing, Love reflected back! For what felt like the first time, I really wanted to honour & love Sam, however he showed up. I went home, & though I knew he would return home angry, I knew I must 'choose love,' as a way of relating to whatever, would appear in my life. I felt aligned with my Soul self, so not worried about, his possible reaction. If I had been agenda driven, my fear of Sam's reaction, would have stopped me, making any move, towards him. He returned, I saw him look towards the kitchen, to check if I was there, then use his muscle testing technique, & I knew he was asking if, he should just go away, for a while longer. I went straight out, put my hand on his shoulder & turned him towards me, & put my arms out. He collapsed sobbing, into my arms. Since then, I have been relating from, this very different consciousness. I felt to pour into his body, all the love, I was not before, able to give.*

Sure, I would maybe feel more relaxed & sleep more easily, if I knew whether we were staying together, & it would be lovely if, he felt to express love towards me, but the timing's not right, so far, there's so much inner change happening for both of us, & clarity will be here for us, when it is! So probably, still some attempt to control.

In a 'Journey' process, on Monday September 17ʰ 2011, I prayed, to become more grounded, in embodied alignment with, who I really am, my Soul self, & to disengage from any old dynamic with Sam, & bring all to Source Love. On the top step of, the flight down, to the doorway, into my inner journey, warning me to tread carefully, there was a strange sort of plastic, uneven coating, blue, black, grey colours melded as on a paint palate, that looked as if it might be easily peeled off, but the rest of the way was smooth & solid. I felt relaxed about going deep. (I want to mention here, - since I have trained in hypnotherapy, past life regression, & many modalities, that many doorways can be used to go on an inner journey, other than down steps. One can go through the heart, up in an elevator, with just a count-down, go through a tunnel of light into a beautiful scene, by looking into a pool, and so on).

A different Mentor awaited me this time, a Nature being, appearing somewhat elfin, with slanted eyes & pointed ears. The green carriage went first to my genital area, then left an energy trail arc, from there to my upper heart, another arc to my throat, then back to my heart. Surprisingly, his part is malevolent, with murderous intent, octopus tentacles, & all the cunning of a creature that has had to stay hidden from everyone's eyes, like Gollum in 'The Lord of Rings,' & will suck the life out of my foe. (This surprised me, as I honour all the Nature beings).

(The Camp-fire of unconditional love & acceptance, is where, you may remember, the suppressed feelings, so long held in the cells, can be released, as the self from that time, *(I was about 60yrs.old then)* can express the pain, not previously voiced &, be heard by whoever, we have been blaming for this, so they are aware, what that felt like. The more totally, we can voice this with full emotion, & feel heard, - the more quickly forgiveness can happen, setting us free)! *However, it was not the betrayal I needed to release, maybe I had released that, in the last process, with my ex-husband Berris. My anger was rather, about feeling I could not be heard, without being threatened, by dire consequences. I had felt dominated by Sam's huge reactions, my truth invalidated, feeling he could see others' beauty, appreciate & find others loveable &, worthy of attention, accept their truth & inspiration, with open mind, but seemed not to want to see, hear, nor love me! "Enough Already!" When I had let 'rip' all this hurricane, or cyclone of energy, no longer willing to be held back, I knew the connection between my base Chakra & heart, was full & healthy, & the raw exposed area in my heart already, had a healing skin forming over the raw flesh, but the connection between the throat & heart, still needs strengthening.*

*

That afternoon, for the women's group in my home, I had decided on 'Choose Love' as, the theme. I felt I was taking a risk, offering a *Maureen Moss's Golden Temple meditation, from the internet replay, something we had not really done, before. As we were relaxing & listening, my whole body started to tremble, my teeth were chattering &, I was feeling terror in my belly. I had had no idea, of the true extent, of my fear about, whether what I want to share, will be wanted, welcomed or, received.*

After the meditation, I shared what I had felt, & every person in turn, reached out a hand towards me. I found myself readily able, to trust everyone, as really being here for me, & so, feel really received. I had had very little trust, that this could be so! I got a strong realization, in that moment, that this is a way, I have blocked receiving, my greater good. I was unaware I was sabotaging, a more expansive flow of, all abundant possibilities, into in my life. After that, the flow of love & presence between us, grew so strong, that I really could see, feel & recognize, Source energy, in the eyes I looked so deeply into, as something I have always wanted to be, see & know. What a gift! I felt utterly blessed. The next day I felt much lighter, very aware of, my whole energy field, being wide open, plugged into an expansive unified field. My intuitive flow was strong, giving me, an absolute knowing, that the future I have been, increasingly aligning with, is drawing near, to show up magically in unexpected ways. Even when one door seems to close, I have stayed trusting of life, and very quickly, another door opens.

*

Any mistrust or pain, from my old life programming, still held in my energy body, seemed to intensify, & surface fast, once I finally let myself feel the pain of betrayal, from my marriage with Berris. It had only taken about 32 years! - before I had felt ready, to unearth what I really felt, more deeply, about the events I have described earlier, during the Rajneesh Therapy training! I thought I had done well, to have our marriage end, & separate from Berris, without feeling too much grief, having 'Voice Dialogued' myself to, enough emotional distance. Because Berris was the first man, I had really opened my heart to, (other than my father when I was very young), his betrayal, even though not done, in a dishonest, sneaky way, left deep wounds in my heart.

Despite 10yrs. between both legal marriages, including the 5yrs.of celibacy, I was fearful from early on, in my marriage with Sam, of infidelity being a possible threat, whereas I had not consciously expected, nor feared this, with previous boyfriends before Berris, nor had I let myself feel affected too painfully, when betrayal did happen, even though the initial cause I am certain, was my initial reaction, to my father leaving me, so many times, in wartime. In 1944, I was just 4yrs & a month old, when my mother said, 'it's good you don't cry at night any more' &, I told her, 'No! - that's not what happened; the last time he came,' - (i.e., my father visiting, on leave from his Regiment), 'he killed me &, I haven't come back since!" Later photos show, a self-conscious, child, not at ease to be seen.

Back in the first months of 2013, year of shift and rebirth, the Chinese year of the Water Snake had come in, a shedding of the past 'skins'. More people were dying or going through extreme changes, than in 2012. My dearly loved friend, Jungleyes, had finally left his painful body too, (not reaching his March 2013 birthday). His very heart-warming Woodland Burial was on the Isle of Wight on March 26th, where family & friends gathered, to honour his life & death, & there was much heart connection & sense of human caring & sharing. I too spoke some spontaneous words, & sent a mango with his cardboard coffin into the beautifully prepared burial pit. I am grateful for our shared spiritual exploration, for his loyalty & integrity, for the Love & depth of our sharing, more recently too, for his child-like enthusiasm & jokes, plus greater openness to touch & human warmth. Blessings, Love & Enlightenment, wherever his path is taking him. Maybe he is on the Star Sirius system, he believed he had recently come from!

*

I seem to have now chosen, to meet the deepest pains & terrors, & let go of whatever has so far, kept me in life-long patterns, of creating suffering & lack. I sometimes had wondered why, these deeper wounds had not yet fully surfaced, to do with Berris or Sam, but suppose, I was not then ready, for the stoppers to be unplugged! I have been more vulnerable & open, my body more alive, with a real commitment to be here for me, living more & more, in alignment with my Soul, living a life inspired by love, for everyone & everything, - for all of Life. As I have moved more fully, into being one with, my courageous, empowered, compassionate, & true self, it has been very important for me, to embody higher vibrational frequencies, being fully present, with my feet very grounded, staying connected with our Mother Earth. I have opened my heart wider again, to Sam, rather than staying protected, by more emotional distance, yet the feelings I was keeping unconsciously, below the level of my mind's awareness, are surfacing very fast. Since my priority became a strong commitment, to fall totally in love with myself, & relate with all beings increasingly, from unconditional Love, I am ready to meet whatever, however painful, has kept me from Joy &, Ease in my being, as much as I am able, without resistance. I seemed to have come to, Peace & Love with my parents, though truthfully, I have a much more intimate & real, understanding of them, since translating their intimate, War-time letters, than when I initially, wrote this book. I was both experiencing my heart, as a blaze of Light, afire with Love for Life, then be feeling as if, I had taken a backward step, being so affected, by my mind distress, after the past weeks of, so many heart opening realizations, so much connection with myself & others, so much knowing and trust, in the abundance of Life. Now I am surrendering more deeply, to the roller-coaster ride, of more extreme polarities!

*

My purpose was always, to walk a 'Path of Love,' to trust the wise purpose of, the unfolding of my journey. How would I learn compassion, if I kept myself insulated, from Life's sorrows & joys, & were unwilling to connect with, my vulnerability &, the aspects I had kept hidden, in order, to avoid pain, as well as my passion, courage, my infinitely creative self? So, this week I have felt the full terror, lack of trust or safety, which was always with me, yet I had not openly acknowledged, nor revealed. I trust it all simply wants to be loved, accepted, recognized, & welcomed, as the gift it is, then it can dissolve. I sure will not continue playing an old 'tape', of dwelling on imagined future pain, such as of Sam moving in, with someone new, & coming back to tell me so. My mind reminds me of the logic of this, Sam being the first committed relationship since Berris. I accept now, it is just what needed to surface, to free myself of more of my past. Listening to Panache Desai, really opened me wide, to the Love & Beauty of Life, & to making nothing wrong. Neither Sam nor I, needed to improve, nor be perfect, for Love without conditions, to be here. I chose to let go of whatever, had been attached, in my energy field, holding me in past dynamics of limitation. I allow my heart to open ever wider, wide enough to encompass whatever I meet, opening increasingly, to powerful, transparent presence, an expression of Compassion & Love, able to offer more of my unique gifts, in service of Life, in a dynamic flow, of receiving & being received. I am less concerned, about Sam's choices in relation to me, knowing my life to be expanding into, the best & highest possibilities, with my full co-operation &, active involvement. With humility, lightly, without the need for drama. Freedom indeed!

No credit nor blame, need be assumed by me, for the dance happening between the strategies of the ego mind, or the voice of Truth, - between Shame & bright Joy, or other polarities. The Voice, the Truth, from the Heart, does not change tomorrow. I have such a Trust, in those messages that come, from deep unshakeable Knowing, through dreams, visions, voices, whereas emotional reactions, change with the swings of moods, with the seasons, & can be relied on to be changeable! I understand Babaji's message, of living in Truth, Simplicity & Love, in a new light, not meaning one should live as a 'Sadhu' in a hut, in poverty but, with the Simplicity which springs from Trust, requiring no struggle, stress, manipulation, nor huge effort. A stronger force does, whatever is required, through our human vehicle, while we allow ourselves to be held in the flow of Love and Wondrous miracles, loving All, resisting nothing. (Even now, that I stay more in Trust, Love & Joy, there is still some deep niggling, core unease). After I sold my Stroud home, I had bought a flat in the Navarra region, in 2020, since I was pretty sure, I did not have enough to buy anything locally. I had not realized what the financial consequences, would be as, the local Council cut off my weekly Pension Credit, because of the flat, so not even the rent, for where I am now living in Stroud, has been fully covered for 18months approx... It is only due to the decision I made about 11yrs. ago, to put 10% of any income, into an 'Abundance account, with the Credit Union', that gave me enough, to buy food & now, those funds are almost gone! And, So It Is! Thus, though I have survived maybe 18months, yet have done so, mainly because of the generosity of loving friends, especially friend Jonah! As August 2022 approached, I contacted the Citizens Advice Bureau, to find out whether, there is any way I can get support, to cover outgoing expenses, until the flat is finally sold. It seems to be my preferable recourse now, to sell the flat, without it ever becoming my home. Renting it out, did not turn out to be a feasible option, as though I had informed the young family interested, that the flat needed a good source of heat, for Winter weather, & though having said they could get a wood pellet stove, perhaps they realized, it would be more costly than anticipated. I believe anyway, as a British Citizen, I would only be allowed, to live there 3mths. a year, & dual citizenship has not been an option, since 2011. Plus, with all the present fear & control measures, by our global governments, travel has become difficult for those of us, who do not subscribe to belief in pharmaceutical drugs, & so would refuse all vaccines. I prefer to live mostly on raw organically grown food, for optimum health, & to stay free of fear, about my future, knowing I am loved by Source Being! Anyway, I was advised, that I should be able to get 26 weeks support financially, from the day, around mid-July, that my flat went on the market. Though I tried to contact the Pension Service, this week, to hopefully set that in motion, & got advice over the 'phone from the Citizens Advice Bureau, from an older, wiser woman, I found that only visiting face-to-face, with a relaxed, helpful lady in the P3 Charity, in Stroud, did I feel supported. She was very calm and practical, & sent off an online application, to the Pension Service for me, to which I have received a response. They ignored my own postal call for help.

Samantha, with husband Mick & eldest son Michael, & friend Martin, made a good start, really setting things in motion, with emptying the first unit. Occasional help from Sandra, on her recent visits. I have recycled piles of A4 paper, no longer relevant to my present life. retrieved some items, especially crystals & books, from my past. Extra expenses have been a challenge, especially paying for 2 storage units, plus car insurance & breakdown cover. I continued emptying & sorting, as speedily as I could manage, recycling many books. I took better books to Oxfam. Once first unit was half empty, Martin did a wonderful job of moving the heavy items beyond my strength to manage, from the 2nd unit, leaving just one sofa & one lovely table, given originally by Cristina.

Yesterday, September 16th, friend Rob, managed with me, him in his 70's, me in my 80's, both of us not so physically strong, but he was willing to help transfer the final two heavy items, a 2seater sofa & oak table, to his car & from there to the Stroud Furniture Collection warehouse)! I hope the strain of receiving insufficient income for my needs, will be relieved soon, now the flat is on the market. Thus, I have let go, of much, physical stuff, much of my past, no longer relevant, which feels wise anyway, as I approach 82yrs. of age.

My other main task is the final of many 'final' re-edits, prior to the publishing of this book. Trying to be sure that the book cover will be my design & colour.

My daily early morning Stargate meditations keep me in Trust, Joy & Love anyway. I am deeply grateful for the new phase of Alcazar channelled meditations, 'Into the Void' promising, to take us even deeper, into knowing our true multi-dimensional nature)! Listening this week, to the Costa Rica replays.

*

My story has not been particularly unusual or dramatic. I have skimmed somewhat superficially, through nearly 82yrs. of my life, aware, that some wise teachers, tell very little of their past story, maybe no longer feeling this, to be of much consequence. I both feel my past to have been a gift, the template that best served me, & yet any identification with this, feels more tenuous as, I have become rooted in more spacious, rich new possibilities, that are forming my new holographic environment. I chose to be born into the terror, of a World War beset environment, a strong karmic challenge for many Souls, but later in the Sixties, was also exposed to the expansive Love-filled possibilities, of the opposite polarity. My awareness was clouded by so many veils, yet some part of me, remained connected to, & listening to, my deeper essence. I accept the gift of the timing, of events in my life. That I took so long, to Trust Life more fully, matters not. If, as a result of all I am sharing, even one person is inspired to find their way, to connect more deeply, with Joy, Peace, Health, & a wealth of Love, in whatever form preferred, - maybe with the deep truth, of our intrinsic Beauty & Divine nature, to finally feel truly at Home, in heart-felt Being, a reflection of the All, it would be reason enough to celebrate. Time to Remember, our true identities. I am not living on any sort of plateau, rather it is a time of contrasts, - those following the antics & fear-mongering in the media, & others at peace though compassionate, knowing we are One, appearing as the many, feeling delight & excitement or trust as, aware of our metaphysical nature, we blink in & out of the Quantum field & the hologram, of the human play, more consciously. During the writing of this book, I have read most of Diana Cooper's, books, including her recent 2nd book, about Unicorns, who are from the 7th Dimension & above. As the Earth's Light frequency increases, they will be able to come back!

However, it is also true, that during the years, I have been translating my parents War-time letters, dated from 1937 to 1946, I was immersing myself, in the many horrific Holocaust books, though reading 'No Place to call Home', by Katharine Quarmby, I realize the many gypsies sent to Concentration camps, & who continue to suffer from discrimination, have less of a voice than the Jews. It is shameful too, how Israel has been treating the people in Palestine. I have read, Paul Preston's Spanish Holocaust books, including an in-depth portrait of Franco! '(At the age of 33, he was the youngest general in Europe, and was finally obliged by his seniority, to leave the Legion. On being promoted, Franco's service record had the following added: 'He is a positive national asset and surely the country and the Army will derive great benefit from making use of, his remarkable aptitude in higher positions.' He was given command of the most important brigade in the Army, the first Brigade of the First Division in Madrid, composed of two aristocratic regiments, the '*Regimiento del Rey* and the '*Regimiento de Leon.*' On returning to Spain, Franco brought with him, the political baggage acquired in Africa which he would carry through the rest of his life. In Morocco, Franco had come to associate government and administration, with endless intimidating of the ruled. There was an element too, of the patronizing superiority which underlay much colonial government, the idea that the colonized were like children, who needed a firm paternal hand. He would, effortlessly transfer his colonial attitudes, to domestic politics).' Always an ongoing War between Fascism plus other reactionary forces &, those inspired to create more equality & well-being for the 'hoi-polloi,' though any War brings so much carnage & suffering. Yesterday, when I was walking through Stroud, I stopped to talk to one of my 'beggar' friends. He is addicted to alcohol & appears 'Caribbean.' I talk with him regularly, but he has just managed, to 'flip out,' as he put it, thus losing the home he had. One day he may learn to love himself better. I said to him, it would be a good idea if all fascists, were genetically tested as, it would make nonsense of, believing themselves to be 'British' & better!

I was born of an 'English' father yet due to the Viking raids on the N.E. coast, York & along the Scottish border (now the site of Hadrian's Wall), plus Northern Ireland, me & my sisters are primarily Basque from my mother's lineage, with some Spanish too, & the rest is mostly from Norway, Denmark & Sweden, even a little Finnish. Some Vikings, are sure to have found their way elsewhere. My sister Cristina has been informed, from her DNA testing, she has a bit of Welsh & Finnish connection too. In the 2022 MBS Show, I have been having increased friendly interaction with African-looking darker hued men & women, & shared with one woman, to whom I gave an aura reading, that as I felt dark-skinned people are courageous, to have chosen to be born in testing times, I had been wondering recently, what I will choose next time!

*

I feel such waves of gratitude for Life, & how, this expresses through the life, of each person I connect with, yet also deep compassion, wherever there are beings, human or otherwise, suffering at the effect of careless cruelty. Still, continuing gratitude, for such a multi-dimensional, wonderful, magic, fantastic stage to act on, so many costumes, exposed to an endless diversity of forms, faces, fascinating peculiarities, smells, fragrant scents, taste, colour, touch, even with such limited senses. My purpose? To fulfil my Soul's highest intention for this incarnation, knowing myself as a multi-dimensional Infinite Being, birthed into human form, from the Heart of Love, from which endless possibilities spring &, encouraging others in the same. Life's so much simpler, more joyful & fulfilling, knowing this, whatever the outer circumstances, playing out. I love knowing myself, as an expansive, limitless, vast self, in heart-open, embodied, intimate, vibrant being. I feel a causeless gratitude ever welling up & bubbling in me. A warmth of Joy/Love, radiating from sacrum, through my heart & throat & out through my crown. Better this, than feeding ourselves, or being fed, the old stories of limitation. So, my Earth planet Purpose? To live at Ease in Life's embrace, with this reflected, or mirrored back in the eyes, words & actions of others, &, so, - sharing my life more intimately & lovingly, with others, taking what actions I/we can, for our precious Earth. I have just been reading, 'The Running Hare' - the secret life of Farmland. Also, 'Irreplaceable' by Julian Hoffman, 'the Fight to Save our Wild places.' 'The Sixth Extinction' & even more dire, her 'Field Notes from a Catastrophe – a frontline report on Climate Change' by Elizabeth Kolbert, spell it out, maybe most alarmingly, especially with regards to U.S.A. & China, & now Russia, still at War, unwilling to forego land grabs for oil, coal, or power, harming all life human or otherwise, within the lands & seas which sustain us. Nobody wins when it spells such huge loss. Yet many are immersed still, in the passing 3rd dimension 5,625yr. cycle of polarized extremes of misery, drama, & dis-ease, feeling victims of past & present, continuing to fight Life.

Also, the belief in pharmaceutical chemical concoctions, so no longer knowing our Oneness with, every particle of Life & Love, nor honouring the gift of our bodies. As we inflict great suffering through poisons, on other life-forms such as, slugs & snails & a host of Earth organisms, so we reap the consequences. Our politicians are mostly asleep, more focussed on personal gain, in almost every country! Forgetting why we chose to be born. Dying anyway, is simply transition to new wonderful, plus challenging, adventures & possibilities. Our Soul selves choose the optimum scenario. Time soon to end this cycle, of this Game!! There is a huge shift, happening for our Earth Planet &, its' inhabitants. Many higher dimensional beings, from realms we've no doubt experienced in the past, are transmitting their Love & Energy. The Pleiadeans being the most recent star system, to have gone through, what Humanity is now experiencing, they are keeping a close watch, on Earth events, keeping track of how it is playing out. Gregg Braden mentioned that, in his talk, in (Dec.2021). I feel relieved that finally, it seems as if Humanity, will (some time?), legally regard Ecocide, in the way we have now accepted Genocide, as unacceptable Crimes against all of Earth Life, including people. Despite ongoing warnings, Shell & Imperial Oil still go on, plus Bayer/Monsanto & Chevron & Exxon Mobil, with Wars & Genocide etc. still with murderous intent, little loving of all of life, including humanity there! Greed prevails.

*

Though I had been 9yrs. on 'The Journey' journey, the two years up till December 2012 had been revealing & releasing, the deepest core traumas, held in my body with, their associated pain. In more recent months, since then, my shift away from an old identity, had rapidly accelerated, helped especially by daily focus with Maureen Moss, (she may have transitioned, as I hear her name no more), & Meg Benedicte meditations, plus many ascension teachings. Helped too, by increasing connection with inner guides, through journey processes often, plus some channelling, where I met Gezra. I knew I was readying myself for greater changes. I had noticed that there was much deepening connection, with so many women, yet as soon as I put out a wish, to see love reflected equally back to me, by more men, with equal depth of communication, this began to happen.

I have been just over 18years involved in 'The Journey' &, it is 11yrs. since my dreams told me to write this book. Also, I now have my translations of my parents' war-time letters, to publish. I have gathered the most likely local publishers' details, & spoke briefly with one of the Co-founders of the Vision Maker Press, however, she has moved on to new ventures, but gave me advice.

*

I received an unexpected email from Mohammed, with whom I had lost contact for many years. Such a joy to speak the same language, to both hear, & be heard. I spoke to him this last week, 2022, still in his East London home. I attracted more male clients for Journey processes, possibly due to their inner knowing, that they are safe with me, now my fight with men is done. The miracles of manifestation Life graces me with, arrive faster and more often. I am readying myself for deeper connection, open to the well-springs of Grace, to the ebb and flow, of receiving & being received, plus expressing in a more powerful way, - seeing Love & Divinity everywhere. Also, since reading 'Dancing with Bees,' my deep intent to honour the world of Insects & help to create an environment to better support bees, is here, once my circumstances allow. Our planet's so deeply damaged & depleted of its former richness & diversity. Women have a stronger voice now too. Such deep long-lasting damage, is being done by the Monsanto-Bayer poisons &, the patriarchal drive, for profit & power, not realising the real cost of this drive, to be 'Someone,' at the expense of our Environment. So much Care-Lessness. The book I was reading in Dec. 2021,

'Working with Nature' by Jeremy Purseglove, is a saddening testament to human 'stewardship' of Planet Earth. I had been fascinated by a recent T.V. advert, wanting to attract people to holiday in Dubai, showing an air stewardess, right at the top of the highest building in the world, so I understood. Now as I read the final chapter, it seems, the sands of Dubai, are sinking into the ocean! I read his 2ⁿᵈ book, 'Taming the Flood.' The most gruelling book emotionally, about human interaction with the Earth, I have read is, 'Irreplaceable.' Governments who should be acting fast, seem too comfortable in their privileged worlds, as if they & their children too, are not accountable.

I am called now too, in my 81ˢᵗ year, as regards raising our vibration &, being voices or activists, for Earth, for restoring Nature. I had noticed a new urgency in many of us in the global spiritual community, (as I'm indeed consciously connected, with various of these, in a very real way), & how others like me, feel impelled to show up, more powerfully in our expression, to make a bigger difference now, in helping others wake up, out of habitual choices, to be & play, the unique part for which we incarnated, & help our Love, Light, & higher awareness, touch every part of our Earth, with intent & wise action, to usher in our New Earth.

*

(In fact, we are well into 2022, (which I believe will be a powerful year of shift for me), - & did indeed turn out to be just that, beyond my expectations! As I read through, I am fully aware I believed in the year 2015, my book would reach completion, yet in 2022, I am on, yet another **last re-edit**! of these pages, ready for publication. Not so long ago, I had finished doing likewise, with my translations, of the War-time letters, though I would still like, to add photos to the latter! I will probably put each of the 5 sections of the translations, into separate folders. I had written a synopsis & had various local publishers addresses. Since then, in the week of the Solar Eclipse, I decided suddenly, to approach Balboa Press, who had contacted me periodically, over many years. They are the U.S.A. equivalent of Hays House of whom I approve! I could have just done it myself via Amazon! My friends who chose that route, seem to have had, a faster, easier process! Yet I am grateful to my patient editor, as I have resisted much of, her insistence on changes, to avoid libel suites!

I am no longer centred on needing to release 'stuff', as this already has just been happening fluidly, organically, as emotions arise. Occasional hiccups, & I would prefer to be living in my own home one day, so it helps I've been letting go of so many things, many of which I've been without anyway, for many months! I am enjoying the constant heart warmth, yet life will be so much more relaxed, when I start to receive enough income to live, & cover all necessary outgoings! I mostly am surrendering to what is, in the present moment, & holding all in Love, judged neither as good nor bad, surrendering to the daily play, at rest in myself, more at Home in me, as if my soul is now more fully embodied, in Being on Earth but, as a multidimensional being. Occasional unwelcome hiccups! Huge waves of new energies are working through or with us, so many Light Beings from Angelic & other realms, such as from the Pleiades, Arcturus, Sirius, Lyra, the Unicorns & Dragons dimensions &, the Hathors, beaming in downloads, of coded information, to help more people, move from Suffering to Love, in sync. with so many conscious global beings, whose Collective Soul Purpose is to raise our own frequencies, to usher in new possibilities. Dolphins & Whales are deeply in harmony with Planetary needs.

*

Back in 2015, an intent had been spurred in me, to experience abundance on every level. As I embarked on my Money Mastery Course, (again with Rikka), I was unexpectedly rocked in the earlier days, by deeper and stronger layers ready to be brought to Light, Love and Truth! Not so comfortable, and noticing too, how I wanted to bring in a different quality, to my creative expression, which can reflect more of, the less seen interconnectedness, with many realms, or the All that is. An upgrade in vibrational frequency! Thus, my sense of Purpose was growing stronger. I feel my new expansive life plus, opportunities to express more of the God Love I am, already in my new field of energy. Even if underlying limiting shadows, with their accompanying emotions, might rock or topple me off centre, for moments or days, I am ready to surrender to Life being exactly as it is! I sent out a request to Archangel Michael to reveal to me what was going on at a deeper level, limiting my level of Abundance & that same night had a dream which took me by surprise. Nonna, (Rammiel's Italian grandmother, who is no longer in that body), had given me some money, which I had stuffed in my bag, to give due attention later. Moments later, a friend of mine, at a Babaji gathering, tells me, he has taken my money from me. I am furious & shouting at him, wondering too, why my friends in a nearby room, are ignoring my distress! When he tells me he first hid the money in his underpants, I fly at him as he sits on the toilet, & feel all around the said underpants! When he gets away, I see other people all ignoring me, or looking at me with disapproval in their eyes. Guilt on some level, that I should have money or riches, when others do not? What a strange pathetically silly dream! I may have mentioned too, Prageet, weeks ago, on Nov.5th, responding to a comment I had posted online, about my 4yr.old self, taking half a crown from my mother's purse, without asking, to put in the empty purse I had been given as a gift, then denying I had done so, when she asked if I had taken money. I had said 'No'! Did that guilt stay with me, adding to my life-long pattern of rich, poor, or 'vice versa'? The memory had suddenly surfaced, during one of the meditations. Later I also felt underlying guilt, that I had not already made a bigger difference, or lit a bigger flame in the world, to address so much that needs people's Love, passion & dedicated intent. I so love to encourage those suffering, to realize their/our true Mastery, the power we are, as one with the All. There seem to be so many selfless warriors, whose riches come to them, from the many who acknowledge, & are ready to receive, their special contribution! We all are & have, a unique contribution to offer!

As I had explored 'Money Mastery', certainly I had met more deeply buried layers, of Shame, Fear, Self-Judgement, Comparison, Inadequacy, Wrongness, & whatever else lurked unseen, which had held me still, in limitation & lack! Life is ever supportive of our Joy, if this is what we truly ask for. We can embody too, the attractive vibratory rate, to open wide to receive & trust in Life's ever-present support. Lack of Abundance has concerned so many of us, I felt my deeper exploration as to how much difference I can create for myself, needed inclusion in this book. Life had blessed me with the tools & means, so that once I had opened the possibility, to purge myself, of whatever had kept me, in thrall to Debt Companies, living in fear of lack, overdrawn accounts, disconnection from multi-dimensional being, - new possibility **was here**. I have & am all I need already, yet still, this pattern continues, on & off. I felt rich, & already know, new realities can come, no matter how often, I recreate old stories of Lack. Everything Is! Today, nearly into Autumn 2022, I still must beg friends or family for help financially! Yet…

I Am! All Possibilities are All Ways Here. I Already Am All Possibilities & feel them in my holographic field. However, if I am pushing Anything away, from Loving Acceptance, in true equanimity, <u>I am pushing away the opposite too</u>! I Can Accept my Financial Reality I have created, exactly as it is, - only then can I make a new choice. Love it All into Dissolution! I am readying myself sooner or later, to move fully into my power, inspiring more beings to likewise let go of personality's mistaken identity, with so limited a vision of who we are. We were not born in a Love-filled Universe to suffer from lack, of love, money, support or, health. The challenge of the last years, has been exhausting & has taken such a toll on my body's ease, energy levels & money flow, especially while with Sam, though magically, synchronous gifts continued to turn up too at key times. It took till September 2019, to finally sell my home. This has been synchronous with living constantly, in deep Surrender & Trust of Life, deep gratitude too for Existence.

Thus, my Purpose is unfolding, as Life reveals the next step! Since my 80th birthday, I had felt an inner 'Quickening'.

The daily meditations, I am doing with the Global Stargate Academy Community, are connecting us so deeply, with the reality of, the Quantum field of all Possibilities. The Journey home, is an inner one. All is Space, vibrating molecules, & everything we experience with our senses as solid, is not! We are sharing an agreed reality which, only has substance, while we imagine it so, thus we cannot see much of what is around us, yet not generally agreed upon.

It is amazing that objects stay so solid, though under the effect of LSD, I could see clearly, this was not so! Our common Purpose, is our evolution into a deeper knowing, of the ever-expanding Love we, & all Being is, continually reflecting itself. I live in the Joyful gratitude & radiance of this being so &, so often, I am now flooded, with boundless gratitude for the miracle of Existence, with such a Love for All and Everyone.

Staying in Divine neutrality, no call to take dramas seriously. My 'work' with clients was, to guide them into their own knowing of this, so the petty dramas no longer hold sway, or power over their own sense of themselves & the intrinsic precious nature of Being Alive & uniquely gifted with a beautiful world of endless Possibility! A Flame of Purpose, to allow Life to express perfectly through each, according to our Soul's encoded blueprint, with Joy, delight & Passion, surrendering to how each moment, presents itself.

I am so inspired & supported in staying focussed, these days, in (2022), by my ongoing global connection, with our Stargate Community, guided daily, through the channelled meditations, into so many dimensions. While we, still 'stay in control,' Life is limited as to how much can be gifted to us, as our free will is respected. Fears of Safety come from past memory & thus, fear of future distress. Realizing who we are, we can let go & Trust or know, we **are** loved & supported, & that means Self-trust too!... a surrender into the Now moment, even if it shows up in a form you do not prefer! There is a Gift in it All. These days, as I have mentioned, my body/being is filled with a heart warmth, which I feel strongly, night & day, from my sacrum to my crown. It is a strongly felt Joy/Love heat, permanently beaming out in all directions.

I feel so utterly blessed yet waiting for my money abundance, to reach me, when I most need this, which I truly trust will do so, sooner or later, before very long at all! We must & will remember that, we are Galactic, infinite beings, & though in linear time, we have been so long experimenting in, these separation nightmares & games, playing so many roles on this 'free will Earth planet, is not it fun too?! That is the fun of outside, inside, as even as galactic beings, we can choose to take many forms & have the delight of playing & interacting with each other. Though I have told my story here, I am aware, it is but one, of many, many roles played, many dreams. I am operating at a higher vibratory rate, have done for a while now, know too, new realities are ever coming, in resonance with this.

I remember how stirred I was in the late 80's, reading 'Gem Elixirs and Vibrational Healing,' vol.2 from Gurudas (channelled through Kevin Ryerson and John Fox), & delving deeply into the world of crystals, reading too 'The Lost Continent of Mu,' by James Churchward with great fascination. I felt very connected with Lemuria. (Many of my beautiful crystals, gathered in my years as a trader, are in my present room, retrieved from my storage unit).

I listen often to, many beings connected into, & sharing teachings from various realms, channelling higher vibrational knowledge &, encouraging us, to reclaim our true heritage. We do not need to carry on with the separation game any longer than we choose. Time to live from our Hearts with Conscious, common Purpose! This mammoth Divine Play, of matter slowed down enough, for the illusions of Time, of solidity, to be sustained, a big clearing house for all the Realms, to come to a place of more integration, free of all Judgements, has just about run its course. Everything that is not born of Love, is showing up, to be healed. Some of us before incarnation, agreed to play the shadow, or dark roles. Our Frozen Light is melting. Realize, dear friends, that we are probably all of us extra-terrestrials, who have experienced the Experiment of Life in many realms, - Love at the Heart of All Creation!! Believe it or not!

The veils of Illusion are lifting, - it is time for Remembrance, a quickening, a heightening of Heart energies is happening so fast. Especially since the Winter Solstice 2016. In 2020, unconscious sickness & fear, has been more visibly evident globally, with much craziness &, attempts by those attempting to control from this fear, impacting on Societies. We are all carriers of the Divine flame & hold the seed of Christ, or Higher, consciousness.

Back in Nov.29th 2015, I chose to take part in a Global Climate March, & would prefer, the Earth be honoured, rather than disrupted by fracking etc. as is happening, with the attendant poisoning of land & water, with whatever creatures were dwelling there, upsetting Nature's Balance. I would prefer too that Bombs are not dropped on Syria, nor War waged in Ukraine nor wherever, - & that men become less War-minded. Still, Cameron, Theresa May, Trump, Boris Johnson & most politicians too, are themselves on personal Soul journeys & represent general Mass consciousness, with Jeremy Corbyn one of the rare politicians, who seems to genuinely have integrity, representing Sanity & Care for people & the Environment. How the Press, controlled by profit-fuelled greed &, short-sightedness, love to discredit & vilify others. 'Positive News' & more recently 'The Light,' are alternative newspapers, for the more consciously awake people to read. Yet everything must show up, which needs to be exposed, in this Divine Play! Surely, all others believing in Separation, believing, strangely, in only **this life followed by 'sleep,'** will take the time it takes, for each person to learn the lessons of Love. Even if actions are harmful, every player on any stage, is not here by accident, though on the personality level, usually this will not be realized, until a later time. They are all Divine, higher beings too. We are All on the same journey into the Heart of ever-expanding, evolving Love creation, sooner or later to know or remember ourselves as Powerful Joyous Creators, part of metaphysical being, gifting the Whole, through interaction with, the vast diversity of a myriad created forms of Light and Love! I AM… God meeting God…

Back on Dec.7th 2015, Judith had come to my home, as I had asked for a session. This may be the last process of this chapter & I sense it will be powerful. (Actually, another one got added too!)

My prayer was to meet whatever, was still holding me bound in any separation, or attempt to hold on to ego control. I pray rather to come into my unique full & potent expression, as one with the All. The staircase taking me deeper, feels very safe, even though there's expansive spaciousness, on the left, no banister. On the right, there is a banister which feels supportive, to my body, & I quickly get a sense of being already very deep. For the 1st time there is no door, just fiery flames with a goddess-being sitting in the flames, no barrier between her & me, other than what my mind might concoct! Feels like she & my expanded Soul self, are one & the same. The magic vehicle is some 'zoom' eco-friendly rocket, powered by limitless energy, moving so fast, after I press, an appropriate fiery button, that I have arrived, before being aware, of setting off, into the solar plexus area, where already, there's strong discomfort or contraction, maybe mind's fear of, letting go of, any remaining belief, it is in control? To the left & above, is a fiery Sun, & the discomfort's located, in the blackness below, to the right. The memory which pops up, shows me, about 15yrs.old, challenging myself, to scale a dark grey slightly sloping high wall, at the old Clay Mill, which I must grip 'for dear life', with my toes & fingers. And I had continued ever since, having to challenge myself, with scary feats, to prove my courage & worth! Also, my unconventional choices as a rebel, not following the rules, nor norm, gave me a subtle sense, of satisfaction, pride even arrogance, despite family disapproval &, rejection. Later, it was maybe about my specialness, as the daughter of a refugee, identifying with being an outcast, or with my unusual, life choices. There had also been embarrassment, & shame recently, at having to ask frequently, for support, expecting to be more likely, less than welcome. I had not admitted or realized this, yet as I drop deeply, into an embrace of every state, such as that, 'feeling nothing much,' is a 'less than an O.K., or good enough' frequency state, than feeling warm Heart-flow & zooming energy, - what a relief, to detach myself from every comparison hook! So, I let go of, any remaining (I hope), Separateness, I have been flipping in and out of, for weeks, knowing myself as one with All. Now I come into a deeper sense, of Sister and Brotherhood, saying within, "Hullo sister Rikka, - Hullo sister Brandon, - hullo Brother Archangel Michael" feeling so much Loving Equality, one with the Totality plus, a loving sense of Community, Inclusiveness, non-separateness. I see an Infinity of Galaxies, in precise infinitesimally small details, patterns, mandalas, Geometry, in every atom, Light & Darkness, & the humour & Honour, of playing &, Being it all!

Still, at the 'camp-fire of unconditional Love,' process, I released the buried pain, at feeling cast out by, my sisters & parents, not successful, not good enough, 2ⁿᵈ class, feeling that every one of, our family, competed for crumbs of Love, as we were all needy, & looking to be validated, accepted & seen as worthy, of being Loved. And 'Mummy' stirred that competition, setting us against each other; I do not know how that served her. Her childhood patterns? I did not realize I had still been carrying, that pain in my body. I cut the cords, together with my guide, between me & my sisters, which were from throat to throat, entered together with her too, into my body to 'spring-clean', or burn out with fierce, fiery flames, all that old 'comparison, not good enough' stuff, driving out beliefs, of 'being an outcast, shut out from Love', then joined with her, in installing the Truth that "I am Love, emanating & receiving Love, in every moment, the more I openly reveal myself, & welcome unlimited possibilities." We were suffusing my entire body with tender, gentle Love flame blessings, so much Love & Softness permeating every molecule of my Being... -like making Love with all of me. I had come to total forgiveness with my sisters, whom I later phoned. Ever since, I have felt a greater yielding softness, letting go easily & more often, into spaciousness, a whole level of resistance I did not know was there, has dropped away. I also breathed in resources i.e.: Self-Love Laughter & Playfulness

Feeling connected Creative expression plus, feeling my voice heard Heavenly help & supported by Life Reassuring loving communication from Heart

When I return to the scary challenge, I no longer feel to, give myself, a hard time, rather test myself in more enjoyable ways, confident that I am loved. Since the session, I feel much softer, like a whole subtle layer, of comparing different aspects in myself, as better or worse, is gone, & in coming to this deeper love & acceptance, of each present moment, I feel confident, strong, staying in a lighter, relaxed, & elated place of deep connection with others, & everything. Nothing to prove! Certainly, feeling myself one with, the wave of Pioneers, in a New Earth, ushering in uncharted territory. Purposeful!

*

My body had not, quite as much strength, as I approached my 80ᵗʰ birthday. I had been months almost entirely, eating raw organically grown food, to best serve my health, yet climbing up a steep wooded & rocky hill, I had a sudden accident. The big stone under my right foot slipped downhill, while my left hand remained trapped, between stones, which twisted my arm & body, resulting in a fractured left wrist. I was surprised, in that tumultuous year of 2020, during my & my friend Sandra's time, back with the Lakabe Community, (8 weeks, partly due to cancelled flights), (in the Navarra region of Spain), how some remaining shadow showed up, maybe to keep me in more humility! Unexpectedly, I encountered negative reactions & a strong verbal attack, from one of the women, - karmic? which felt wounding, in my heart, as mentioned. It had been many years, since I had had, that sort of interaction, i.e., verbal attack. This may be, because I had decided, as I approached my 80th birthday, to try to buy a property, in Spain, to leave to Samantha & Rammiel, in my will, (not yet written & signed, - a pending task). Not having my own transport, this necessitated, my being more dependent on offers of lifts, even though I paid more, than the petrol cost, & expressed deep gratitude. (I have never yet driven in Spain, & years back, staying with relations in & around Madrid, the traffic seemed so chaotic, with much aggressive, horn blasting.) So, though I only had 3 lifts for this purpose, I then had to have 2 hospital visits, for my wrist! It is interesting, weeks later, during the week of the Eclipse, everything in fast motion, with my book, I received an unexpected email from said lovely lady Clara, who had felt to upbraid me, apologizing & extending a hand & heart of friendship, saying maybe, she had been hard on me! I am happy, Clara, has now delivered her darling son, Alain, months later, in her home, in the heart of the Lakabe Community. I hope she read the book I gave her, 'The Children who Lived on the Hill,' the best book I have ever read, about, relating to, & teaching our 'offspring.'

After I had spent our obligatory quarantine period, in Sandra's home, in the Welsh mountains, on our return from Lakabe, I then went by train, still assisted, between trains, back to Stroud, where Ish met me at the Station. Back home in Stroud, I had been weeks, with my left arm in plaster, managing as best I could, with my right arm & fingers. It has never fully healed, so far, over a year later. I had made an appointment, with Gloucester Royal Hospital, where my plaster was removed, & I was given a light harness instead, as my arm healed & grew stronger. I have been plaster & harness free, many months, but still, there is a little lingering pain in the wrist, when strength needed for physical tasks. I still cannot lift the same weight, with my left hand, as the right one. My left shoulder, is strong, following the fracture in Jan. 2017, but my right shoulder seems to suffer from years of repetitive strain. Sandra has continued to serve me, as best she has known how, when we see each other, for which I am truly grateful. We have really come even closer.

I feel much of this is happening, through great blessings, from daily Stargate Alcazar meditations, journeying into Quantum Field Expansiveness.

I look forward to receiving, live Journey sessions, one day, **not** via online zoom, as the control measures, provoked by Corona virus 'pandemic' suggest might be. The 'Journey Community' unexpectedly gifted me, with a free Journey event, (an Abundance & Enneagram one), at the end of January, 2022. When I asked myself why, since a child onwards, I have manifested bone fractures, I remembered how I hated, the hardness & solidity of houses, roads etc. My skeletal structure, including ribs & teeth, seems to have taken many hard knocks, since youth (at 12yr. old), onwards! A cracked right pelvis bone, which caused me, to limp a bit for 7yrs., followed 3 months in bed. For some reason, I have never since, liked nor eaten, marmalade nor navel oranges! In fact, it was a surprising revelation for me, to find that zoom processes, we exchanged, were every bit as powerful & real, & much easier, having our partners chosen for us!

I have decided, to insert one last process, (from the Journey Practitioner's Mastery Event in Elspeet, in Holland) from Sunday, Nov.20th 2016 for this chapter; - *I partnered with Dalia, from Israel. The descending stairs, were like glittery & sparkling jewels. I drop down quite deep. I am so much more trusting & relaxed about these increasingly deepening, inner Journeys. Along a passageway, there is a solid, wooden door, with a window in it, & my black-skinned guide, who has appeared a few times, in other processes, is here though, it is the 1st time, I have seen his gleaming, white teeth smile, especially by the end of the process. I feel his joy &, he is more visible, than other times. An unusual vehicle again. It has a long giraffe-like, though wider neck, giving more of an overview, especially as the whole vehicle, seems made of reinforced glass, with a side door. We travel quickly, to my heart & throat area, where there is a strong beam of light, shining into the right chest area, so, generally more space & light, though not in the Left, where it is a darker, brown goldish colour, & less spacious, with a staircase, going down, inside the left of my body. I go down to the bottom step &, it feels these are the beginning steps, of my new life. Panic arose, recalling the invitation, offered back then, by Stuart M., manning the stand, opposite our Aura stand, (whom I think managed the Birmingham Holistic Health Centre). He had been drawn to speak to me, asked too, if I would talk to people in his Birmingham venue.*

I had replied yes, without much conviction! Now, in my 'Journey,' I am feeling as if I will faint, like when I am surrounded by snow. My partner suggests she guide, me through a phobia cure. The usual dizziness has arisen in my head, at which point, I would usually lower my head, between my knees, to avoid passing out. However, Dalia tells me to stay totally present, with every sensation, without resistance. Next, I also find, my feet feel paralyzed. I sense the 'weakness of my skeletal structure' (!) needing support, sense too, isolation, but soon, this shifts to Quietness, & Stillness. I relax here & it feels comforting. I begin to fully land in myself, breathing deeply, able to slow down, & relax into my authentic Being, arriving Home in my body, (after all, the situations where I faint, are often lack, of sufficient oxygen,). It happened on the underground, when I was pregnant, crowds of people hurrying past me, probably imagining I was drunk. Here, I am more open to, my intuition & inner Guidance, more playful with my voice, learning humour &, also honouring the step, the ground I stand on. Now the idea of speaking publicly, to others, feels easy, or easier, even exciting. I have noticed that Fear, is *quite close to the energy of Excitement, but the former, can paralyse me, whereas excitement, propels me into action or, appreciation of the moment, where fear of the New, <u>might</u> have shown up! This requires conscious breath, honouring & enjoying my Self, to allow Ease, in the joy of relating, so this, will be reflected, back to me.*

I found myself fainting, after arriving back in Stroud, unloading my car, after the recent December2021 travels, but found it easier to put my head down low, for the blood to return to my head, rather than be still.

And so, my Purpose unfolds, as Life reveals the next step! The Journey home is an inward one. From the perspective of earth-bound 3rd dimension seemingly separate reality, Heaven or other Realms & Galaxies are imagined above or be-low, yet in Truth everything is contained within us, within who we are, - one with, the vast, Infinite Quantum field. All is Space, vibrating molecules, & everything we experience, with our senses as solid, is not! We share an agreed reality, which has substance if, we imagine it so, thus we see little of, what **is,** around us but, not generally agreed upon. In truth, I understand that everything is 99.9% empty Space! Patrick Sterry, from Star Trek, is well aware of this! I believe he is part of the Resonance Science Foundation & has written 'The Connected Universe.' The entire Universe is connected. Creation happens, from the Quantum Field &, we too, are the Field! Scientists, have been catching up too, with the fact that everything here, is a holographic reality &, every particle, is blinking in & out, from the Quantum field of reality. We, are always **in** the Quantum field. As soon as we get to know, more of our reality, our whole ability, to have more influence increases, to become stronger & stronger. Alcazar, (the name for a group of Masters, channelled through Prageet & Jules), has been leading us gently, to know more of our true nature &, our new phase of his teaching, is called, 'Into the Void! My recent favourite meditations, have been journeys into the Blackness of the Quantum field of all possibilities! It is amazing, that objects stay, so it appears, so solid, though I noticed with LSD, that this was no longer so! Our common Purpose, is evolution into deep awareness, of, an ever-expanding Love, we & all Being is, continually reflecting itself. I live in the Joyful gratitude & radiance of this being so. I am flooded mostly now permanently, with boundless gratitude for the miracle of Existence, with such a Love for All & Everyone. (In fact, in 2022, since the last week of the 'Becoming Superconscious' meditations onwards, & continuing with the 'Into the Void' meditations, I physically feel a constant warm expansive glow, which brings me joy, from my sacrum chakra to my throat, & beyond, & which has become constant)! It is possible that this permanent expansive warm love flow, is one way the rising of the kundalini energy, can manifest, if I understood a conversation I heard recently online, between Julieanne (Stargate channel) & Barbara Blum.

Staying in Divine neutrality, no call to take dramas seriously thus, any 'Journey' 'work' with partners, has been to guide them into accessing their own knowing of this, so petty dramas no longer hold sway or power, over their own sense of themselves &, the intrinsic precious nature of Being Alive &, uniquely gifted in a beautiful world of endless Possibility! I did not expect as powerful an impact, from the recent 'zoom' Journey event, - (I was gifted with, - since I had no money), as meeting in a physical venue. In truth, exchange of processes, with my daily zoom partners, was every bit as powerful! I also had not anticipated, the cut to Pension Credit, since Nov.2020, as a result of buying the flat in Spain, which is why I have had no money to cover outgoing expenses, yet been so gifted by friends & family, that my needs have been met. Now in 2022, since I have put my flat on the market, I may be able to receive income again, so I was told by a better-informed lady, I consulted, from the Citizens Advice Bureau,

While we 'stay in control,' Life is limited in how much can be gifted to us, as our free will is respected. A Flame of Purpose, allows Life to express perfectly, through us, according to the Soul's encoded blueprint, with Joy, delight & Passion, surrendering in trust too, as much as we are able, to how each moment presents itself. Fears about Safety come from, past memory &, fear of future distress. Knowing deeply, who we are, we can Trust we are loved & supported, & that means Self-trust too! ... a surrender into the Now moment, even if it shows up in a form you do not prefer! There is a Gift in it All. We may remember we are Galactic beings, & though in linear time, we have been so long, in these separation nightmares, playing so many roles, was not it fun too!! That is the fun of outside, inside, as even as galactic beings, we can choose to take many forms & have the delight, plus every other emotion, along the way, of playing & interacting with each other. Though I have told 'my' story here, I am aware its but one, of many, many roles played, & is all past. (I have read that our higher Self, splits into 12 different parts, having different experiences in different realms. Since operating at a higher vibratory rate, as I have done for a while now, new realities come, in perfect synchronous, resonant timing.

An earlier real & most life-changing shift for me, came as I entered my 70th year, Oct.25th2010. I had felt for quite a long while, that my 70's were going to be particularly significant. I asked for a 'Journey' session, prior to my Birthday, yet for the first time, experienced 2 sessions, I could not complete nor, could I come to any resolution, which seemed to show up, as never-ending grief. I woke up on the morning of my 70th Birthday feeling so low-spirited, I did not even want to get up. Eventually I decided, I would bring up any Birthday cards. The 1st one I opened, from dear Parvati & Pete, said 'One precious Life, one precious Planet'. I burst into tears & the words which erupted from me, were "I'm all wrong!" I was shocked, but the impact was so strong, I realized, so, that is what is really going on, "I **still** don't love myself." From that moment, my focus became, to honour truly & love, my **body**, & my **personality** self, as well as the **divine** aspect, seen through the eyes! I started to speak daily, to myself, in my favourite wall mirror, telling my body reflection, I loved her. Some days I did not want to look at myself, but as I persevered, all these aspects, began to trust me, until, days later, my mirror face, became my best friend. My life felt, in fact **is**, deeply transformed.

Now, I delight in myself, whatever age, with the love & delight, with which I now equally experience others, no-one better nor worse, in essence, **whatever reality**, they are choosing for themselves. Now in my 80's, my intent to fulfil, my highest potential, on my true Soul path, on Planet Earth, is a strong ever-deepening, ongoing focussed intent. There is a strong quickening.

We are All on the same journey, from the Heart of ever-evolving, expanding, creative Potential, seeded in the Quantum field Blackness of the Void, thus sooner or later to know ourselves, as Powerful Joyous Creators, gifting the Whole, through interaction with, the vast diversity of a myriad created forms. Let there be Light! I AM... God meeting God.

I so appreciate speakers, with Alicia Power's depth. She works with very high levels of Creator Beings. I love the ongoing inspirational support from Rikka Zimmerman & Michael Beckwith. Very recently too, I have listened to delightful women such as Masami Covey, Mahalia Michael, plus, Xi Earthstar & so many more. They interact with the higher dimensions, with fairies &, other non-terrestrial beings, such as Mer people, with light-hearted joy and respect. Mahalia has links with beings, from Planet Lyra, with which I feel connected too, without remembering why this is so.

Since my 70th birthday, Oct.2010, & onwards, I felt much softer, like a whole subtle layer, of comparing different passing aspects in myself, & others, as better or worse was gone. In coming to this deeper love & acceptance, of each present moment, I feel strong, confident, staying in a lighter, relaxed, & elated place of deep connection with others & everything. I have had too, a personal vision, for years, about having enough land, for a cabin, with rain-water harvesting & solar panels, 'innovation t' technology I have been told of, free energy, trees, serving too, as a haven for wild-life, Nature, & visiting friends. Plus, a car which does not pollute the environment. I could be in this body, for another 10 to 20 years, (**or** more), which gives room, to new possibilities! Certainly, I feel myself one with, a wave of pioneers ushering in a New Earth in uncharted territory. Purposeful!

Chapter 3

One Hundred percent Responsible

I have mentioned, I was in my mid-thirties, before the idea trickled in, during my first taste of therapy, that I might in some way, have been responsible, for how my life unfolded; having so long believed, like so many of us, in my victim role! 'God,' - (also my father), in a controlling seat, certainly would have little reason, to particularly notice, an insignificant creature like me, unless to visit misfortune, or criticism, my way if I failed, to measure up!

I now believe, as the 80 plus, multi-dimensional being I am, who has had many Earth lives, though I will have had countless other adventures, in other dimensions, that I may still have, at least, another couple more Earth lives, especially now more people are waking up, as the light frequencies are increasing. Only another 10 years till 2032, the year Diana Cooper's Angels predicted, harmony would prevail, in every Country, - China last. A great time to return to Planet Earth. I have no fear of Dying… I expect it would be an exciting journey.

Responsibility…. a word some shy away from, in a Society of victim mentality. Societies like ours, with increased tendency, to cast blame. YOU are responsible for my/our misfortune, or suffering. If you changed, my world would improve… It is your fault! OK? Many businesses have been created, specifically, around suing others, wherever there is a chance of 'getting even', of compensation, resulting in gain, more control, money, or power. How common too, it has been, for people to say, or think, "How can 'God' allow…?" especially, "How could any God allow something like that, to happen to, an innocent child, like her (or him)?" This mentality arises, from the idea of Separation, separate individuals. Yet a great shift is happening, & I trust there are enough in our global human family awakening, that I feel 'all manner of things shall be well.' The shift, may not be evident till 2025, maybe…, onwards.

This human experiment we have chosen to experience on Planet Earth, impacts <u>all</u> life-forms, bees & birds, grasses, trees, insects, dogs, cats, farmed animals &, domestic birds such as hens & turkeys, or parrots & other caged, distressed creatures, like bears & lions. Unless we are good clairvoyants, or remembering from a young age, (as has happened many times, in the earliest years), we consciously know nothing, about the past experienced by, any baby, nor, any other being, human or otherwise! Sometimes a child remembers, in the earliest years, 'I had a different Mummy before,' then as this life, gets imprinted more strongly, in ones' psyche, usually forgets. A baby, a cat, dog, or horse, may have more inner wisdom & knowing, than the adults 'in control!' A vulnerability too, dependence on others, for food, love & caring, since we have destroyed or control so much of their preferred habitats, where crying, whining, or other signs of distress, may be responded to lovingly or not. A newly incarnated soul, has chosen carefully, in consultation with one's Guardian Angel, or other guiding Beings, to come into this dense, material world of polarity, making surely, for a huge adjustment, - having chosen, to come from spacious infinity, into the challenge, of living this, particular life, in a world of duality, which best serves his or her Soul purpose; though I've heard that the Soul, is separated into, a dozen different aspects, simultaneously living different lives, maybe even on different planets. Each being will have chosen to fulfil a particular purpose, by choosing, where to incarnate, into which exact circumstances. This dependence at birth in some species, for physical survival, seeming helplessness, equates for some with being ignorant, - dependent on its 'betters' or, adults, to give them the 'facts' about 'reality'! My parents also thought, somewhat like this, & both being teachers, were prepared, to educate us, so we would learn their wisdom, or lack thereof.

We children, no doubt have our own agendas, as to why we choose to incarnate, into a particular family, at that very time, in that environment in the chosen Country, in that Century. We may have agreed to come also, to help the parents learn life lessons. Many more awakened, light beings are currently incarnating, knowing from a young age, why they are here, with a strong intent, for a big Quantum Jump, as it were. I find it better to focus on, Wonder & Gratitude for Life, rather than feed dramas & horrors, though feeling compassion, for those caught in horror, unaware maybe, of their true heritage! Reincarnation is widely accepted in many countries, & for anyone open-minded, there are so many accounts, which give credence to this, where children have remembered,

who they were, where they lived, and how they died, even what relationship they had at that time, to those who are still alive, especially if they maybe had, a sudden brutal or shock death! I read since my younger years, so many, many accounts. Most recently I read, 'When I was Someone Else' by Stephane Allix, in that genre. A special book!

I will have mentioned, in Chapter 1 or 2, probably, how I have had my DNA tested, & sure enough, the Basques I have identified with, in my heart for so long, have given me the biggest part of my DNA, through 2 or 3 of my mother's grandparents I believe. Vikings were responsible for most of my remaining DNA via my father, as they battled & settled, from the Nth. East Coast, York, the Scottish border & Northern Ireland, from Finland, Norway, Denmark & Sweden, & obviously must have impregnated many women, along their warring way. My Chinese astrological Birth creature is, a metal Dragon &, I <u>was</u> pulled out, by metal forceps, or were they plastic?

It is said to be the 'Emperor Justinius,' in the year 553, who declared a ban, on teachings about reincarnation, at a meeting, the Pope of that time, had refused to attend! Yet this ban, became adopted by the Church, for good Catholics to accept, like it or not! "I didn't choose to be born!" is so unlikely a scenario, in a Universe of vast Intelligence. Though personally, I did hesitate, not feeling totally ready, & being pulled out by forceps, is not a gentle entry! When, as I believe, we have played such myriad roles, it certainly makes a total mockery, of any discrimination, based on choices regarding religion, sexual attraction, race, skin colour or gender. Yet even now, there are many far-right Fascist extremists, anti-Jews & 'black' people, gypsies, plus whoever else qualifies, for being on their hate list. (As I mentioned earlier, genetic DNA testing, would make a mockery, of people's belief in the purity of one race, they believe is their heritage). Mostly we have forgotten, who we were & are, & why we chose just these, life circumstances. Many of us certainly do believe, we have arrived with a definite purpose, or agenda, that we are here to fulfil, yet we will all face too, the obstacles that have impeded us, in former lives, so, have carefully chosen our parents, & the life circumstances, to best assist us. In some ways we do indeed, arrive with a 'clean slate', yet already, we have certain tendencies, differences, & likes, plus whatever has come as a legacy, from our chosen present parents &, ancestral heritage. Our radio & T.V. programmes, newspapers too, will mainly scoff at any belief in re-incarnation, or anything not mainstream! Recently, & once or twice since, as my Stargate meditation, was drawing gradually, to a close, I have seen, with my inner vision, a bearded face, with chin-length black-hair, gazing at me &, after a while, an older version of, I think, the same face. I guessed they were Vikings, & wondered if they were me, or relations. Also, our vast earlier experiences together with our specific agenda for this body experience, will attract the key people & triggers to provide new opportunities to face &, master whatever is intended; - yet, most of us will not remember who we really are, nor why we are here! I've both remembered lives, where I was a victim, of others abuse, & also, as the abuser, such as believing myself, superior to my wife &, all women, & most likely, through the aeons, I have done much worse, even though I was stuck, identifying myself as a victim, for too much of this life. I remembered too, a more solitary life, in Europe, I chose, closer to trees, to the

Nature world. A Viking life? I heard long ago, we tend to be given information, or occasionally remember details, about lives which relate to what we are here to learn, or accomplish, in this one. If you cannot really accept 'past' lives, (*viewed in linear time reality, - yet actually could be concurrent lives!*) - as being as real as, the present life, even so, images which surface, seemingly of' past' lives, could be very insightful. *(Read 'Soul Survivor'- Resources Page).* I've read & continue to hear many, many of these accounts of NDE's & past life memories.

*

Although I always believed in, a greater Reality, & life before & after, incarnation, yet I had a low level my of trust, that life was 'on my side.' This did not change significantly, until my 'Sannyasin' days onwards, when I began to express myself, with more life energy, then even more so, as my heart opened to Berris, allowing more heart expansion. Of course, LSD was significant, in opening me up, to a much more expanded, view of reality, as well as so many years of inner therapy 'journeying.'

I have been able to live, in greater integrity, than I had briefly, in the past.

I like to see myself honestly, thus have shared, with closer friends, with neither shame nor embarrassment, choices I made in the past, things I did, which were not in alignment with my higher self, nor integrity, & less than honest. Mostly I have been very aware, when I have chosen to do things, that, I was certainly not proud of. In my mid-twenties to mid-thirties, I felt particularly unsupported by life. My relationship with men, with myself, & everyone else, had not always been guided by inner wisdom, nor by transparent, open-hearted compassion! I do however, like to observe myself, as honestly as I am able.

Initially, the whole following episode, was triggered by Bob's disappearing periodically, sometimes for weeks at a time. He was the father of my daughter Samantha. One time, one of the men in our East End Community, a homosexual, (he used to take 'Purple Hearts,' - I am not sure what effects these were supposed to have), was mocking me about Bob, having left me, & not loving me. I've no idea what investment he had, in wanting to needle me in this way, but it was one of the few times in my life, when a red-hot rage, tore through me, to the point, where I was jumping up & down, with the force of the energy, before grabbing a chair that, I would have smashed down, on his head, if others had not come into the room &, restrained me, seconds before the chair's downward trajectory! (Even though I did not love Bob)! Anyway, I must have been about 26yrs.old, soon after Bob & I were finally apart, & one day I found myself going into a shop &, taking a packet of baby muesli. Within memory, (except that half-crown from my mother's purse!), I had never ever, stolen, - nor even thought to steal. I am guessing I felt the world, owed me something, my self-esteem being at a very low ebb. I remember too buying a 'bra,' - (I had not been wearing bras around that time), feeling, it might boost my worth as a woman, in some way. I certainly, felt myself a victim of, scarcity, lack, & deprivation, - God & the world not on my side!

*

I believe I have made clear how, through my beliefs, & habitual thoughts, I created my reality, affecting how others, in fact, how all of life responded to me. As my consciousness has transformed, so the life I experience, the way others relate to me, has transformed. By the end of this book, it should be clear how I, (& I believe this is so for us all), came to see, my own responsibility, for every pain, betrayal, or situation, in which, I had believed myself, a victim. Of course, as a child, I would not have known, how the seeds had been planted in me, nor what would be, the resulting harvest, but these are part of the Soul path!

*

I have felt strongly, against having injections or medication, since I was a child &, was so happy, when I learned enough about natural healing, in my 20's, to avoid the best I could, ever taking medication again. I avoided subjecting my son to vaccinations or medication, while he was in my care. Of course, as an adult, he makes his own choices. I studied natural health, in a 'College of Natural Nutrition' too, & learned, both through study & experimenting with myself, the effects of different diets etc. I will have mentioned this in the previous chapter, as it has been a big part, of my life's focus.

Victim mentality, blaming anything or anyone, outside ourselves, is very prevalent around health, such as viruses or germs, "I caught a bug from...," food allergies, our partners, our family, life, weather, childhood unhappiness, dissatisfaction, the social services, the government, experience, work colleagues, & work-place, & so on & so forth, for our own state of health, or happiness. A big theme these days, in adverts & News, is a War on germs, on bacteria. In truth, we would only be 'adversely affected' by 'germs,' good & 'bad,' from a natural healing perspective, if we are already providing, a more toxic environment, inside our bodies, thus creating a stronger internal reaction, i.e., we are already dependent, on needing Nature's healing. Our bodies will **always**, attempt to restore Nature's balance. Germs are neither good nor bad, in the sense that, different ones thrive, in different environments. The more we have challenged our health, through processed food, tobacco, alcohol, pharmaceutical synthetic drugs, negative beliefs, plus lack of Self-Love & Care, the more vulnerable we will be, to adverse or uncomfortable consequences. I have witnessed over & over again, the level of fear, people carry, when disease, or ill health, happens. Even the naming of symptoms, has given these, more substance plus, power to manifest. Most people in 'the West,' anyway, trust the orthodox mainstream medicine system, & give responsibility for their bodies' health, into their doctors' hands, giving them almost a god-like status. Doctors have invested so many years, so much focus, in training in a particular set system, which does not allow for the possibility, even, that there is _no_ condition, which cannot be healed! Thus, any recovery, that happens outside the 'box,' is a fluke, or near impossible miracle. It is also true, that a day will come sooner or later, when a soul will leave the body. Sometimes, more often than many will realize, the soul returns, after an experience of other realms. Of course, it could feel threatening, to doctors adhering to a certain belief system, having given that many years, of one's life, to learning one such set approach, to health, to even allow, that there are, so many other possibilities & keys, to living in vibrant health, (while this is in alignment, with an individual's Soul's choice & intention, in this life). It is seen almost as a criminal offence, to question the established system, in which the 'cure', often has worse 'side' effects, than the original complaint. I learned this, when I worked as a Carer, where I was obliged to hand out, pharmaceutical pills & liquid medicines. The side-effects enumerated in a many-paged medical Glossary, sounded as dire, as the original complaint!

My wrist, broken nearly 18 months ago, has not mended as it should. Two men nurses in Spain, took hold of my hand, pulled so hard, I was crying out, in pain, - to bring the bones into more alignment, I suppose &, it is mended, as best as it is going to mend, but I am doubting it will ever recover, the strength of the other wrist!

I do know there are many more doctors nowadays, who have a broader perspective & accept other healing systems too, even question their own indoctrination. Yet, with so little awareness, about how we create, our own health, or lack of it, through our beliefs & relationship with ourselves. Maybe we have little love, for the body we are inhabiting, thus comparing it with anyone else's, (especially of our own sex) &, looking at our image in a mirror, for flaws, or harbouring toxic emotions, maybe too, lack of optimum food & drink choices. Recently, this so-called world-wide, Pandemic happened, labelled 'Corona Virus' or in short, 'Covid 19'. I personally regard it, as both carried & transmitted by Fear, & being the result too, of the weakening of one's body, using synthetic drugs; the so-called remedies, sold by the pharmaceutical industry, which suppress or weaken, the immune system; - this is not healing. Rather, health is compromised, when the body's attempt to throw out toxins, is supressed; - though people's belief in them, could also reduce symptoms, like a placebo, yet still make the body, less resilient in the long-term! Since I deeply trust in Nature's remedies, live strongly in a place of Surrender, & feel no fear, of contagion, I know, I will not get sick. At present, I am living on fresh, uncooked organic fruit & salads, as I have for longer or shorter lengths of time, since my twenties, though at Penny's recently, I did try, unusually for me, raw milk from a local micro-dairy, for a few weeks, though I had not drunk milk for many years. Certainly, dairy products, create mucus in the body, more so if pasteurized. Suppressed life energy can result too, in less enjoyment, of our physicality, less walking, dancing, running, jumping, swimming, climbing, all in all, not much love, getting directed to this wondrous body.

(I have continued to enjoy walks, hill & tree climbing, swimming, dancing, the joy of physical agility, though less running. I do have less strength in my body in my eighties, but no sickness, just an increase of mucus, or nose-blowing, if I eat dairy foods, long enough).

It was fascinating to read 'Molecules of Emotion' & learn about the mentality of the world of scientists, in their search for how Body Intelligence functions! Also, just as fascinating, & very relevant, 'My Stroke of Insight' by Jill Bolte Taylor. I do also totally honour every person's free will right, we have been gifted with, to make our own choices in every moment, so long as it does no harm to another. Part of the Divine Play! I recently ordered her more recent book, 'Whole Brain Living' & lent it to my neighbour Bea, though I enjoyed it less than the first book.

Many of our most powerful moments of decision, continuing to create our reality in this life, happened before 7yrs.old. So, what are the key moments, of creating, the reality we have settled for? We have already incarnated with certain tendencies or programmes, embedded in our psyche, from ancestors and, their inherited patterns, (from at least 7 generations back I have heard), from our past lives too, or whatever historical past your mind can believe in. Time to create new neural pathways, energizing those beliefs & thoughts, most in harmony with, a fulfilling, joyful, life. I may be repeating, what I have already been clarifying, throughout this book, but often we do not take in, what we read, or hear, until that moment, when resistance has dropped away so, we have shed our chosen style of carapace, whether it is a hard, protective shell, or many layers of 'cotton wool', or veil upon veil. I choose to no longer energize, thoughts telling me, I am not enough, not to expect too much, keeping me in fear or doubt. Although so many loving Beings stay close to us, they will not interfere with our free will. A lot of our powerful, creative programmes, may be operating, below the level of conscious awareness, so maybe we will not know, when, why or how, conclusions were formed. It can seem easier to stay in the reality we are used to, even if our habitual comfort zone is discomfort, or never feeling safe. Unknown possibilities, may seem to be 'pie in the sky,' seen from a sceptic standpoint. Eventually our Soul gives us a big enough push, nudge, or knock on the head. Anyway, enough of that! I am hoping belly laughter, jokes, and lightness, will become more a part of how I express!

The higher the vibration we can rest in, the stronger a force we become, for healing ourselves & others, maybe broadcasting by being Love, with charged intent, through hands-on healing, or by sharing oneself through inspired life-changing communication. I know too, it is possible, to have strength in one's body, living from light & love. I have read various accounts, of people who stopped eating, including a family man, though the rest of the family ate physical food. He even subjected himself, to allowing laboratory supervision & testing, since it is outside the realm of possibility, in most minds. He had 'normal' strength & well-being. (I have just recovered, my couple of books, about such beings, from Storage). Jasmuheen is, one such lady. Michael Werner, the father of three children, very active, is another. I have not read 'A Year without Food,' by Ray Maor. Naturally it would require strong spiritual knowing & trust, thus, a higher vibration, - thus not emotionally hungry! Maybe with the help too, of the many beings seen or unseen, (such as angels).

(Diana Cooper, one of many through the ages, has been given information, about world events to come & much else, by Angels, who suddenly appeared, in her home. She shares much about Unicorns too, in a couple of books she has written). The whole of life, is energy vibration, so each one of us, affects everything & everyone. I have studied this whole field, in some depth, in the last 60ish years & continue to open, to new ways, such as all the different proliferating, 'quantum' energy healing modalities, that are being taught. We can choose Health. I did qualify, as a Quantum Touch healer, in Sam's last years, as previously mentioned. Richard Gordon has written 3 or more books, listed in the Resources section. We are living in a holographic reality, birthed from the Quantum field of all possibility, (which is continually I believe, blinking in & out! (A 'healer' does not do healing, but by being a channel for, a strong transmission or flow of energy & love s-he is able to broadcast, & the body receiving the healing, is invited to match the frequency, thus allowing healing to be received). I forgot who wrote that! Probably Richard Gordon.

I have always had, a strongly felt flow of healing energy, going out from my hands, when I direct this. Now it is joined by a much stronger force from my whole being, a warm fire of love/joy beaming out, from sacrum, belly, heart. throat & out through my crown too, & Ja Karuk has assisted, with a 'woosh' of this energy, down from my sacrum, through my legs, into the Earth.

*

In England, weather is a circumstance, commonly complained about &, to add to this, we believe the weather to be fixed, so, accurately predicted, through weather forecasts. That, could influence, what weather follows. It is too cold, too hot, there is too much rain, it could seem indeed, that we have no control of this. Yet the truth is, the weather's affected, like all of life, by the emotions & consciousness, in the environment, & can be immediately influenced by any focussed intent, to bring about change, such as when rain is needed, or sunshine. Everything 's so intricately intertwined & linked with everything else, that when we consciously connect, in heartfelt evolved knowing, aware of the environment & oneself as One, with no separation between all the energies involved, synchronous 'magical' wonders can happen. Yet now, when we know that as a human race, we have messed up badly, in our interactions with our Planet Earth, we are anticipating & responsible for, many extreme changes, for the ground we walk on, the air we breathe, the water we drink, the food we grow, all at the effect of our irresponsibility, selfish uncaring & worse. This Summer of 2022, there is a real heating up on our planet. Fires in hotter Countries, the U.K. too, - the hottest Summer I have experienced in the UK. More so than in 1976.

*

Michael Roads, one of my teachers, who makes many metaphysical journeys into other planes, has the following conversation with Pan, his 'Guru,' after being catapulted by Him into the midst of a storm:

(*Michael*) - "The strongest impression I have now -- having had a chance to simmer down - is that human negativity is a creative force. I had always assumed that anger, bitterness, greed and, our other negative feelings, merely dissipated when they left us, somehow dispersed into nothingness. It is a real eye-opener to learn that such energy, builds into a destructive force, that is eventually expressed in violence."

(*Pan*)- "What else?"

(*Michael*)- "Well it is rather shocking to learn that negative energy can only be expressed by returning to its point of origin. I had no idea that cause and effect worked within atmospheric levels. Knowing our mental garbage can accumulate, in the atmosphere and then, be dumped back on us in the destructive fury of a storm, is rather frightening. It is the sow-and-reap effect! Just imagine the effect if we could create that much love and joy!"

(*Pan*)- "That *is* the human potential. And?"

(*Michael*)- "By yielding to my own inner negative fears, I conquered them. Without doubt, negativity is born from all our many little fears, and those fears destroy the quality of our lives. Yet I am not really aware of surrendering. I do not feel I did anything."

(*Pan*)- "That is the whole essence. You did nothing. If you had tried to surrender, you would have created resistance, for surrender is a 'letting go,' not something you can force. By giving in, you give to your inner self." (- quoted from Michael's book 'Journey into Nature -A Spiritual Adventure' Chapter 6 - 'Within a Storm.') He, plus his lovely wife, have become friends over the years. Michael's happy for me to quote him & add his photo.

In Autumn 2012, in the United Kingdom, there had been a great surfeit of rain, which coincided with the huge release of the emotional, mental baggage of the five thousand plus year cycle which is coming into completion, before ushering in the new unknown, though anticipated, Lighter reality. So many emotions are being projected, intensified, mirrored, & resisted, so much emotional drama, is being enacted, that floods & extreme weather conditions, are to be expected, & are indeed happening world-wide. Coming back to their place of origin! We have been carrying family & generational patterns. What if it will be finally, time to let go of the Dream of Separation in our Lives!!!! 2025 will supposedly be a turning point, of greater awakening. Though I have always felt an uneasiness, about so much discarding of 'unsightly' rubbish, this has become much more toxic, since plastic & other more poisonous waste, has proliferated. Whoever invented plastic, no doubt has his part to play, in our learning! What is worse is, once the damage is clear, no real action taken on a big enough scale so far, to undo the effect of plastic in our oceans as well as on land.

The ground, maybe country-wide, was indeed so saturated with rain, that the flooding in our home, (in Nov.2012), was coming up from the ground, rather than from the swollen stream or torrents of run-off, down the valley slopes, to our valley 'basins.' Yet nearly 10yrs.later, still more and more housing projects are continuing to be pushed onto our beleaguered Earth, increasing flooding risks. Plus, toxic attempts to wrest more oil & coal in life-destroying ways such as fracking, from the source that nurtures us! There was such an increase in the heaviness, the intensity of suffering & emotional release, I imagine this will be, what brought us this flood. I did an energy clearing process for our home &, whilst also deeply honouring their function, asked the Water spirits if they would avoid bringing in further flood water & silt. Although the ground is still saturated from continuing rain, our home has stayed dry ever since. Finally, too, by 2015, the Environment Agency had finally, taken effective, hands-on measures to slow down the flow from the surrounding slopes!

*

I am going to **repeat** here too, what I quoted earlier from 'Zero Limits' by Joe Vitale and Dr. Hew Len:

'I operate my life and relationships according to the following insights:

1. The physical Universe is an actualisation of my thoughts.
2. If my thoughts are cancerous, they create a cancerous reality.
3. If my thoughts are perfect, they create a physical reality brimming with LOVE.
4. <u>I am100% responsible for creating my physical universe the way it is.</u>
5. <u>I am100% responsible for correcting the cancerous thoughts that create a diseased reality.</u>
6. There is no such thing as out there. Everything exists as thoughts in my mind.

So, 'To be an effective problem solver, the therapist must be 100% responsible for having created the problem situation; that is, he must be willing to see that the source of the problem is erroneous thoughts within him, not within the client. Therapists never seem to notice that every time there is a problem, they are always present!'

I heard someone say the following recently: "I'm only ever playing the role that you, asked me to play for you." i.e. for any 'problem' to be attracted into our field of play, there must be a corresponding resonance within us, or it just would not be here. I realize that when we are habituated, over most of our life time, to feeling a victim of 'outside' circumstances and actions, it is difficult to accept the above truth. If we came to accept, we possibly did choose our birth, our past & present too, & were able to realize too, how we are creating both present & future, by the thoughts & beliefs we energise with repeated focus, at every moment, we would give attention, to what we are repeatedly thinking, to which life is responding all the time, and most likely, choose differently.

*

There's so much inspirational help these days, both offered from the heart, in accessible ways, even sometimes, generously gifted free of cost, for many of us who, want to plunge deeper into teachings & training, from so many spiritual luminaries. Much of this reaches us via the internet, an empowering tool for so many. I realize, someone living in a very expanded, unified field, like Anastasia, in Siberia, would not need mobile 'phones, nor computers. We human beings who, are using such a tiny part of the capacity, of our brain-heart minds, design our computers, as very poor copies of our human potential, obviously so!

To find out about her, read the series written by Vladimir Megre, published in Russia by the Ringing Cedars Press. (It <u>was</u> possible to get these through Cygnus books, or directly from the publishers, *through Ringing Cedars UK Ltd, phone 0115 9738 073, or online www.ringingcedars.co.uk), though I believe there is no longer any U.K. office.* The books would widely expand your minds, to appreciate the real greater potential of human beings.

*

'You,' have your unique path to more joy, more love, greater health. If like me, it becomes a priority, to look deeper, into what created the life, you do not so much want, if at all, - surely you matter enough, to choose a new possibility. <u>First</u>, love your present creation, <u>then</u>, you can make new choices.

We have often been stretched to the brink of what felt bearable, which had been so for me, many times, yet this yearning for something different, propelled me into faster transformation & deeper opening. In one of my yesterdays, I connected deeply again, with loving myself. Nowadays, in my 81st year, loving myself & all other, has, become my norm, for the last 11yrs! You will maybe have realized, I was more disconnected, more resistant, to receiving my greater good, than many people, before my 70's. Since I did not expect any better, I accepted as normal, to live in a state of lack; lack of safety, lack of feeling loved or connected deeply, to my heart, or to people, in a relaxed way. I grew up so serious, not knowing how to play, nor laugh from the belly, yet I have noticed when I know clearly, what I am ready to have, or be more of, in my life, I am blessed with the next step, that will lead me here. Even asking my spiritual sisters, or brothers, from deep within, why I **was not** experiencing, what I yearned for, seemed to propel rapid change. Many will do this faster than I did, yet every moment carries its own gift, & creates the unique flavour or fragrance, you can then share with any, who will benefit from your sharing. If we were to make our heart-centred command, but once, very clearly, in the Theta state, i.e., connecting oneself intimately, with the Light & Love at the Heart of All, like speaking to our best most loving heart companion, as that is what it truly is, it is already heard &, coming into manifest reality in perfect timing - as in 'The One Command', (Asara Lovejoy).

*

Whenever I am feeling intimately connected with the Truth, or Love I really am, the energy moves from my heart, down my arms to my hands, as active extensions of the heart, if I am offering physical healing. I can increasingly feel & trust, the acceptance & good intent, I see in others' eyes: - though, I am no longer a beggar for love, not looking outside for this. I felt a huge blessing moment, to be one in which I connected, with total soul presence in a friend's eyes, like connecting with God, with no separation at all between me & her. These days, I feel a strong heart warmth, throughout most of my being, whenever I am fully present, in the now moment, more so, now I am so alive to, the multi-dimensional energies, in the Quantum field, as well as rooted in the Earth. On the Summer Solstice 2021, I was focussed on my morning meditation with the 'Stargate Academy,' where thousands of us connect globally, when I really got it, that the 'Alcazar' being, (a name for a group of masters guiding us), really is, connecting lovingly, with each one individually, all the time! There is only NOW! I was suddenly re-inspired that week, to take the steps to get my long-time written book published! And it is happening! I know I could have self-published easily, through Amazon yet, once all the contentious issues I was reacting to, are cleared with my editor, my dream can finally be manifested. I felt that heart warmth spreading to my left side equally, in my meditation, as if I am feeling seen in a new way. This is surely what we are all most wanting, to find & connect to, the love in ourselves, & see love reflected in others. In one of my Yesterdays, my Soul's message was, to stay connected with this heart Love which is who I am, stay in love with this me, which surely is my safe abode! It is never too late for this deep connection with oneself, nor is it for others but 'not me', meaning you, as whether you remember or not, we are all on the same journey, by as many different routes as there are people. The Infinite Soul Being that we are, chose this Earth experience, of separating ourselves into many bodies, to experiment with Free Will!

Since the energy, of what we call Love, is experienced in a myriad of ways, this warm, potent, expanding, yet nurturing, tender, very full & blissful state, plus Joy, long-time so elusive, which radiates out from my sacral & heart area, up to my head, or pineal gland, is very recent, yet seems permanent now in my 81st year, ever since we started connecting with our multi-dimensional being, in the Void! About 6 months, so far. Why, am I describing this, not so easily describable? -... because **feeling Joy/Love/Warmth beaming out permanently, is a very recent state of being! Recent, as in a few months already!** - especially as, I could be worrying, about having insufficient regular income, now & for the foreseeable future, to cover outgoings, considering my present precarious financial dilemma, thus my trust, that I am cared for, beyond any predictable certainty, is a blessing in this life! Regardless of whether I am financially abundant, which will change, once I have sold the flat in Spain. Hopefully, this book too, will generate ongoing income! I trust, this rapidly accessible, sense of warm spacious Being, is guiding me, to open to a deeply transformed life. I am home, in a physical sense, as well as emotional, yet I do not yet know how, this will manifest, nor what form it will take. I have had so much love & support directed to me, throughout this uncertain time, & have survived for a year, since my income was slashed to less than half, of what is needed to cover outgoings, rent & daily food. I have re-edited this book again & again, - & again! yet I will very soon, re-submit it, once more. My patiently exacting editor, is doing what she must, in order to avoid libel disputes, so I trust & hope, for harmonious resolution, regarding all technical issues, (having entered the 2nd half of 2022)! I really want my book cover, plus inside script, to be as I have visualized.

*

Certainly, there are challenging issues on our planet, regarding survival, from so much human plundering of our planet's resources, as well health challenges for so many human beings. I enjoyed a big boost of energy, love & support from the Stargate Community in our London, mask-free, hugely love-filled **physical** Gathering, within this last Christmas period. (January 6th is the 'Day of the Three Kings' in Spain, when gifts are given)!

I am living in Ish & Daxa's home now & Ish, has a great full body laugh! He is good at playing, too. Yet it is not my ideal home, which I trust will one day be. Sandra asked if she could sleep on their sofa for about a fortnight, but Ish said 'No!' His blood family have priority. Daxa has just been in India, near the West Coast, in Monsoon season, for 2 months, to be close to her mother, who needs, in her 90's, support, from wheel-chair and family. Sadly, for Daxa, it was a sister, who suddenly left her body, during ecstatic dancing to Ganesh! A Blessing for the sister, but a shock for Daxa after she returned from India!

Having read Diana Cooper's Unicorn books, in the year 2021, now drawn to a close, the Winter Solstice, Christmas celebrations enjoyed, I have welcomed higher vibration light & love around. I was visualizing being graced with, the presence of a Unicorn! Not long after, I begun to get the sense of connecting with a Unicorn, called Rebecca, & had a fleeting glimpse of a 2nd white shining one too. Rebecca is very friendly, white with light grey markings. In celebration of this, I went to a local Faery shop &, bought a Unicorn, I had been noticing in the window, the third of the 'Faery lady' owner's wonderful creations, to grace my home. The first was a Faery, the 2nd, a female body lying 'lifeless' with, toadstools growing out of her, to help break down her body into the Earth. Most recently, I bought a dragon, stretched out in repose. Most of my crystals, - also a dragon emerging from an egg, had been mislaid, in a storage container, which my daughter, her husband & their eldest son, Michael, helped empty, a long-awaited big task. More recently, Rammiel helped clear much more. Much to let go of, - we are halfway there! This week, final emptying of unit 4A!

*

I doubt there is any one of us, who has not loved, wanted too, to feel loved, & thus felt the sadness, of finding so little love in our world. I had felt sad sometimes, while with my husband Sam, that the love I was connecting to within, so deeply, more & more, was not being reflected by him, yet my heart went out to him, knowing how disconnected, he had been feeling still, from his true being. Yet I am surrendered, to letting Life orchestrate itself, in resonance with inner Heart Love/Light. I am 100% responsible, for staying deeply connected, with the Heart of me, to transform what is drawn, into my field of possibilities. I could interpret, what I meet, as dense, slowed-down energy, so, choose to take it personally, react to, or judge, or I might instead, focus on transmuting heavier energies, which 'belong' to all of us, or none of us, surrounding them in an embrace of love & light. We carry them & identify with them, if we are attached!

Over 30yrs.ago, I kept being told by clairvoyants, that I would be doing hands-on healing, & was told too, that a 'Chinaman' would join me. Later a psychic artist gave me pictures of some of my guides, among them was 'Lu Yin' as I call him. I call him in, as a Healer guide in Journey processes, (as earlier mentioned), & other healing processes. Ever since I declared out aloud, with full intent, that I was ready!... - for whatever beings were waiting to work with me, to come in, - (the prayer which precipitated this Book-to-be dream!), I sooner or later, remember to call in Lu Yin, (also Gezra, ever since the channellings where, I connected with him, which felt so light & love-filled), for any hands-on healing. This was synchronous with my regular Vortex meditations (with Meg Benedicte), since 2011, ongoing for months, which precipitated more energy, moving through my body, hands & feet, making them tingle, with even more charge, whenever I focus from my heart. I really trust them, & very often, invite in St. Germain with his violet light. Babaji of Haidakhan, is ever deeply heart-felt. Mother Mary, Yeshua & Mary Magdalene, (of the Essenes), Quan Yin, Tara & Dragons, are ever welcome. Nowadays of course, I feel the Alcazar group of Masters, deeply supportive & loving too, in our global daily meditating, as earlier mentioned. When Carmen had a tumour in her colon &, I asked her if she would like me to do some healing, - we used St. Germain's violet light, & focussed too, on the tumour dis-attaching itself, from the wall of the colon, so it would be removed easily, during surgery, the following week. Sure enough, it came out easily & there has been no further problem.

When my focus turned strongly, to restoring all balance between, my male & female aspects, feeling it was time to move into, a new dynamic in my relating with men, to clear too, whatever, was still playing out, from the third dimensional matrix, Lu Yin appeared, as I described, near the end of the forgiveness chapter, together with my 'male counterpart,' and between them, created a healing ritual for clearing collective shame around sexuality. I have described too, after that, how very recently, I finally cleared the anger and outrage which erupted, no longer allowing my expression, my truth, to be suppressed by whatever threats etc. feeling myself, having finally completed my karmic past story with Sam. I will come soon to that account. Somehow, there is a connection in my mind, between my male counterpart who appeared, & Gezra. Whenever I travelled to the Golden Temple (in Maureen Moss's meditation), where healing Masters come and go, I had been finding Lu Yin and Gezra there together, both very supportive in my life at that time, & so loved in my heart. *Anyway, I had decided, in mid-October, to try channelling on my own for the first time. I decided to start with the Golden Temple meditation, & ask Gezra to lead me from there, to deepen in our connection. Once I was ready to, leave the Temple, it felt that Gezra, though seemingly more light-being, than solid, took me by the hand. The Nature realm he took me to, was much more light-filled, than last time, with a green, beautiful, glowing ball of light before me. He told me I have related to Earth for many life-times & Ages. He is encouraging me, to become fully embodied in my Heart courage, my Power & Inner Safety, as until I do this, I will be delaying, my fully opening to my greater good, potential & Abundance -* (which hopefully, will include a beautiful solar-lit new home-to-be, geo-thermal under-floor heating, set in land which is a Nature wildlife haven, allowing me deeper contact with this realm. My flat in Navarra, is powered by, a mainly green energy company, using wood pellets. Whether I will get to live there, even a few days, is uncertain).

Gezra is also in similar contact, with my male counterpart, whatever reality, or dimension he is in! A beautiful pink ball of light, enters my Heart. I ask him about, how to engage in, my relationship with Sam, while staying in Love & Peace. I get first the impression, of sadness to come, (as I felt earlier), but he says to focus on, the highest aspect of Sam, & to pray that, Sam's denser aspects, I was struggling with, be transmuted, without judgement, the best I can, yet that I stay focussed too, on the courage, to be authentically truthful, from Compassion & Love, not from any battle stance. I agreed to connect with Gezra more often. When I returned, he did not lead me by the hand, but was following behind. As I was arriving back into my rooted, embodied self, I was suddenly flooded with a huge influx of light, more than I had ever received, within present memory. It felt so all-pervading, I felt I could have stayed bathed and immersed in this, with no more needed, for a long time. My mind eventually re-asserted itself, but I continued to feel expansive and light-filled. This still was not, being reflected, in my interaction with Sam. I still was not sleeping well, sleep patterns having been unpredictable, and erratic, for about 3 months. Five days later, I arrived at the Sheraton Heathrow hotel in London, for a 3day Journey Intensive event with Brandon. I had decided to focus, on all 3 days, in my swap processes with partners, on clearing from my being, whatever was keeping me, in self torment! I started in the 1ˢᵗ process, in sadness & grief, connecting too with my fear of future 'unbearable' pain, in the event of, Sam's future infidelity, - how self-destructive is that?! I connected too with feeling discarded by Sam, feeling angry, like "it's not fair!" I felt the pain in my heart, not wishing any further mangling, of this vulnerable place, to happen. However, by opening totally into vulnerability, I was able to come, to strong self-acceptance & a renewed intent to stand tall in my courage, & stay, in my heart's expression of truth & Love, no matter what. I feel the power, of the feminine creative impulse behind me, and a vast compassionate awareness, which holds both light and dark, within its embrace. I then dropped, into unconditional acceptance, & gratitude, having let go my puny scrabbling, to maintain some control over others choices! From here, I dropped into awareness of. a deep well of stillness, that I might have dropped into more deeply than I did, but still felt, the utter peace of that. I slept more deeply that night with no tears, nor troubling thoughts. *Gezra was more light-filled than I had seen him, other than in that last channelling. Our carriage went first into my solar plexus, then on to the heart, totally refusing to move any further.* The 2nd day, was a *physical 'Journey' day. The stairs down, were different from usual, ebony wood, lovely & carved, with bigger gaps between both side bannisters and, the staircase, narrower too, much more perilous! I chose to go very deep anyway, & the bottom two steps were wider. Also, even before reaching the door &, my same two Mentors, Lu Yin & Gezra, I had to walk through fire to reach the door. That has never happened before!* (When I say 'heart', I have found when I have been clearing pain with my daughter, or mother, I have landed in the left of my chest or breast, whereas concerning my relating to my father or other males, the focus has been beneath my right breast, & when it is about my universal heart or, relating with the whole, from a higher-self or Soul perspective, my upper chest's involved).

There is a blaze of fire I have never seen in here before. I am drawn to the right side of my chest. The whole area, beneath my breast, is more light-filled than the last time, I was here, & though it feels safe in here now, with no mangled heart, nor precipice, there is, a smooth metal chute, or slide, down to below the ribs. I squeeze my way through any obstructions, like sinews or tendons, but my attention is then brought, to a pale section of my gut (no special bit), and a word arises, "indigestible." The surfacing memory involves a 24yr.old me, weak legs, a general feeling of lack of strength. I was 3 or 4mths. pregnant, not handling it well, with much nausea, unable to prepare nor contemplate food, some bleeding so, needed much bed rest. (I did not begin study of diet & health, in depth, till I was 28yrs of age onwards.) …However, I was feeling I would recover, if I went to Spain, and sure enough, as soon as I got south of Bordeaux, my appetite returned. - (with hindsight, this is maybe because of my predominant Basque heritage)! (The Basques & the Catalans inhabit the lands on both sides of the Pyrenees). We ended up under the pine trees in Formentera with Jose, where he fed me goats' milk & rice milk. Jose was aware, of Bob's seeming lack of care & concern towards me, plus his increasing inner tension. At some point we left Jose, but also money, seemed to be running out, and Bob started revealing his more hidden fantasies or proclivities. He disappeared, & I found myself, feeling very unsupported and distressed, wandering the island. Some fishermen gave me shelter, in their stone cottage, & then I managed to find some English-speaking tourists who lent me enough money, to leave the island. I found Bob near the boat, & somehow, I got drawn into my rescuer, giver role, offering to stop at a Paris hotel, & let him act out his sexual fantasies, thinking this would be a therapeutic release for him. I do not even recollect, what these fantasies were. If he was speaking these out, I have blanked out all memory of this. All I remember, is one moment he was unzipping his flies, & the revulsion showing, in my face, led to his suddenly trying to please &, reassure me, with cuddles & normality. *In the Journey session, I really saw the extent that my needs & worth, were largely non-existent, like I was worthless &, could be trodden underfoot. Nor was I giving due thought, to my unborn child. Yet I was still trying to fix & rescue the world, to prove there was love, even though I could not feel much love for Bob, nor anyone much. My over-riding sense about my role in this episode, is, I can be sacrificed like a victim or martyr, to rescue him. I am of little consequence. Degrading desires directed at me, though totally disliked, can be tolerated! A nightmare, shocking relationship at times, that I both don't & do accept. I breathe in resources which would have helped at the time*: Deep knowing of, the boundaries I must maintain. Feeling connected to &, compassion for, all the souls involved my heart, full of Love.

Deep acknowledgement of the child I am carrying, seemingly disregarded

When I replay the scene, everything unfolds more calmly, even agree to spend a night, in a Paris hotel, on our way, though I maintain my boundaries, while giving him space, to share his inner turmoil. I self-disgust &, feeling of unacceptability. He cannot handle being himself. I feel my own compassion, fullness & love. He wants to feel loved & accepted as he is. I can see him as a teacher, who is helping me see more of myself. At the camp fire, I have Bob, my/our daughter Samantha, & my son, Sam, as well as my two Mentors, my 24yr.old & present selves. Although I had asked about healing my present marriage, I believe the memory surfaced of Bob, because he was the first sexual partner, whose behaviour I had found extreme or shocking at times, so though this was acted out, or expressed, in a totally different way by Sam, (a beautiful soul, I continue to love), still I saw his seeming emotional torment, & desperation, which I was then drawn, to fix or rescue, accepting my suffering.

I express now, how this is no longer acceptable, to put what my partners want, before what I need, thinking I do not matter. How did I even allow this!? All my anger had turned inside, so much self-anger! My mentors cut cords, between me & those, with whom I played this out, cleaning out, the accumulation of self-disregard & anger, to throw into the fire of unconditional love &, acceptance, & filling my cells & all the spaces between, with love. My mentors remind me to stay connected to their support, & not just when I travel in higher realms and vastness. The connection is always here. My responsibility, is to create what I really like! The whole gut area is now healing, has more colour & life energy, & it is up to me to stay, in loving relationship, with all my body.

Again, I had a good sleep that night, & throughout the day I had people coming up to me telling me, how beautiful I was, how they saw just light, as they looked at me, or saw me as holy. I saw how important it is, to hold that perception of myself, & to align with and, honour our divine expression, rather than hold a limited, false, shrunken vision of who we are. The next day, I was feeling, there was still, some attachment to suffering, to clear. Even if I had held doubts, about the existence of Love, for so many years, I had still felt impelled to prove, the existence of caring and Love, to others. *Today, I find this impulse held in my solar plexus. From here I dropped into more of a sense, of my own worthlessness, that I should allow myself, to be treated in ways I found unacceptable. Part of me felt, I had no right to protest, but my heart does protest, yet there was still, contraction, in my solar plexus. I found here, this real expectation, long-time ongoing, that others would not see, anything good, when they looked at me; I felt all over my skin, as if it is going to erupt in boils & pustules. I know too in my guts, this is not true, yet I notice, there is a part that wants to be seen, at the effect of this suffering drama, & share that story, a sort of self-flagellation. I had been living out this drama, I had thought directed from outside, for so long. I feel suddenly a 'real' pain in my heart, about whichever part, is still holding on to the story, yet another part, remains totally unaffected, knowing it is time, to totally trust, who I am. I feel ready, to receive all my good, all my abundance of love & joy. My usual two mentors turned up, but Gezra seems more light-filled, less solid, each time I see him now, & something in me relaxes &, feels strengthened, yet my body is suddenly racked with pain &, there is a fear, of not being able, to go on feeling safe & empowered, even as, I increasingly __am__ trusting, that I am one with Life.*

As a 3 or 4yr.old, both parents were giving me a strong message, that it was not OK, to express the aspects of myself, that were not nice &, I was imbibing too, their general terror, also from the whole War consciousness prevalent, in the wider environment around me. My swap partner encouraged me to breathe in an extra influx, of appropriate resourceful energies, such as:

Innocence Purity Beauty Light Really be my own best friend

Self-regard Safety Knowing my connection

Self- honouring with Love, and self-love

Strength of knowing Source & maintain boundaries no matter

I was born with who or what I must let go of

After receiving these added resources, I was invited by my process partner, to focus on "Who am I?" which I do for a while, then went to the camp-fire, where I had present, those I had sacrificed myself for, plus Brandon as someone I had been imagining, did not want to look at, or see me, not liking what she saw! The whole me, who does feel aligned with Truth, wants to speak to that part, which has believed this, as I am now choosing to embody, my full true essence. Even as I ask if that dis-empowered self, is ready to let go, & tell a different story, so we can stay strong, in the truth, fully forgiving the past, & merging as co-creators, I suddenly experience myself stretched out, on a sacrificial marble slab, and following this, I am aware of other past lives, often as a nun, where I have played this same sacrificial role, annihilating myself, for others! When my mentors come to cut, the connecting cord to these lives, it is so thick, absolutely the thickest cord I have ever had cut, with so many hooks & attachments throughout my body! My Karma Mentor appears, & says my Life's lesson, is to come to the full realization, in my Heart, of my real essence, & to trust, that Heart essence, is whole in others too, thus I can be reflected truly back to myself, in my embodied life with, everyone on Earth, no matter where they are, on their journey, &, to recognize once & for all, the Truth, - what is truth & what is not. A huge award to myself for playing the martyr & sacrificial victim, with such dedication, & now I have the extra bonus, of showing others, it is never too late to wake to, this sense of excitement, gratitude & the joyful exuberance of being present to Life, in this body, in a magic Universe, - to One Self! I recognize Bob & Sam and everyone as my teachers, & see how I orchestrated my part in the Play. My Mentor's last words remind me, we are one in Source, but others are willing to play their roles in my drama when called upon. "We are You." Much more light-heartedness after the process, in fact I have continued to feel elated, & freed from, that whole self-created, painful scenario, & though on the surface, I cannot predict whether my path is, to stay with Sam in our marriage, I am no longer concerning myself with any need, to control life, noting how the dynamic between us, has changed anyway, & trusting the best & highest possibilities are already being seeded. It is for me to choose my focus, & release any hint of, fear or self-punishment, if that should appear. I do not have to limit myself with false beliefs, poverty, nor suffering.

*

Though in Essence we are each other, we have choice, as to which thoughts we energize, & how we operate, in our way of relating with ourselves, & all else, preferably from open-hearted self/other, acceptance, tenderness, Love, & authentic expression. No-one to blame, just seeing behind the illusion, & becoming aware of, who, is creating, the Life we, are experiencing. Who is the choreographer, & how, do we attract our co-dancers? It is All, perfect, so I welcome all with love, including feeling uncaring!

Weeks after the Journey session, I am still feeling in harmony with, Life in the present moment, no longer host, to old suffering dramas, playing out through me, grateful for the miracle of life, the exquisite beauty of experience in every moment. Nothing to have any problem about. Feels light, playful & easy.

Brandon has sometimes said, that releasing what is held in the cells is like dropping one pearl at a time, off a necklace, until finally the whole consciousness beneath the pattern, is truly gone. That is how I feel now, after nearly 72 yrs., plus many former lives, playing out the sacrificial victim, busy rescuing & fixing the world, until increasingly I did not! Feeling myself free, I feel an even greater compassion for, the ways so many of my clients, & friends, still play out, their own version of 'not enough,' or 'not good enough', when I so know the truth of, the beauty & gift of their/our being. Emotions that feel more blissful, or heavier, may show up at moments, but there is no attachment to these. I am integrating still, the lightness and differentness of this, compared to the past!

Well, I went deep in the process I received, back, near the end of November 2012, & the Mentor is one who appeared once before, 10mths.earlier, a black-skinned male, very silent, with a very potent presence &, like last time, I can only see his face & eyes, not the rest of his body. The chariot is more solid, than last time he was with me, but again winged. It went straight into my vagina. My impression in past sessions, has been of a narrow, darker tunnel, this time the right-hand side has energy, colour, - pink too, & feels a more welcoming, loving expansive cave like place, yet the left side seems to be holding itself more stiffly & protectively, so, no movement of energy. (I am very aware that, as a younger woman, when my flesh was young & firm, i.e., youthful beauty, my level of deeper distress, was nevertheless with me. Years refusing to compete, yet feeling any man I might wish to claim as 'mine,' might be attracted away from me, by other women who, were competition! In short, I had little confidence, in my own beauty or perfection, as a wonderful part of creation).

In an earlier Journey Process, I described how Babaji guided me to experience, no solidity of matter, neither my body, my chair, nor the floor seemingly holding these in place)! Such a gift. What I uncovered in this week's Process, were many beliefs I had been continuing to hold, about the unattractiveness of my older body, in anyone's eyes. Such as, "Sexually, in a man's eyes I am of little value, if my skin is more wrinkled, less supple, or my vagina not so easily moist, since menopause, thus I would not be in any way, even recognized as an attractive, sexual, being. As I am re-reading this, approaching 82yrs. of age, & though I have less strength in my body, my sexual energy is strong, & at moments when I might feel to experience orgasmic bliss, I can pleasure myself. I feel no need of a sexual partner. I realized too that, identification with the body, as being 'me' had been generally so strong, that this had brought immense self-rejection &, rejection of others, in the past. Now, instead I feel how every molecule of my being, is always part of Life's beautiful expression. Older trees, horses, lions, deer, birds, dogs, anything, are so beautiful in every stage of life & people too, need to be both recognized &, fully recognize themselves as this! I feel so elated by this awareness. By the end of this Journey session, my whole vagina was full of colour & energy. It has taken me till my seventies for my Creativity, my Heart & my Vagina, to feel so open to the inflow, of Life's Abundance and Goodness. I trust I will stand in my naked body unashamed, glorying in my perfect expression exactly as I am. Sexual pleasure continues to delight whenever I should choose!

I feel such Compassion for, everyone in my Life, who is in the deep, most painful meeting of, every part that has been unloved & unmet, in themselves. (This was extreme as we were moving fast into the month of Dec.2012). I was blessed to be able to hold all my 'clients,' (such an inadequate word for each beautiful being I worked with), in a strong embrace of Love, of Healing energy, simply reminding each one, of who we really are. I know Lu Yin & other beings currently assist me/us whenever I offer healing. I am willing to stand for me, to speak for my sexuality, my woman self from, a place of love and honouring.

I am coming near to the end of this last chapter about responsibility, with a 'Journey' process received before, the momentous 2012 Winter Solstice. *In this process I was praying, to Love and, move towards a still deeper surrender, opening ever wider into living from my Heart, in an ever-deepening Trust, that Life's holding me always, in her embrace. I wished also to see if there was a lid, I was holding in place which, though allowing immediate needs, always to be met, in unexpected ways &, in exact timing, still allowed only, a restricted flow of wealth, so I did not always know if, nor when, the next extra expense, would be handled in time! Outside my control! For the first time, it was Lord Ganesh, who had turned up as my Mentor!*

I have never known how to relate with Ganesh, throughout my many years of Temple practices. Lord of material realms, remover and, setter, of obstacles!

An Angel with large wings also appeared. A very ornate, magic carriage, came, drawn by a team of horses. It landed in my belly/solar plexus area, though I could feel a connecting energy, with my throat too. My 5yr.old young self, certainly could not believe any adult, could support her in her needs, so how would she believe in any 'outside force,' as remover of obstacles, to allow an inflow of goodness & abundance, into her life. The first rising emotions of panic & despair, relate to feeling, I cannot find the resources to adequately, defend or protect myself, yet even as this residual drama, is playing out, I am simultaneously all the time aware of a spaciousness, within which, everything else plays out. Sure enough, soon I find myself falling through blackness, a familiar environment, except this time a metal post protrudes, just where I must fall so, I cannot avoid being skewered, with the threat of annihilation. However, though my body disintegrates into many fragments, it makes little difference, there is no sense of any death, as I continue to fall, then just wait in Stillness. The Blackness I am in, is a very neutral place, yet still, I feel the coldness, of being an unprotected child. Yet as I surrender completely to, just how it is, a warmth begins to enter my body &, expand in my heart. It seems this place of not making anything happen, just stopping and being alert, has a lot of potency, as if life's greatest gifts arrive when we stop, & drop any conditions about how life should happen. The Love intensifies as well as expanding. It has happened to me before, that when I did nothing but open &, surrender to the Present, without agenda, nor any judgement that anything, should be other than it is, nor any attempt to exert control, even unconsciously, Life came rushing into this empty space, with more exuberance or intensity. When I take another look at the metal, which appeared so dangerous, I am very aware of its molecular structure, which appeared so solid, in its separate distinct form, yet in essence is the vibrating energy of Love, disguised as a metal post! I had felt so unsafe as a child, in a world none of the adults, were able to improve. I could depend on no-one for real safety. At the camp-fire, where I had adults, my parents, also Hitler & Churchill. Franco probably should have been there, as wielding power over who to destroy, with Mussolini's or Hitler's bombs. I accepted my parents did all they could, to make a less mad world &, protect me as best they could. The Angel beamed Compassion, on the whole situation. I could accept that, when I let go & let Life, I am supported in Love & Safety.

*

I had been focussed, for months, on working with Asara Lovejoy's 'The One Command,' a powerful, yet simple way, of opening to our unlimited potential realities. As I had been moving, into greater alignment with, my expansive being, through this daily practice, I had been feeling, more confident, that the reality I invite into my life, of financial abundance, and, freedom from karmic and financial debts, is imminently here, especially too, with the co-operation of angels, two of whom I have invited to be part of my financial team, & who brought me some work very rapidly, this week. I briefly mentioned in Chapter 1, the deeper underground rumbling, stirring in relation to Sam. I had still not always been having the courage, to speak my truth, with whatever is yet to be met, deeply pushed down for many years. *My last Journey session addressed this long-standing issue, on March 18th 2013*, as, though so much improvement, had happened, in that I have been speaking out, much more freely &, standing much more in my power, I had still felt at some level, cowed & threatened by Sam's huge emotional reactions, to anything he did not want to hear, or he could translate as meaning rejection! It is so important for me, to come to deep inner safety, growing in my Heart Courage, to be authentic, truthful, no matter what the consequence might be, as, when we speak from the heart, the outer response is going to reflect this back. I was guessing I was still holding on, to deep anger & lack of forgiveness with Sam, deeply buried, & had noted this, the 2nd time I practised the One Command with Sam, Fear strongly surfaced in me, which I suspected related also to him. In fact, the underground eruptions could no longer be silenced, by the time I met with Judith for my session. Unusually, this could only happen after the Woman's group, in the evening, when I was feeling sleepy, particularly, as I am going through another Expansion cycle which, is disrupting my sleep patterns. Yet I felt I had to do this now. *The 1ˢᵗ steps down had, what seemed like a heavy warm blanket draped over them, which I pushed aside, to create a safe soft buffer. The rest of the stairs had blue light, playing over them, so I guessed Lu Yin must be close, maybe Gezra too. I go very deep as I descend, & find Lu Yin & Gezra indeed present, behind the door, but in a misty background, while an Angel (maybe my Guardian Angel who, turned up in a previous session), is in the foreground. For the very first time, my magical carriage has an engine, high powered, with a "Vroom, Vroom" feel about it! It moves very fast into the Solar plexus, seeming firmly jammed there, with no intention of moving elsewhere, yet my body kept signalling, the strong connection with the throat, via various sensations. My prayer for the session, was particularly to bring my (potential) intimate, relationships, into alignment with my true expanded being, & to meet whatever, is still there from any old story, around LACK of LOVE! The memories which surface &, are put for a while on a screen to be dealt with, at the 'camp-fire', show Aradhana, then a succession of different women, chased by Sam, often in my presence, as if I did not matter &, would be immune to feeling pain, or lack of worth. Right at the start of the session, I was already feeling the subterranean rumbling of anger, coming up, with no intention, of being in any way shut up, any longer. There was murkiness in the right side of my solar plexus. The emotion nearest the surface, in my belly, was Outrage, through which I dropped quickly into Power & Strength, & an unshakeable, unstoppable intent never ever, to allow myself to feel, in my life again, controlled or cowed, by threats. Yet deeper still than this powerful resolve, was a very young, maybe 2-3yr.old, feeling fearful, not wanting to feel threatened, very protective therefore, of my/her totally Undefended, Vulnerable, totally Exposed being, most felt in my belly, solar plexus & my whole skin area. Surprisingly quickly & easily, I dropped from there into Mother Love, then total unconditional Acceptance. Still, I was so motivated, to have my chance to voice my truth at the camp-fire. That younger me, is in her early sixties. The power of her anger & outrage is unstoppable. This is the angriest I have ever felt at the camp-fire. This felt so timely. So long awaited! I wanted to be as horrible & truthful, as I liked, fuelled by so many, many years of being shut up. My throat, which for so many years, felt pain & strain, from strangled expression, now was feeling so strong, with this resoluteness to never, ever, tolerate this in my life again. At this point I felt nowhere near forgiveness, so Judith had me do an 'Inside/outside' & outside/inside' exercise. I navigated my way, in Sam's body, through so much feeling of rejection, (which is not mine to heal), & has pissed me off so many times as, it diverts attention to his story, & away from, whatever I am trying to share, so, I am never heard. Behind his fog of rejection, I meet his loneliness & feelings of isolation, but eventually reached the same vulnerability &, feelings of being exposed & undefended as I had felt. He is needing to feel loved, yet seems so disconnected from, the deep Well of Love in his Heart. I let Sam also enter my body, to witness & feel the extent of pain &, my feeling of being, deeply disrespected & dishonoured. After completing whatever little else was left to say, I was in a place of more understanding, & totally open to forgiving both him & myself for what I had tolerated, i.e., my inability, too often, to stand up & strongly speak up for Me. When my Mentors did a 'spring-clean,' it was also of false beliefs. My very young self, decided, "If I fully express what I want, I'll be threatened & rejected." Also, another old belief which, in my limited mind-set, seeming confirmed by Sam, was, "Whatever I offer is not valuable," plus a deeper Fear; "What if I could never live totally in abundance & freedom, can never have the Life, I most would love, as I'm not good enough, & I haven't got, what that takes;" i.e. I am Lacking! My Mentors, install new Truthful ideas: "If I fully, express what I feel, think & desire with authenticity, my partner & Community, will be delighted to encourage me, see me, include me & fully respond to me, & really want to get to know me, which creates incredible closeness & intimacy. It is my very existence, the Love that I am, that is the most precious & valuable gift, in whatever expression or form it is given. I am the Love, the Child &, the mother." Afterwards my throat feels so strong, & pink Love Light & gold rays, are entering the murkiness in the Solar plexus. The words of wisdom offered from this area are, "Be in a place of Honour, Respect & Love, with Me & All." I felt so solidly grounded, so energized as, the former tiredness & sleepiness, from the lateness of the hour & my recent nights of little sleep, were gone (which seems to happen when, my being is moving into, an increased vibrational frequency, as happened in 2012), & I felt such relief & gratitude to have finally liberated myself, with help, after previous unsatisfactory sessions which seemed, to just scratch the surface of what I needed to meet, embrace & voice, to do with my past with Sam. Thank you, Judith, my Angel, my Guides, Gezra, Lu Yin, & my own Soul, for being so ready to step out of the old story, & be with both my Empowered self, & my undefended Vulnerable Self, which needs no defending, but is always, tenderly, safely held & loved. The end of this cycle of accumulated Karmic debts?* I noticed a few days later when I 'phoned Sam, he seemed critical still of me, which made me wonder, if I had completely, cleared all our past, yet still felt I had.

The next morning, as I was doing my daily One Command practice, I realized I still held, some remaining belief, in lack of Love from others. I have since been focussed, on settling into Ease & Safety in my Body, feeling totally held within the Earth Mother/father Love & Heavenly Father/Mother Light rays, creatively joining their energies in my whole being & Heart. I sensed I needed to sit intimately with inner Ease, Love, & the Tenderness, that is me & see this &, the Innocence & Beauty of every Being, myself first, & to love whatever I meet, not making it mean anything about Me, unless this resonates with the Truth, of who we are. In our Women's group last week, we celebrated each one of us in turn, honouring each other's unique fragrance. I was able to receive the loving, appreciative words, spoken by every woman, so fully, I felt very deeply affirmed. Feeling seen, I am getting to see every other being, with more depth, as if, whatever veils of protection, were keeping me disconnected, are gone. I am much more aligned with, my multi-dimensional self now, rather than seeing my good as outside me. And yet so many, beautiful men & women, are embroiled still in the self-torment of, believing the dramas, the roles they are enacting, thus creating more suffering, for themselves, not yet being aware that We, are the Divine directors of our 'Movie'. We are <u>self-responsible</u> &, oversee our own lives. Remember who we Are!

In Rebecca Tope's 'Fear in the Cotswolds, the following words grabbed me, "Suicide is, by definition, an expression of immense suffering." So much inner torment & self-attack, it seems most of us, opted for slow, long-term suicide, through attack on our bodies, in our attempts to avoid discomfort, by over-eating, drinking, smoking, lack of exercise, or rest, i.e., in a multitude of ways. Deep Love of myself is a primary prerequisite of a Joyful Existence. Love for everyone is then a natural outpouring, from a Full Heart.

Though I went through several days in April 2013, where seemingly I was in some sort of 'bottle-neck,' with weeks, of less food or money, I knew all was well. I soon realized it was a birth canal I was squeezed in, and this feeling only lasted a few days. Feeling disorientated when the shift came, I was struck soon by the realization, I have now reached, the uncharted territory, I had, months before, seen in a dream! - (as mentioned earlier in this book).

My sense now is, that I am One with Love, with Light, my whole vast holographic field beaming in new impulses, in a higher Love frequency than before. The energy flow is strong in my body. (This has accelerated into a permanent, beaming out of warmth, Joy & Love, in 2022). Life is fun as I play with being All, with 'others' who are this, even if they have not yet recognized this is so. Response- Ability!! I am very focussed too, on disconnecting from any passing judgement or, limiting distortion, choosing rather, to co-create my reality, in harmony and alignment, with the immense Heart-Love within, all of Life. Life is wondrous! However, though there has been more abundance & well-being in my life, with a more expansive future approaching, I had realized I will be called upon, to relate and express in a bigger way! Truly fulfilling my Soul Purpose? This, resulted in much panic arising, even though I did not yet know what form my 'work' would take. *My 'Journey' process, this week connected me with my unborn self, just prior to birth, about to be propelled into a seemingly unbearable world of wars, suffering, pain, and horrors. So huge a 'NNNOOOO!' was filling me, afraid I would be unable, to stay connected with my expansive awareness. No wonder the 'medical system' decided to be pull me out with forceps, before I felt ready. At the start of my process, it is interesting, no steps down appeared as such, so, I had a choice between, either a gently undulating slide into a 'known' future ahead, or letting myself fall into fathomless blackness. I felt very supported & loved, throughout the whole process. As I considered dropping into the black sea of energy, I went much deeper down, than I had ever before chosen. Babaji appeared in the blackness, sitting in lotus position, totally relaxed, so before any door appeared, I sensed he was holding me & all, in a protective embrace. Behind the ornate carved Chinese sort of entrance, Lu Yin's presence added to this sense of feeling loved & cared for, by my guides, by Life. The chariot had for the 1st time landed in my Womb, & again the environment here felt friendly, with a golden glow in the upper part. I intuited this was to do with my birthing into, an unknown future which, will require new expression, from a greater depth of Love & Passion. Reaching out from the right side of my womb-cave, were sort of arms, but the redness in them suggested effort & stress. In the left of the space was blackness, & I sensed, I was not confidently rooted, in my feminine being. Not such a surprise then, that the surfacing memory, was of me just prior, to Birth. I was seeing my foetal being from outside, surrounded by spacious awareness, feeling her Panic, in my whole body. As I entered the core of this emotion, I fell quickly into the utter helplessness beneath, or, lack of control, but found no resistance to letting go into Surrender, relaxing easily & rooting deep into the ground of my Being, feeling strong, in the Potency of Oneness with the Love, the Creative force which I truly am. Any action will stem from this Ease, & fulfil itself, through my unique expression, a gateway, a channel of endless transformation & change! Judith wisely guided me at the camp-fire, to meet my worst monsters, e.g. - the S.S. Nazis (from 1938), armies programmed or expected, to torture, rape & kill, plus any other rapists and torturers: sensing their extreme Heart & Soul disconnection, such inner nightmare brutal hells, of numbed down pain, fury, fear, guilt, even a burning need, to receive praise, be admired, to be adulated, 'SOMEONE', in control, soon gave rise to my Compassion, my Forgiveness. I have also realized that although these beings are playing this role in one dimension, they are also living higher aspects of themselves in other dimensions.* As I am re-reading this, I am recalling the 'Mount Shasta' book by Machaelle Small Wright too, & all her books, starting with, 'Behaving as if the God in all Life mattered.' I have just been reading, 'People Like Us' by, Louise Fein. A powerful book set in Germany, in the build-up to War, starting with the War on the Jews, or any non-pure Arians! I will have mentioned too. 'When I was Someone Else,' by Stephane Allix. A great book for extremists to read! For Nazi horrors in Poland, 'Little Bird of Auschwitz' - How my mother Escaped & found our Family by Alina & Jacques Peretti. (See Resources page). Every day, life teaches me. Since this session, I have been very aware of how my child selves, were running the story of my life, based on accumulated false conclusions & beliefs, about life, but also, I have now been mothering, my early baby self, the 5yr.old too, reassuring & encouraging her, to let go of all these limiting perceptions, to allow greater freedom & joy. Simultaneously, I have been aware that, though I have reached the end of a cycle, of the old story, I am just a baby myself, at the beginning of this new cycle. Humbling, yet also a relief to let go of any ego mind idea, that I have reached somewhere special. I am just where I am. Many have gone 'before', & many are coming 'after', in 'Time' reality, & my present awareness senses, a little more of the truth than before. There is though, an end to feeling identified with, my old version of my story, of not being 'enough,' of playing insignificant & small, from my shrunken idea of who I thought I was. Fear of future Pain, future failure, of seeing myself as, a Victim of circumstance, is over! In truth, Life has been happening so magically, with so much synchronicity, since that process. I feel so wonderfully blessed & grateful. My creative ideas have been flowing, my painting only occasionally, had been unleashed onto cards & murals, but is now wanting to be set free to paint in Nature again, as I much enjoyed in Spain, in the 1970's. I spent a few days in Kew Gardens, on my (more or less) monthly visit, before all the current restrictions, & found what felt to be a magical, less manicured area, except for grassy avenues, through wild borders, where I sat in the sun, sharing my cherries with a squirrel, by a grove of Atlas Cedars, a Cedar of Lebanon nearby, not far too, from a tall Stone Pine, as well as several Black poplars surrounded by their white fluffy seeded carpets. I lay too looking up at the sky, at the sun seeming, to scud through the white clouds, carving a light trail as it sped. I was filled with joy, at the prospect of spending hours connecting with sky, sun, earth, trees, plants & flowers, translating what I see into paint, colours, onto canvas, hardboard, or cloth. Wherever I go too, on 'JOURNEY' journeys, involves opening to those, who wish to meet themselves more deeply, through these processes. Not only have I had many unexpected clients showing up, wishing too, to see me next time, but people have been going generally, direct for their core issues, and having many breakthrough sessions! I so acknowledge these people, who are going into the fire, & darkness, their pain, meeting resistance, numbness, feeling stuck, yet leaving familiar comfort, to let go into greater depth, connection, and, Freedom. Having surrendered fully to being 'Born', it seems I have opened a doorway for others to come through too! Up in Snowdonia, I realize there was both the power from the surrounding mountains, also a beaming to Earth, of powerful new energies around July 26th & 27th, but I have noticed too, every time I sit with someone, prior to their receiving a 'Journey' process, I feel a surge of energy through my body, stronger still, when their process is going to be particularly powerful.

Here in the U.K., in 2022, we are enjoying, a glorious Summer, in Stroud, though the unusual heat, is resulting even in the U.K. in fires, on the parched earth. We human beings, are faced with the consequences, of uncaring, unwise choices, yet in any case, it feels so many light beings, are so much closer, responding fast to all those willing, to make a shift into a Life of more Joy, Presence & Magic, the more we trust this, especially. I am living more in the moment. I have been listening to my own energy, as well as aware & responsive to all of Nature's messages.

I am no longer in the world of problems &, blessed as I feel, seem to have moved into, my 'Elder' role, teaching, sharing & encouraging all the beautiful women, some men too, to know the Love, that is our Essence. Self-Love is, realizing this! What an immense difference, in our responses & choices, knowing just this, - we would so gladly come to love & trust Life deeply. Even so, we must first welcome, with loving acceptance, the various layers, of whatever may be sabotaging our opening, to unlimited possibilities, to fall more deeply into our creative Potency, into Ease in our bodies, & birth into All we truly are, conscious co-creators with Life in Love and Gratitude. I have truly somehow emerged into a body full of JOY/LOVE/BLISS streaming out all the time.

*

I loved 'The Never-Ending Story', (not mentioned in my Gratitude section), of which I enjoyed the tale, but loved the title better...... Yet, for so many months, no remarkable challenges arose. I thought my book was complete other than technical book Cover concerns.... However, ...!

*

I had put out a call asking to come even deeper into Intimacy, - knowing Self, in Love &, Being One with All. Life responded, stirring deeper shadows to come to light ...! Or maybe simply shades not quite cleared nor recognized, which are part of what has been in the main, cleared & released. Maybe!! So many months I was identified with being part of the All, Stardust, Air, Water, Planets, Light, Fire, & Earth, Universes, Galaxies, & all of Creation! I felt centred in my Heart, in Compassion, no problems, no emotional Dramas, instead streams of energy coursing through my body, synchronous unfolding, Miracles, Ease, less doing, rather Life orchestrating all perfectly, & my letting go of so much of my former need to control.

*

I was aware back during the 2nd half, of 2013, that my husband Sami George, as he had been calling himself more recently, seemed to be losing his short-term memory. He had given up chasing, over-night enlightenment which, seemed to promise an escape, from his present life, yet still Fear was a near companion, especially with physical problems he seemed to believe, were life-threatening, though he avoided any medical diagnosis. He was finding his gardening work more taxing, so could never do 6 hrs. in a day, but needed to go back 2 or 3 times a week. It was not till mid-October 2013 that, I became aware he was in a worse state of imbalance than

I had realized. I had paid for him, as he had said he would like, - to attend a Quantum Touch Healing Course, (though he did wonder about the required hours of practice necessary, to fulfil all the Qualifications to become a certified practitioner, saying he might not be alive that long!). He had expressed wanting to open his life into a new direction, so I assumed the comment about not living long enough, stemmed from his habitual victim-fear mode, anticipating the worst drama, so less than compassionately, I suggested, learning to offer so much healing, would be a good preparation for death! I needed to leave for London, a couple of days earlier, (I sleep in my car when I travel), so left clear directions, in writing, text & by 'phone, of how to reach the venue for 10a.m.; it proved beyond his capabilities, to follow these relatively simple details. He did not arrive, & finding he was unable, to follow any instructions, I had to track his progress, throughout the day, though I was participating in the training, as he got progressively more lost, & further from the venue. Eventually, I persuaded him, to wait to be rescued from Kings Cross St. Pancras station, 10p.m. that night! Though I took him to the 2nd day's training, I realized it was beyond his ability, to focus on the workshop information. Back at home however, he could function safely & cope with, his challenged body & mind, following usual routines.

*

Early November 2013, I worked in the Brighton MBS show interpreting aura pictures, as always, saw some clients, then went home for a few days, however, in order to keep my Practitioner status, I then drove the 'Mennorode' Conference Centre, near Elspeet. Holland to, for a Journey Practitioners' Mastery Gathering, plus more commitments in London after. On my return to Stroud, after these 3 weeks, I saw a marked decline in Sam. I returned to the St. Luke's Medical Centre, (an NHS practice working together with 'anthroposophical' medicine – i.e., Rudolph Steiner based system of treatments). I had asked Sam in October, if he would agree to have blood & urine tests, but these tests had revealed nothing. I got a 2nd appointment organized therefore, with a different, young, energetic doctor, in order to get things moving fast. Happily, a Chest X-ray, Brain MRI scan etc. were quickly scheduled, in Gloucester Royal hospital, where abnormalities in the lung & a big mass on the brain, led to Sam's fast admission for the next few days. The diagnosis was, Sam had advanced Lung Cancer, (from smoking?) &, as often happens, this had metastasised to the two tumours, in the (left) brain. The pressure of the biggest of these on his brain, was causing the loss of physical balance (i.e., feeling dizzy, wobbly &, falling, with inability to focus, or relate to time, such as the month, year, or day, nor even location. Also, incontinence. I had been very suddenly plunged, since my return from Holland & London, into the role of full-time 'Carer,' with constant washing & drying, of clothes & urine-soaked bedding, & was soon exhausted. Rammiel arrived about 10 days before Christmas, proving an enormous help in sourcing elasticated waist trousers, mattress & duvet protectors, etc. & any other support Sam needed. Refusing surgery after considering the risks, so, unwilling to go down the radio or chemotherapy route, Sam discharged himself from hospital. He was steering a course between steroids, (which avoid the above symptoms by keeping the swelling reduced, yet caused other strong side effects, he was having to live with), plus alternative treatments, to turn things around. Meanwhile I continued feeling exhausted, as even when Sami was in hospital, I was travelling there almost daily, & before & after his hospital stay, was ferrying him to appointments, plus liaising with family, friends & all the relevant official channels, as well as setting up, a new source of income for him; plus, a Palliative Care team, District Nurses, Stroud Carers and so on. I had had to postpone work commitments, to stay balanced between, my and Sam's needs. Before the steroids, when he often seemed absent, yet more surrendered, it was easy to feel compassion for his stressed, unloved Body. Now, as his ego mind, with his habitual fear, frustration, & resistance to Life, reasserted themselves, I was meeting this Ego bravado, with my own 'bolshiness' or refusal to be railroaded. I got to feel more disconnected from myself, with unexplained bursts of sadness or anger, deep yearnings for a deeper connection or intimacy, which eluded me, except in moments of meditation where for instance, I met once with a beautiful female being, maybe an angel, who held me, in a deeply healing embrace, of much Love, allowing me release of some of this sorrow.

*

It was February 17ʰ 2014, before I received the Journey session I had been wanting. (The last ones, had been in Holland, where the focus seemed to be on clearing & healing, past-life victim scenarios but, I knew at that time, there was deeper to go, to come to a more intimate connection with Love. Isn't there always?)! In this process something deeper did emerge. Though black mists were swirling around the left banister, my descent felt safe & colourful, down the solid steps. I noticed, the door into deeper connection with, my shining brilliant Soul self, with Source, and my guides, was less solid. Lu Yin was present, a loyal friend always on my 'Journey,' plus a less solid very large male presence. My chariot was a special golden-winged large Moth-like being which landed in my vagina very fast and clearly, was not going to move anywhere else. I was surprised to find much resistance in me, to being here, and tried moving our vehicle, but it seemed to be firmly jammed, with no intention of moving. I looked up and, was aware of the connection with my womb &, though blackness was all I saw, this felt like a potent & creative source. My vagina appears alive, in the sense of good colours, yet a certain vibrancy &

softness, seems to be missing. There is like a slippery slope down, unsafe feeling, & rather than my usual more detached curiosity, & fascination, I have a definite feeling of non-acceptance, feeling my vagina is not an honoured nor, loved place. I had been having disturbing war dreams surfacing during the week prior to this session. Especially the night before. Murky, desolate gloom, & though in the dream, I know I am to be rescued by Winston Churchill himself, with others, I find myself alone, first by a harbour, I feel will attract bombs, & then, as I visualize the cavalcade of cars which will transport us, feel these will equally attract bombs. Bursts of Anger, with this combative need, of War-mongering men to dominate, in a relentless, brutish & ruthless drive to be top dog, also using women & children, to inflict punishment, on their enemies, had been surfacing in me, when Sam's more aggressive drive had been showing itself. I had also been having bursts of unexplained sadness & tears, & was puzzled by it all. Since June 2011 I had moved into a deeper healing of my rage with men, -felt too in a Journey in May 2012, I had really forgiven men, & realized their essential innocence. I felt I had met, my inner male, divine partner, & had come to Love & Forgiveness. So, what was happening now? Letting myself relax & welcome, the layers of emotion, I met much sadness, followed by a sense of, deep wounding in my heart, under my left breast, yet surprisingly, I clearly know, this is not personal, but reflects the collective wound of dishonoured femininity. Feeling so vulnerable, like there is no protection, I then find myself falling into spaciousness, & feeling that, though the wounded part is still here, there is nothing to do, nothing to get right. Yet some part of me feels too I am not allowed, not to get it right, not allowed to say, nor even to feel what I do! A rebellious growling anger arises in me, but it is not explosive, nor fiery, instead I feel an immense Oppression bearing down on me, frustration too, which is paralysing me. It was with great relief that I agreed to Judith's suggestion, that I ask my guides to spring-clean my body, of all that oppressive disapproval, pressing down on me, for not displaying the correct nice emotions! Afterwards I feel spacious inside, but it is a restful blackness, very safe. It is not a neutral nor cold place, but deeply embracing, and, deep acceptance is here. I am happy to stay in this dark, restful safety. It had been my 2yr.old self who showed up in the first memory, who was still real in her expression, full of life's energy, power & vitality. She was angry too with my mother, for only approving 'nice emotions, not allowing sadness, nor anger. Not surprising that years later, my mother was diagnosed with Cancer, - & we were not allowed to have any emotional outbursts, which would then be deemed by her, to make her Cancer worse. I realized that Sam's Cancer, with everything revolving around him, being the special victim, & people also expecting me to be in victim mode, attributing to me the emotions I should be feeling, had been triggering the story with my mother, & I had been totally unaware of this. The specialness & manipulation conferred by Cancer. Not that Sam lays that number on me, but it **has** given him special status, so he now finally, can feel he deserves, to receive all the attention he always wanted. I believe we are each the Master creator of our present *reality; it is what we have chosen at some level, & we are the ones who could, choose differently. I breathe in different resources, now allowing my little 2yr.old to be assertive, playful and herself! My Guide reminds me, to stay connected with Life & speak from the truth of me, no matter what.*

*Afterwards, my vagina feels more honoured, connected, throbbing, vibrant, rather than held, in contraction, or a sort of slippery unsafe slide, to danger. I feel this is a healing of, **the deeper Collective Oppression of Woman, the Feminine, by Men, by the Patriarchal system**, over so very many generations, & life-times. Yet I am sure we too, have sometimes played that male role! I have just read a book, entitled 'Breadwinner' by Deborah Ellis, about a girl's life, under the Taliban!*

My vagina advises me, to stay connected & vibrant &, honour Being. I noticed in my meditations since, I have been connecting with more still, deep, moments of Being, less Doing, allowing whatever wants to appear, to do so, with no attempt to visualize differently. I have felt the Earth energy & Love, move into my Heart, with myself as an observer. Less colourful maybe, but more Presence. My prayer to come more deeply into Love, Connection & Intimacy with Life, with All, had stirred a response, of feeling deep dishonouring of Women &, feeling opposition, to Man's Warring, Brutal & Competitive attack, on human 'Enemies' often using, Women & Children to vent their Punishment &, Hatred of Life. It still goes on, but Women including me, are now connecting with their Power, & Creative expression, which holds the Unmanifest Potential, ever-birthing new possibilities. Every Woman is part of, this unique ever-creative force, held in inner Being, birthed from the Wombs, in varied Life expressions.

I bow to the Feminine so long oppressed, in many Countries still so, & welcome Balance, Harmony, a Loving relationship with the Earth &, all her Creatures, being restored. Each one of us must play our part. I acknowledge with Gratitude & respect too, those men who honour both their male aspect & the outer & inner Feminine, of their own Being. It has been part of Evolution, to meet every shadow, to better bring Healing Light, to every disowned, rejected aspect, including any emotions, we have identified as bad, or unacceptable, in a tender Embrace, that they may dissolve & leave us lighter, more Joyful & unencumbered by the weight of suppression, oppression & Disease! Free will has allowed us to kill, to maim, to hurt ourselves & each other as part of our journey to know, who we are in Truth; what is, & what is not, Love's Voice. Every Stone, every blade of Grass, every Insect & Leaf, every Planet is ever changing & Evolving towards its finest Expression & its unique Soul purpose. An honouring & Blessing of our Motherland. I am inviting my energy to be light & love-filled enough, to attract Unicorns, since I read 'The Wonder of Unicorns' - Diana Cooper. In storage, I have a book by St. Hilarion, 'The Nature of Reality' explaining the different lessons being learnt by being grass, or chickens, or cows or whatever!

A couple of weeks or so later, I was in bed and had a sudden urge to touch my vagina & stroke myself. My Body, not Shameful! I was hit by the realization that I felt very different about my vagina. I got the sense of it being a Sacred gateway, both linked to my Womb, in its creative impulse to birth, - linked too, to the whole of Creation, the birthing of planets, creatures & Universes. I was filled with grief & found myself deeply sobbing in sorrow, for all the years of my own dishonouring of my vagina. Unloved by me! After these tears of release, I felt that my vagina will now be free of pain and know it is loved by me. It is important for me to come into this relationship with every aspect of my body & personality selves, not just love my expansive Self, who is Star-dust, Earth, Water, Sky, Cosmos & All. So, I acknowledge once again, my part in having myself co-operated, or abetted, in dishonouring the Feminine, either in some of my lives as a man, (& I have remembered myself as an Arab warrior with my curved sword & curved shoes, driven to ride on horseback through the desert, ready to mow down any obstacles in my path), or by co-creating this story, as a woman too. It does not serve Life, for me, for us, to direct rage at Men, rather let that wild, fierce, Feminine energy transform into a passionate intent & fierce Love, to be part of the change to Harmony & Balance between Male and Female. As usual, no-one to blame, just good to recognize my responsibility, for my co-creations, & to act & live from integrity, as a Heart-open Warrior Goddess when this is called for.

One day, in the right timing, in this Life, (or another), I may experience making Love with a Beloved man, a partner who equally feels supportive & protective of me, committed too, in a deepening journey of Intimacy & Love. First, I will need to be sure I have opened wide, to receiving Life's support, through People, with no more shadows reaching me from my 5yr.old's decisions & beliefs about people & their ability, or not, to be supportive! The Feminine Wisdom is Rising, or being heard!

*

On Sunday March 9th I planned to be in London. Sam had been fearful about my leaving, & found himself hardly able, to get up from his bed the night before, which meant, I had to do much more, to leave him adequately supported, with plenty of spring water, easily prepared food, etc. as well as getting me & my car, ready for my journey. Thus, I arrived much later than expected at Nubia's. I was tired, but still willing to receive the Journey session she was offering me. *In my session, I felt the insecurity & vulnerability of just being with my personality, my ego-mind self, felt sadness too, a yearning in my heart to be deeply met by a partner, plus mistrust that any person can come to that Unconditional Love, in a world of Duality & free will. However, I then felt strongly throughout my body, the need to really stand strong in my commitment to rest in, an even deeper Loving, Compassionate Acceptance of every aspect of myself, as, only then, will this be mirrored back to me. This had become more obvious, since that last Feb. session, showed me the hidden truth about my relationship with my vagina. Also, my present life challenges are showing me the need to love & fully meet the character I am playing, not just my expansive cosmic self, & to truly love every molecule of my body, judged as 'imperfect'!*

I had cut my time away from home to the minimum, though gave myself Monday free, to enjoy Kew Gardens. Even so, I zoomed to the fruit market (near Southall Western International Market) early, from Nubia's home in White City, got Nubia two boxes of avocados, plus a small box of blood oranges for me, yet was parked back by Kew Garden main Gates by 8.30a.m. in order to enjoy the Gardens till evening. I drove back with the avocados to her home, then left, to park by the usual Mosque, near the Market, before sunset, as I enjoy hearing the sunset & sunrise prayers, feels a good place to sleep, - between there & a park. Next morning very early, I loaded my car with pallets, boxes of fruit, plus all the broken bits of pallet, then drove to Ascot, where I worked with two clients, before driving to Chalfont St. Peter to give a third Journey session. I slept there as my 'client' has become such a close friend and, her husband too, is lovely. By 6a.m. next morning I was on the way back to Stroud, where I spent much of the day emptying the car, of the many boxes of fruit, avocados, pineapples, oranges, & pallets, sorting shopping, preparing food & whatever, then drove up to Minchinhampton Common, to collect Sam from his kinesiology appt. I was feeling pleased, my body & back could handle, all the lifting. The next day, I worked for hours in the garden, lifting heavy compost bags, rebuilding the wooden compost heap structure, enjoying the strength in my body, then reached to lift something not so heavy, but from an awkward angle, without my body weight behind, & was suddenly in pain. This, has not healed very quickly. I received a massage, & immediately after, felt in worse pain, but it brought near the surface, my sadness & the 3 to 5yr.old me - which longs for support, & for human mothering & fathering. I realized part of deepening my intimate connection, with Life, is to open wide to receiving the support through others, which my 5yr.old did not trust was possible. This was confirmed for me when I dreamt, I was with a male friend, sharing our interest in crystals & whatever else. In the morning I thought of one or two men, trying to remember who, it was in the dream, then thought of Durgadas & knew immediately it was him, because of how much I trust him. (I have certainly had to open to being supported by others, this last year, since my Pension credit was withdrawn, so I have been reliant on help to cover all my bills, as the pension does not even cover the rent).

Back to 2013, for many days, my body was under strain and pain. I had been taking pleasure, in my ability to be strong, to be able to handle it all physically even if unable to emotionally be, everything Sam, is looking outside of himself to me, to provide. He still seemed to believe, that if enough people showered him with Love, support & attention most of the time, he would be whole & healed. After months, of feeling myself centred in my overflowing Heart energy, strongly coursing through me, particularly noticeable in my Hands, this has been somewhat diluted, since I came back in December, to unexpectedly find myself, back in the full-time role of 'Carer.'

My recent experience had been, that I have been sometimes exhausted, though mainly tired. I am assuming I am learning a deeper lesson. I did put out a prayer, to come deeper into Love, Connection &, Intimacy with Life. After finding out, the degree I had distanced myself from loving, my vagina, I also realized how easy it has been, to love myself as being the 'All of Life', yet hadn't acknowledged as equally important, to love my physical body-self deeply &, my human ego personality, even if this has been formed with such limited understanding, or born from illusion. After so many years, of unaware suppression, of my 'not nice' self, there's purpose in my being brought again, into close relationship with fast-surging emotions like anger, zooming through & leaving quickly, less detachment definitely! At the same time, I knew all was well, so did not get into suffering victim mode any more, but simply looked to understand, my part in my co-creation. Knowing myself as the expansive Heart-Being I am, seems to have taken me, into more presence, plus real acceptance of all facets, of this personality self I inhabit, in such an intimate way, not fully acknowledged, nor appreciated before. I am connecting with my wild, energetic, alive 2yr.old self, more fully, reclaiming who I am in my physical body as well as my cosmos self.

*

I have again just taken some days for me as, to be a Quantum Healing Practitioner, I must attend further training in Derby, in the Midlands, where I'll stay with my sister, Cristina, whom I've not been able to see for about 6 months. She is still opposing the many less than compassionate, would-be badger killers and politicians, though focus on such horrors, does not bring as much light and sweetness or joy & love into her awareness & being, as could be! Still, I love & acknowledge her dedication & caring, about the suffering of many beings. Again, the day before I was due to leave, Sam manifested being more unwell & incapable, but I had spent much time, organizing much support from people, who would bring him care, food, and healing. I had realized I needed to open wider, to support from people, rather than still fall back into my 5yr.old's 'I can manage, I don't need, nor will I ask for Help!' This will open me to even more of

Life's blessings & abundance. So, I continued packing the car, doing all I could, to leave plenty of easily prepared food, ignoring too, a little arising guilt. Sam stayed in bed. Just as I was ready to go up to say, I must leave, I heard a slight noise & noticed, he had come down. I sensed he was trying, to encourage my break, though he felt weak, & unlike the last time, I did not sense he was trying to manipulate me. So, I was drawn to give him some moments of healing Love energy, before leaving & still was able, to reach my sister's, before dark.

Eileen Strong, the Quantum Touch Trainer, was to pick me up from outside my sister's home, early the next morning, Friday April 4th, to take me to her workshop in Derby. The venue was a Friends' Meeting House, & had small Gardens, with a nice mossy lawn, which left wild cowslips untouched by lawn mower! Just a cat joined me while I sat there, for the lunch break. With only four trainees, an intimate, more in-depth training was possible. I had more opportunity to ask questions and, understand better what we were doing, than in my previous training with Karina, as there was plenty of time. Also, I was not repeatedly having to leave the room, as in the earlier training, (to check on Sam's progress, as he attempted to find his way to Brent Cross)! I felt a good connection unfold with Eileen, & everyone, & intended to keep contact, especially for practice with Maria, as she lives in Derby, but it feels good to keep in touch with Eileen too. (I was interested to find I was the only one of us trainees, with my hips aligned. I guess it is because they were aligned in my first Level 1 group in mid-October with Karina, after someone worked on them. No wonder I have not quite known how to stand in my body since, except when focussing on being supported by Mother Earth & rooted in her body). When I received healing, I focussed on my lower back, experiencing deep healing around Support! As my partner held her hands over my lower back, first I felt some discomfort on the left, then felt it move over to the right side, & heat shot from above my hip down to my sciatic nerve area. At the same moment, a memory came up. of the time when Sam was in the throes, of his affair &, I felt the least supported ever, every day sitting on the ground crying to God. I had manifested the worst sciatica I have ever experienced, (worse than when I was pregnant with Samantha, and Bob my partner would disappear for weeks or days. Sciatica, as mentioned by Louise Hays, relates to fear of future lack of abundance. I manifested this recently too, due to the present lack of funds. Only the Stargate morning meditations & ever-deepening love & trust, despite any lingering insecurity, keeps me relatively peaceful, sciatica gone, legs getting stronger with so much walking, plus I have nearly finished this final re-edit of my book, before publication, the sooner the better!). This time, with Sam, I could feel my spirit leaving &, would imagine sitting in the desert letting my spirit go. (Remembering now, how unsupported I felt when carrying Max's child too, who was still-born in Spain, where I had escaped to sleep under trees and sky, & feel Nature's support!) So much abandonment & lack of support I created for myself, holding true to what my 5yr.old believed, about whether her needs could be met. I reassured my whole sciatic nerve area as, clearly it still carried the trauma, and I now held it in an embrace of love and tenderness, with assurance that I and others, are now here to give support.

*

On Sunday morning I left Cristina's home, (the home our birth family lived in from when I was 15yrs.old, till I left for University and my London life; - Cristina has lived here more recently for some happy years with her 'late' Welsh husband). I still enjoy the lovely large garden, & Cristina has created an extended, much enriched inside space, she was sharing, with her two, golden-white Labrador retrievers. She has restricted her present dog Sky, to the top part of the garden, to allow, badgers & foxes, to use the bottom, wilder part.

<u>She has given me many folders of letters, written between my parents, from 1937 to 1946, to translate from Spanish</u>. In case I would like yet another project! Some letters very brittle & crumbly, difficult to handle. (Took me 14mths.to start reading them properly)! They are all duly translated now.

I intended to reach Snowdonia that afternoon, but was so tired, stopped so often in lay-bys, Parvati had almost given up expecting me. Nourished by so much good, in-depth sharing with Pete and Parvati, especially talking about death with Pete, I felt reassured, that like me, he feels anyone who dies, is never far away, and is connected eternally. Parvati gave me a special book of Shamanic stories by Manda Clements, which felt so apt at this time. Her first tale is very relevant regarding my 2yr.old vibrant, young self! I left for Dolgellau, where after visiting a family on their beautiful land and sharing from the heart with Tracey, I carried on to Sandra & Jonathan's mountain cottage, where they are so near the land, busy with their spinning, carding, dyeing, knitting wool from the Welsh mountain sheep, craft making & selling, & other earthy, creative pursuits. I was made as welcome as ever, but again could not stay long, as so many places to reach next day, Tuesday, before getting back to Sam, as I had assured him I would. I went via Machynlleth, & Aberystwyth, first to track down Vibha's cottage nr. Mydroilyn, before calling in on the warm-hearted family in 'Blaengors,' the beautiful land we had intended for, the creation of a true Sanatan Dharma ashram. Sam and I had focussed on much energy-clearing, in co-operation with our higher selves, with Pan, the Christ consciousness, the White brotherhood of Light, plus the Deva of the land of course. So much joy, focus, heart energy, mantras, and intent went too, especially from the core group, but from many others too, into wall-paper stripping, painting, digging, the planting of hundreds of trees, lovely gardens, into buildings and land, <u>which has</u> <u>continued</u> with the new owners, to blossom into beauty, craftsmanship, an extended, light-filled home, flourishing plants, animals, and people. They gave me two eggs from their geese, for Sam. I continued my journey to Lampeter, via the Organic Food Stores (off the Tregaron road), and onwards home, which I did not reach till late evening in the Dark. I had driven so many miles, that day, connected with so many lovely people, with little rest, but with plenty of healing and deeper sharing, so arrived home feeling inspired and, not tired! Back with Sam, he is generally resting much more, needing more support, eating lots of eggs and fish, which he scarcely ever ate, before, throughout all the time we had been married, i.e., over 23 years.

*

On Sunday I was to lead the Women's group in Barbro's home. I was choosing some music & came across 'Dear Self I Love You' on You Tube, from a CD by Amanda Marshall, which linked me too, with Dr. Cha-Zay. I have been finding out more about her fascinating life, and read her book, (title) - 'I'm Dying: Shit! Not Again!' In the group, I read us the 1st story from Manda Clements book, 'There was Once a Land where Children were Persuaded to Trade their Beauty'. and here too, is a short section I would like to quote from the story; ... "Her pulse slowed, her breathing stopped and then one day, the civilized woman died. There in the woods her body rotted and she became food for the acorn she held. As her energy seeped into the ground, she at last realized, what scared people – the wildness of its children's beauty, that smelled of exotic dew-touched flowers, also smelled of death. To be fully alive, one must also fully accept death.... they had tried, to tame their own true natures so that they could tame death. But in fearing death, they never truly lived.' When there was time later, for each one of us to ask, for what we wanted to receive, I wanted it affirmed to me, that I really deserve to receive abundant support, & later asked too, for my toe nails to have love beamed to them, as I had felt embarrassed for them to be seen. I never gave thought to appreciating my body, when young! Since realizing, how little I had embraced, as it were, my vagina, I'd given more attention, to any of my body parts, I might not be accepting as fully as I had believed. At least not with my ego-mind which prefers, not to experience peoples' disgust or withdrawal. I love the song, 'Dear Self......',

Then approaching my 80th Birthday, I felt deep & grateful love, for my body, even while I feel no fear of death, which I expect to be a special adventure. I also ordered from the Stroud 'Faery Shop,' a creation carved from different materials, of the transition from body to Earth, now situated on my windowsill; many toadstools are rooting into the woman's body, rotting into the Earth!

I have been reading so many books about people's journeys with Cancer, and will quote too from 'Grace and Grit' by Ken Wilber, ...'everything is impermanent, everything passes, nothing remains, nothing lasts. Only the whole endures eternally; all parts, are doomed to death and decay.' I am feeling a fresh sense of this with my own body, plus a deeper acceptance, whatever the future may be. It seems so much energy, is expended by so many of us, in keeping fear at bay, warding off the possible judgements from others, avoiding pain, or thoughts of decay and death. I have been exploring options regarding disposal of my dead body, & am most attracted for myself, to Jae Rhim Lee's Infinity Burial Project and the mushroom spore body suits she is developing, (soon to be on sale, I hope, in production in 2020 onwards), which break down or eat the body tissues rapidly, & also clean up any environmental toxins, thus better serving the Earth and the planet, - superior I think, in that respect to cremation or normal burial procedures. In fact, now in my 81st year, I intend to buy one. Otherwise, a shroud.

Tree Pod Burials are also being developed by, Anna Citelli and Raoul Bretzel. Very much in resonance with this, and what I have always felt in my heart, is the following story and poem. I was kindly given permission to include the following lengthy quotation from the 'Tibet Foundation Newsletter' no.64 (Spring 2014). It is a free verse poem by Datsenpa Gonpo Tsering, written in the Tibetan language on the website www.khabda.org on Sept.7th 2008. He, left his body in the Summer of 2013: 'It's Sunday morning. The father, mother and their two boys aged thirteen and three are as usual, seated around the breakfast table and talking. However, unlike the other days, today the father is talking about his preferred funeral rite. He says:

One day, I will be dead.

No one can tell when.

But after I am gone, I don't want you to incinerate my body.

I have no wish, to have the face of the sky, polluted with smoke.

I have no wish, to have the pristine air polluted, with chemicals.

I have no wish to have, the invisible spirits disturbed, by the smell of burnt offerings.

One day, I will be dead.

No one can tell when.

But after I am gone, I have no wish to have my corpse interred.

I have no wish to have, the bosom of mother earth dug up.

If we all did that, one day our beautiful earth, will surely be filled with tombstones.

And in particular, I have no wish to, have my dead body left, in some faraway foreign land.

One day, I will be dead.

No one can tell when.

Even whilst I am alive, I do not have the right to freely go, to the place where I was born and have grown up; the place where I have played and laughed.

I cannot return to my fatherland, whose relief resembles the breastbone of a proud ram.

Now it looks like when I am gone, even my body cannot, be taken back to my fatherland.

One day, I will be dead.

No one can tell when.

But when I depart, I wish to have my body carried, somewhere on the border of Tibet, be it Ladakh, Sikkim or Bhutan.

There, let the vultures feed on my remains.

Have my flesh, skin and cartilage chopped into pieces, and let the vultures feast on them.

Pulverize my bones with stones and let the vultures, feast on them.

To protect yourself, from getting splattered with blood, keep adding flour-powder, as you pound the bones. Bless them!

The hungry vultures satiating themselves, feeding on my remains, would bring peace to my soul, after I am no more.

You needn't be apprehensive about that.

Along the long journey of my soul, this physical body of your dad, is nothing more than a dilapidated inn, where wandering souls rest only overnight.

When one is dead, then one is dead.

Don't betray foolishness, by covering the useless corpse, with expensive brocade or coffin.

That is like decorating, the dilapidated inn, after the guest is gone.

This funeral rite is the custom, of your father's homeland.

This also happens to be, the funeral rite I like best.

This is one of the most ancient, of funeral rites.

This is one of the tidiest of funeral rites.

After the father finishes his last testament, a crystal-clear single teardrop, rolled down from one eye.

The father logs on to www.khabda.org website and, starts typing something.

In the midst of typing, he actually passes away.

Funeral rites are being conducted for him somewhere on the border of Tibet. His acquaintances, both in and outside Tibet are reciting the mani mantra for him. At the funeral site, some monks are droning, "May all sentient-beings, who at one stage or other of my past lives, (have) been my mother be blessed with happiness and the causes of happiness..." and such prayers in a tune unfamiliar to him.

Before long, a flock of vultures come swooping down from, the folds of the clouds and finishes off, what remains of him. Even the brain in the skull is picked dry, with their sharp beaks.

Nothing is left except his skull.

Fully satiated, the vultures fly off towards Tibet.

Bearing his flesh, bone and blood they soar heavenwards.

Mere specks bobbing in the azure sky, they disappear further and further towards Tibet.

His consciousness, too, mingled with the flock of vultures, goes towards Tibet, visible now and then, almost like a real vulture.

A year has gone by. Somewhere in a nomadic encampment, a child is born. Faintly visible on the child's chest is: 'Chinese, get out of Tibet!'

People are amazed.

As someone says, 'Surely, this must be the emanation of a Lama!' the child opens his eyes.

And then with a look of disdain, starts crying.

A single loud wail from his three-year-old son, wakes up the father from his reverie.

So, he has to stop his writing. Once again, a tear drop wells up in one eye...'

*

Since mostly, we do not remember we chose birth, nor why, it seems too many of human-kind, can clinically observe, with indifference or lack of empathy, all else in our surroundings, in Nature, & even each other. Whatever we can use for profit, control, we do, or assume the right to trap, subject to torture, sacrifice in experiments in laboratories, out of greed, in attempts to safeguard our youth, health & strength, enhance erectile potency, or alluring flesh, rather than accept all of life's processes, with compassion for the impermanence of matter, in every species or body form. Of course, we have been as heartless, often men more so, to each other too, in the Concentration Camps & other prisons. Some of us attempt to boost our ego-selves, by presenting the most perfect image, & when someone is attracted, crucify ourselves with thoughts of, 'he only loves me for my looks, not really for myself,' the self we are so self-judgemental about, 'she only likes me for my money,' or whatever our pattern is. There is always someone to compare ourselves with, who is 'better'! Bhutan, is the only Country I know of, where success is gauged by, the 'Gross National Happiness' of the population, rather than 'Gross National Profit.' How sad!

*

In the last months of 2013 and the earlier months of 2014, I was 63yrs. of age. Reaching age 60 had held, no special significance for me, unlike with my sisters &, often in Society. It was though, a time, when it became increasingly clear, that as Sam was coming closer, to leaving <u>his</u> body, that, would be a big change of focus. Some part of me however, clearly knew, my 70's would be more consequential in my life. Though I have mentioned the idea, or imagined that, I would welcome meeting a sort of twin flame, in fact, since my 70th year onwards, I am very happy being with myself! More restful.

After so many months of feeling seated in my Heart, & feeling so much compassion, for the people I was helping through Journey sessions, my prayer to come deeper into Love, Compassion, & deeper Intimacy with All, had brought exactly what I needed, to test me, showing me, how disconnected I still was, from even deeper Compassion & Love, for All of life. The strength of my physical body has certainly been tested, & found sometimes unfit, for the demands I was faced with. Looking more deeply now, I am seeing, that I came together with Sam, despite initial resistance, (i.e., "Sam? that's not the sort of man I want to be with!") - yet I paid heed to what my dreams had indicated, plus increasing Soul urges, as I have earlier described in Chapter 2, & ended up, in this most challenging, & maybe most growth-spurring relationship of my life. Though we loved as much as we were able, we were not truly connected from our hearts, both living in mistrust & lack, of deep intimacy & connection. We did make love, mostly in silence, & after orgasm, my spontaneous response was to burst out laughing. I believe the carefree, joyous me, must have been long suppressed. I do not have much memory of former lives with Sam, except, as I have mentioned, the first time I touched him, when we lay down on the floor of Ambika & Gopal Hari's living room, when I flipped into a former tepee life for a few moments. I was told, by Patricia Sterry, of his anger, taken out on animals, so a horse kicked him to death, in one of his lives. In another life as a Nun, I loved the children in our care, one of whom was 'Sam, - (treated mostly with unloving strictness, by the other nuns). '(I do not know what name that child, now Sam, had then).' There was a fire &, I was unable to reach him, nor the other children, so they died, as the fire, got out of control. I felt responsible thereafter, for their Souls.

As my primary focus became, a journey to heart-felt love &, acceptance of myself, during my deepening inner explorations, Sam felt increasingly abandoned by me, & lost. I had had enough though, of our habitual ways of relating, but did come to forgiveness of our past, totally aware of my part in co-creating that, & felt by 2013, I had completed, why I had come into our time together, no longer feeling such attachment, nor need to control, what Sam would, or would not do, in terms of relating to other women intimately. I knew it was no longer appropriate for me to relate in this way with Sam, as we had not been able to really honour each other deeply, meeting as equals, with honest sharing, speaking the same language, & standing rooted in Love of Oneself & All, in the way I now realize is, what I would have deeply welcomed, when appropriate. We did try.

*

I had voiced plenty of probably unhelpful, opinions about the causes of Sam's Cancer, plus what he now needed to practice, yet he seemed to understand very little, maybe due to the tumour in his brain, of what I was in truth saying. This was puzzling for my mind to comprehend, at the time, after so many years of my offering guidance, the support of inspirational books, courses. and therapy sessions. Also, Sam had finally entered the world of computers, for at least a year, even got his own lap-top, & spent many months, day, and night, receiving energy-clearing, after energy-clearing. He bought packages offering transformational strategies & healing support, from the presenters of inspiring teleseminars, talking many nights by Skype with spiritual teachers or leaders, mostly from U.S.A., who engaged in helping him with his blocks, his difficulties, or feeling stuck. He expected to be transformed almost overnight somehow, & transported into a new reality. I kept my thoughts to myself, that having everyone else do it for you, avoids going on a deeper inner journey, to meet oneself. On the surface, he was saying the right words, seeming to understand our essential nature, voicing too his opinions to others, don't we all! Yet still here he was in the same inner discomfort, the same persistent, habitual, underlying thoughts, habits & beliefs, his body still challenged, as had become evident. He gave up suddenly, this attempt to transform overnight, & was again faced with his depression, anger, & frustrated resistance, to Life being as it is. Especially as his inner dis-ease, displayed more noticeable symptoms. It is sad, he did not come to love Himself &, Life in the now moment, while he lived in his body, plus come to greater inner peace & surrender, able even to embrace pain & discomfort. He did write in a gratitude book, I found after he died, expressing how grateful he was that I shared so much with him, ideas etc.

That last Summer, Sam was not really drawn to be in the garden except to smoke, or walk via the garden to town for tobacco, or cake, or whole packets of biscuits at a time, (though this time with the biscuits, he experienced the consequent pain of his legs swelling up, from overdoing it with the sugar, enough so as, to make him change that almost life-long habit. When he was younger, his mother Ruby, used to say, 'Never mind dear, have a biscuit). Outings with anyone must include, this oral kind of stimulation, plus really being listened to, or appreciated. Steroids & Paracetamol, then slow-release Pain relief patches, became his pain fighters. Sad that he did not delight in the wonderful fragrance of the Rowan & Lilac tree blossoms, the air such a delight to breathe. I have spent many, many hours giving long overdue, much needed attention to, our beautiful small, insect-friendly garden.

I was finding Sam's need to blame, complain, oppose & argue about so many things that I, as Carer, was expected to keep in hand, burdensome. The fact too, that though he had no energy, to go to the nearby pharmacy, go shopping, do any housework, make phone calls to St. Luke's Centre or to Jane, (his main palliative care nurse), he was motivated & had energy enough, to go to buy Tobacco! Air is life-giving, inhaling tobacco tar, is not. I have had 3 days totally resistant to Sam's smoking addiction, which suppresses his anger seemingly, but then actually, this just bursts out more forcefully later, his anger-fuelled energy, a good excuse to march off to smoke, turning self-destruction to blame. Otherwise, his poor beleaguered body can mostly, hardly move around, but he is seemingly too addicted, too disconnected, from body & heart to listen. It will be obvious here, that I was not sitting in my own heart & compassion. Later today he was crying in despair & self-flagellation. Compassion arose, & as 'Carer', I cannot easily remain detached & removed from Sam's choices. Do I just say his choices are not my concern? I see the amount of stronger pain, he is driving himself into, even faster, often very early in the morning, as well as throughout the day. Sam is in an advanced stage of the effects from his tumours, with a confused mind. I would not leave alcohol around an alcoholic ...?!

*

I am learning a lot from Treya, in 'Grace and Grit' written by her and Ken Wilber, her husband. After years of practising Vipassana, Treya, with Ken, met Kalu Rinpoche, an 'altogether extraordinary teacher, generally thought to be one of Tibet's very greatest modern masters', and under his guidance, deepened her practice to include too, the next of the three main levels of transmission, Tonglen, which extends one's awareness to the suffering of the world, rather than staying focussed on one's own enlightenment. I had reacted one evening, to Sam's tobacco smoking, as it seemed insanity to be paying a kinesiologist to dowse, what his body should drink or ingest, for increased beneficial body balance, & then continue poisoning his body & lungs. I retreated to bed & read about Tonglen, which involves on the in-breath, drawing in someone's sickness or pain, first through the nostrils, then into the Heart, envisaging it as 'a black smoky tar-like cloud'! (I thought 'God! No! Just like tobacco!' I have worked on a farm in France with tobacco plants & even when growing in the Earth, their 'sap is black and sticky). On the out-breath radiating out Love, Goodness, Peace, etc. in the form of liberating, healing light, then continuing to do this in ever widening circles, until one is breathing in, the Suffering of the World! ...& breathing out Love! It seems no-one gets sick from doing this practice. Seemingly, I have way further to go, in deepening into more Compassion! Given that my & Sam's vibrational frequencies, seemed so disparate, we have not really been able to truly meet. I believe the yearning in one's heart that seems, for a very short 'honey-moon' stage to be met, by another, is really the longing to meet Oneself, or the Source of our Being. I was strongly drawn, for a while, to invite, in appropriate timing, by virtue of falling in Love ever more deeply, with who I am in Truth, a Twin Flame relationship, with another who had equally met more deeply with himself, & life, - when appropriate or - if I am some time ready! In fact, now, since I fell in love with me, I have totally lost that desire, though I do nowadays, love relating more deeply, with many Beings! (Meanwhile, I will read Cha-Zey's 'Quantum Love: Twin Flames - Myth or Reality' when it comes in paperback format, if she in fact, writes it. I never did find that book)! Maybe she died a 5th time, & did not return to Earth. I did read, her book 'I'm Dying, Shit! Not Again', followed quickly by, reading Michael Road's, 'Stepping...Between...Realities,' both mind-blowing. Mixael metaphysically travels into many, many realms, worlds, galaxies, wherever in all time and space his vibration allows. Thus, he can connect in an immediately intimate, more 'real' way, with Beings & energies, beyond what most of us have been open to, or capable of, experiencing. The name Mixael used during these journeys, was his 5th dimensional name, before he came into Michael's body, more fully explained in his previous book. Hopefully those two books helped blow at least some of my mind's limitations & beliefs to smithereens. They certainly, expanded my vision. Anything truly Real, is beyond mind interpretation. However inadequate <u>this</u> book may be, yet I will trust it has a role to play, & may serve as a path or, small bridge, towards heart-centred, galactic or quantum field awareness, even beyond my limited conceptual awareness of expanded reality & my cosmic self.

*

I went again to London, (April 2014), connected with my journey clients &, bought boxes of oranges, avocados, pineapples & 'Alfonso' mangos, from the wholesale market, where I have been buying fruit from many countries, for nearly fifty years. I planned to eat just mangos for three or so days, to help heal my body, which is again hurting from lifting 7' by 4' (at least), heavy wooden panels. (I learnt that though this is the start of the Indian mango season, they have now been banned from the U.K. because of some insect. I so hope this does not mean further war on insects I am pleased in 2022, to have connected with 'Buglife', though I am unsure how they support insects). My best days, Saturday & Sunday, I lay hours resting in the grass & hot sun, in Kew Gardens, by my Cedar Grove favourite place. (The one time I did not find my way straight there, was when I tried to show Sam, - obviously I was not meant to share my special sanctuary spot with him, at that time, if at all). My body felt so much better lying there, & reading those 'Wake up!' books, & brought me back to feeling centred, open, with my writing flowing again. I am so busy at home, in my Carer role plus, with house & garden tasks. I returned Bank holiday Monday, April 5th & on Wednesday, today, while Sam was most of the day, in the Hospice, I was able to listen for the 3rd time to Matt Kahn. I was in tears listening, as I understood more deeply, the ways I have related to Sam & his sickness, from my Ego-mind mentality. I have been attempting both in my Carer role, as well as throughout our relationship, especially since I had left behind, the problem, fear, martyrdom & suffering mentality, to point out he need not live, in his habitual resistance, suffering &, ego-based determination, to change how every moment is showing itself. Matt Kahn suggests, this is the worst way to relate with him, rather than accepting & loving him where he is. It is important when I am around Sam, to be totally comfortable in my own body, to slow my breath, thus his frequency can entrain with mine. For my own protection too, rather than my energy being pulled down to his, as has seemed to happen. Last night in bed, as I tried to rest free from pain, by moving into different positions, I realized it is one of my lower 'floating' ribs, that must be cracked. About the 5th time! Bones represent protection, or rebellion against authority, - maybe other's ego-wills too! - (according to Louise Hayes). Probably including, our neighbour Maurice's, who played a part in, my excessive load-lifting, rib-cracking, garden dramas! His wife Jane, told me the other day, that Maurice misses me living next door, plus the beautiful trees, all cut down by the new neighbours. I so wanted the trees to remain protected, but it was not to be! The birds, so loved the rowan tree. Also, I was listening to a teleseminar where Edward Mills was interviewing Jennifer Mizell, & when she shared powerful insights about what she calls 'Evolutionary Burn Out', or a unique burnout she attributes, to those of us on a conscious spiritual, mystic path, I immediately felt inside myself, that that, too, was going on for me at that time! Thus, the energy comes through, whenever I call on it, for supporting my clients, while they are delving deep in their 'Journeys,' & for healing, but is not zooming through my body with the same force, which is why I'm so strengthened, whenever I connect to bathing in streams of Light. Meeting Sam's resistance, I found myself less centred in my Heart, with less compassion, & disconnecting from, my Joy & Ease, feeling I would not usually choose, to stay around such low vibe energy, Sam's pushing & controlling Will, complaints, his ever-present anger, frustration, very little softness, or appreciation. I am not even attempting 'Tonglen'. Yet, I totally acknowledge, how Sam's my teacher, in learning a deeper unconditional Love.

Low vibe is not bad, nor high vibe good. Simply different. Higher frequency energy is simply faster & lighter, more conscious. All is as it is. There's so much caring support for Sam & for me, in our community network locally, further afield too. I feel so blessed by Life, anyway. Life is gifting me, with whatever best fulfils, what Sam and I are choosing to co-create. No uncaring forces are responsible! I am feeling as I am! I have asked Judith for help. I do feel my rib healing, day by day, which makes it easier to breathe. I have felt saddened by Sam's seeming inability, to prepare more deeply, for his possible fast approach to leaving his Earth body.

*

Gopal Hari's funeral was a week ago, but Sam would not have been capable of sitting in the Crematorium, nor for the hours, of Memorial service & the journeys. Gopal Hari has been so ready and happy to leave, for some time, with such deep trust in Babaji. Ambika suggests my going to spend time with her & family later, though I am not sure Sam is able to handle travelling. I am feeling the need to talk with her, about what it was that exhausted her, looking after Gopal Hari. He & the family have been so much a part, of my Heart family & still are. He co-operated as far as I know, with medication, & did not attempt to smoke, nor eat, all that was most harmful in terms of health &, increased body pain. I later learned that his grumpy, difficult reactive moments, were experienced more often by Ambika than anyone else! I have always felt strong enough, to handle whatever. I am definitely meeting limits. Durgadas, Hari Sudha, Prem Das, Dinesh & Bharati all visited &, told us more about Gopal Hari's send off, the painting of his white cardboard coffin, his body's anointing with vibhuti, perfumed oil and flowers. We had already heard about the 'Mundan' (i.e.- close family mourners shaving their hair, males anyway), for Shambo, Veda, Tom, Prem Das, & Ambika, too. Prem Das helped Ambika take care of Gopal Hari for so long. It has been at least a 3yr. Journey for Gopal Hari, for his family & friends, with his brain tumour. He had been so impatient to leave his body for some time.

*

My Life's now restricted, as far as travel's, concerned. From early morning, till I go to bed, I am needing to be aware of Sam's needs & attend to them. When I do travel, there is a lot of organization involved, to have a friends' support team in place. Sam's close family plus, the palliative care team, (especially Jane) see me, his wife, as the main 24hr. Care & Support, as I generally am, except when I travel. Sam's chosen, probably because of the level of pain he is now living with, to go with the medication route, pain suppressants etc. Sam's needing around-the-clock care, yet given his lung Cancer, tobacco would be better avoided. I choose not to buy him tobacco. Such substances, are to be avoided, more so, when not in one's right mind, but still, I do not stop other people getting him tobacco. At least, Sam never smoked in the house.

Before, in my focus to invite in my new Life, I had asked for what I thought I desired, though without need, to control the timing, nor how, of this. Now I felt, I had put out such a strong prayer to fall more deeply, into Compassion, Intimacy, Trust & Love with Life, & invited Life to hold the reins, I am consequently faced with deeper challenge than I anticipated or expected, into ego-knocking shaky new territory! Having just travelled again, to work in the Mind Body Spirit show in London, to interpret Aura pictures, offering guidance.

I recommended Cha-Zey's book to all whom I thought, could be open to it. At the start of each day, I prayed to be a source, or channel, for Life's wisdom to flow, to help every being coming to me for feed-back, in the highest & best way, for Truth to reveal itself. It resulted in a lot of people feeling really met &, happy. Later I was given very positive feed-back. Even though I was tired by the 4th day, still the energy flowed whenever required, which was very rewarding. I stayed resting in the Princess Diana Conservatory, much of the next couple of days, since there was little sunshine in the Gardens outdoors. Not surprisingly though, I had to call on the A.A.'s assistance later, for the car battery or alternator, as the power had died. However, I still got to my 'Journey' client, & all worked out perfectly. With a new battery, I went early next day, to the Fruit Traders Market, then drove home, my 'Journey' appointments for Friday cancelled. As usual, after greeting Sam, I emptied whatever needed from the car, & began restoring order, in the kitchen. Sam, seeming to resent my return, began by being very controlling & hectoring in tone, so much so, that I retreated to sit in my car, with a bowl of food, feeling "I can't do this!" Help arrived on the Monday with a *Journey session I received on June 2nd 2014. While I was in this process, it seemed so deeply revealing, I even thought maybe this could be the end of my book, yet to my logical mind, as I wrote what happened in this session, it seemed this is just a deeper level of the lack of Self-Love I thought I had already met, (especially so in the session when I looked at my legless, armless, useless self, & said, "Throw her on the rubbish heap!" I still did not realize, how totally we are held in unconditional Love, just for existing, with nothing to prove nor do, to deserve this). Near the start of this latest session, my uppermost feeling was "I can't handle this!" yet the stairs were straight away, inviting me to jump down deeply, & were bathed in a pink Love light, I totally trusted. Seeing the door, very black on one side, I was aware there was great light on the other. Babaji was further back on left, my mysterious almost black guide, to the fore on the right. Judith asked if he had a name. Abdullah, came to mind, possibly an Arabic-Muslim connection. The carriage, again had wings, mating dragonflies, I realized. They made themselves solid enough to take me astride, with Abdulla's supporting embrace from behind.*

My throat felt very involved as, I kept experiencing nausea, plus strong throat discomfort. However, the Solar Plexus was where we landed. It seemed a very crowded space, full of obstacles & diagonal chutes sloping down, so I look downwards & find myself, protectively clutching my vagina, plus a memory of my mother telling me, when young, not to sleep with my hand, between my legs, as it is bad for me. I never understood why, nor ever asked! There is still a lot of discomfort &, energy in my solar plexus, right through to my back, plus nausea in my throat. The accompanying emotion is one of my pushing away, rejecting. (Though it is my mother showing up, I am aware the same dynamic operated between Sam & me, as between my mother & me, so what I pushed away in him, was the same. I 'married my 'mother' not my father,' though Sam & his family, are from the North of England, like my father was; & Huddersfield was 'by chance', my birth-place, though Cumberland my main home, for over 5 ½ yrs. anyway of my life (not the last months of 1940 and 1941, due to my mother being displaced, by War-time moving about, from Brampton to Huddersfield, then Scarborough and back to Brampton). Having my DNA heritage info. I now know the North of England, was over-run by the Vikings, which is much more dominant in my DNA than English & I suspect it is the same for Sam. In fact, when I have guided him, in past life regression, one of the lives was, as a Viking). The feeling is concentrated in my right upper-chest, like heart pain. The dominant thought that "I can't handle it" relating to my 'Carer' role with Sam, reflected the same role with my mother too! She was the child wanting my Love, but using our strong attachment to each other, to control & manipulate, so her hugs felt like steel. (Contemplating when my recent body discomforts first really began, I realize that though the recent rib damage & extreme back pain has been concentrated in the last 2 months, my first experience of cracked rib came from being hugged by Sam in my 50's! Then too, began my exhaustion, plus arm & shoulder repetitive strain, from commuting between London & Gloucestershire every week. Plenty of exhausting control & manipulative dramas too, throughout our relationship!). Sure enough, I drop next into a layer of total exhaustion & tiredness, throughout my body. I really embrace this tiredness deeply with Love, & the spontaneous words which come up, are "I really want to rest in undefended-ness." I am surprised to notice a little Fear & Mistrust arise, (unusual these days for me), & some words erupt strongly, "Who are You! to believe this is possible" i.e. -for me to rest, in Unconditional Love, that needs no Defence, - as if it is the ultimate arrogance of my Ego self, for me to believe this. A feeling of despair and deep Sorrow in my chest, feeling the seeming disparity of this Spacious, supporting Embrace of Love and my 'broken' body. Suddenly I realize how persistent & deeply embedded, is the rigidity of my pattern of "I cannot expect support from others. They have no way, to make a safe world nor, to look after my needs." Looking now at my battered body, I am so deeply aware, of how hard I have been on this body, repeatedly injuring my legs, my ribs, my back, time after time, particularly so in the last 2 or 3 months, even a week before my 80th Birthday, I fractured my wrist, never fully, (in the 6months since), recovered, though slowly I find the strength returning, I've noticed this very last week of September. So, having come to so much acceptance & self-love, a still deeper layer of that same theme, seems to be playing out, from before, I was even 5yrs. old! It has pushed & worked on my body, to be able to manage without help, ever reluctant, even to ask for directions, when travelling. My body's protesting big-time. I feel & see myself lifting, this broken body & holding her, with tenderness & compassion, coming soon after, to a deeper receptivity & thankfulness for Life. I now drop into spacious 'Isness' & I feel I have a firm, solid but alive, sort of muscle or membrane down from the top to bottom of me, that sends roots deep, deep down, into the Earth, but also upwards into the Heavens, powerful, supportive, helping my body come to healing, able to support itself, while being supported by Life's Love. Love is Here & whatever Is, I am! I feel myself prostrating in Gratitude & Awe of this Vast, powerfully loving Embrace. How are such notions, such patterns, I believed I had met & released, still exerting a hold!? At the Camp-fire of Unconditional Love & Acceptance, I invite my mother, - & Sam, since he represents too, the way my mother interacted with me, - to a Camp-fire of Unconditional Love & Acceptance. What I push against is the way they have been controlling, in a way which does not honour & respect, the value of my choices, for me. I DO NOT WANT TO BE HELD BACK by THEIR FEAR & MISTRUST! I LOVE ADVENTURES! I invite to the fire too, my friends such as Parvati & Louise, who have been destroying their health with Tobacco & lack of Self-Love. Parvati, also Jonathan, (Sandra's partner), have now stopped smoking, I am delighted to hear. Judith realizes that one reason I shy away from, asking for official support, has been the fear they would take, my choices from me. I am surprised at the thickness of the main cord attached between me & my mother, & how much anger was still in me, about her not trusting that, my choices come, from my own integrity AND, the right, to make my own mistakes as part of, my own learning and growth. My guide also cleans my being from, any persistent beliefs, about not being perfect enough, i.e. - "Who am I to believe I could love unconditionally & be a channel for Love & Presence in the World. I suppose there is a deeper layer here, of mistrust that I am enough, i.e. "I can't handle it," regarding my intention or even the strength, to serve Sam in his sickness, without a need to defend. Can I stay living in unconditional Love, Intimacy with Life, Compassion, & Connection, knowing the transience of my & others bodies & personalities as energy, simply appearing in form for a very brief time. Judith helps me install the Truth, throughout the molecules of my body, in place of any sense of worthlessness, wrongness, or imperfection: i.e. "The Gateways are open for Love, Intimacy, Support, Connection, Abundance &, Joy in being who I am. I fully accept all of myself & all my choices. My body heals, in perfect Timing." My Mentor says, "Support is eternally here from all of Life." There's now Space &, deep yellow-gold Sun rays in my Solar Plexus. The pain in my heart, & throat nausea & discomfort, are gone, plus the Solar plexus pain. A deeper Trust in Life is here. I am truly the Bigger Expansive Being, &, my body, my humanity, are included. All, is Source Energy. Judith told me a story about a lady who for many years was living in Bliss & Expansive being, then gave birth to twins who were both severely disabled. She did her best with this circumstance, but felt she could not handle such a challenge. On the point of committing suicide, babies in arms, Life called her back from this act, of choosing the death of their bodies, & she was able to hear, this would be a mistake. She found the renewed Strength & Trust to handle the Life she was experiencing. Judith reminded me, "I" (as the limited idea of who I am,) cannot handle this, but Love can! I am still integrating my not having realized, there were still more deeply hidden shades of that old consciousness, still in operation. Reminding me yet again, of the folly of coming to any conclusions, that I know anything! The truth is, although my mind could not fully understand, why this session seemed so important, during the weeks since, I have continued to feel light-hearted, haven't felt exhausted &, have renewed energy, for dealing with doing whatever, seems a priority, trusting my intuition, to make the right choices, in alignment with the flow of Life. Probably this same pattern, with my present financial challenges!

*

Soon after, I was listening to Darius Barazandeh with Rikka Zimmerman. I was so resonating with her words, to the point of tears, as it answered all I had been asking, as she answered other's calls, for help. I had wondered why this 'old' issue continues to reappear, & she pointed out that, as we move to higher vibrational levels, so we will meet next, its matching opposite, at the equivalent lower swing of the pendulum. She suggests too, that creating more story & significance around our emotions, holds them in place. It is unnecessary for the mind to know why, we feel what we feel - the body knows already &, will reveal this anyway when we look more deeply. We, are the Source Energy beyond all the separation, & can connect with Light 'brighter than the Sun'. Our choice. All possibilities are here. Regarding Body pain, it is important, not to see the body as separate. Rikka suggests speaking the following sort of words; "Thank you, Body. Without you, I could not be on this journey. Thank you for returning me to Love." What if, my Body is part of the Creative potential, at the heart of All Being, what about if I treat it, as if it is 'God,' because it is? (As is all of Nature…) I now focus on rebuilding the Body of 'God,' &, I relate to others, as 'God,' from Myself as 'God,' not abandoning Myself, to be with another, whatever challenges they are experiencing!" This is more Compassionate as, when we remain in a higher vibration, other's bodies then entrain to match **our** frequencies, better than our choosing to bring ourselves down, to a lower victim mode frequency, in sympathy, helping neither oneself nor them!!!

I have been learning that, & feel so much better now. I have found when I choose to ask for, & open to my being One with All-Being, as the Source of my support, rather than struggle, Life quickly responds, mirroring me back to myself. If I moaned or complained about the unfairness of Life, believing Life, does not love me, so it would be. The nature of this Universe is so Supportive & Generous, & when we know & open to this Embrace, it is here! We have been creating scenario after scenario of Loss Neglect, Abandonment, & Rejection dramas, through our underlying beliefs about Life, - "God's punishing me, & always lets these things happen to me," seeing ourselves as victims of an uncaring Universe. When I have met sadness with Love, it has dissolved into compassion, my bitterness or anger has dissolved into Peace, Forgiveness, & Gratitude.

Another body challenge happened 24hrs. before I was due to drive to London, when I nearly fell off, the top of a ladder through inattention, so strained my body, during the effort to save myself. Changing gears, was painful during the drive, & when I reached my parking spot outside the mosque at nightfall, my body could not fully relax on my thin car mattress. I arrived just in time, to hear the last prayer call of the day &, 3.15 a.m. was awake with the Dawn prayer call. I drove to the Traders' Market, bought oranges, pineapples, cherries, nectarines, peaches & avocados, then spent most of the day in Kew Gardens. When I 'phoned Sam, all I heard was groans & growling noises. I went to a 'Kirtana' Concert in Kew, happening in a beautiful Church, met too, some of my 'Journey' friends there. The whole focus was on Connection with, the Truth or Source of who we are, & it was good, to be in the company of, those who relate from awareness, of being Oneness and Love. I 'phoned Sam, after the Concert, late in the evening, when I had reached Nubia's, & he sounded human again. He said he had collapsed trying to get the 'phone so had not been able, to get up for a couple of hours. I got back, after a night, in a very soft, comfortable bed, & found the driving was much easier on the way back. I found Sam had been confused about meds. remembering little of any instructions, given by me beforehand. His increasing pain is not helped, of course, by his tobacco smoking, his strength is lessening too, making him more frustrated, with not being able to pretend he is fine, as he is so challenged to stay mobile.

*

I turned up at Judith's home 4 or 5 days later, as she had asked for a 'Journey' process. It turned out to be powerfully transformational, not only for her, as she found how to stay, seated & rooted in Truth, when those around us are steeped in, or relating from, the Illusory Lack & Separation mentality, but also a key one for me, in my understanding, on my own Self-Love journey. I felt propelled into a renewed sense, of Approval and Love of myself, staying free of resistance and resting in, the Truth of Limitless Possibilities, rather than getting caught in judgement around Sam, when he relates from the Density of Illusion, then judging myself, for not Loving enough! I would rather rest in the Infinite Energy of all Possibility, than energize any idea of, Separation from Source. It is not my concern nor responsibility, to Love someone else, but to Love me, without condition. In the infinity of being in intimate connection with me, there is no separation from all else. Love naturally overflows, in relation with everyone & everything. The idea of Judgement, surely could only stem from belief in, the Illusion of Separation, that anyone or anything is judgeable!! I found Rikka's Self-Love Mastery teachings, helped enormously, which felt very freeing as, I let go of long-time guilt, if I was not being loving enough. Now I am simply present, without judgement, in the flow of how it is, in each moment. I believe this guilt had maybe, created my frequent injuries & strains, during the last 3 months, inflicting further damage, on myself, as soon as the previous body pain was healed! It seems as if Sam is now meeting the pain he was so much trying to avoid, for so long, & as for me, I am meeting unseen hidden layers, of lack of self-love, I had maybe, refused to see. Such a strongly challenging journey for us both. Certainly, I had been avoiding, as insignificant, the ways I so often avoided me!! In truth, I have missed Myself, not realizing how much I mattered, ...as if my relationship with others, I felt connected to, mattered more!

*

Since the early hours of Friday 4th July Sam came into a new phase, with increased pain, much more groaning, but his body strength gone. I was not strong enough to move him, nor could he relieve his bladder, so his clothes & bedding became urine-soaked, to his distress. This continued all day, as he could not even roll himself onto a temporary mattress, I arranged next to his bed. Finally, early evening, I looked for support & called on Maurice, my next-door neighbour, as the strongest-looking nearby help I could think of. Maurice helped me remove Sam's sodden bedding & clothes, roll him onto the other mattress, after sorting out incontinence pad, dry t-shirt & sheets, then he returned to the job he was doing. I could not get Sam back onto his hospital-type bed, my body still recovering from strain, so he had to stay on his make-shift bed all night, until Dinesh arrived next morning, to help him back up. He also bathed him & changed his pad. I felt so supported by his care for Sam, I was in tears downstairs. He encouraged me to 'phone an 'out of hours' surgery number. This led to a lovely Indian lady doctor, coming to assess the situation. So, for the last fortnight of Sam's life, emergency assistance was arranged, i.e., two Carers coming in, early mornings & evenings to change Sam's incontinence pads, bedding & clothes, plus keep him clean & dry. She also gave me a bottle of liquid morphine, to add to his daily steroids, to minimize his increasing pain, when necessary. The last days he is no longer even eating, just having water. I began looking on the internet, to quickly source & order a Burial Shroud, in preference to a Coffin. Organizing a funeral began to seem daunting, but to my relief, in perfect timing, our friend Girish offered to help: "Would you like me, to be your Funeral Director?" "Oh Yes!!!" I had neither asked him, nor imagined he could. He certainly could! By Wed.16th Sam was drinking very little, though I had been giving him water & juice, but his groans persisted, even with extra morphine doses, (within safety guide-lines), with occasional stronger protests or curses, aimed at his compassionately efficient Carers, when they needed to change his pads. His breathing rhythm noticeably changed that evening. Early on Thursday, the Shroud had arrived from Devon & Sam's breathing rhythm had altered even more. Minutes of laboured faster breathing, followed by seemingly ceasing to breathe, continued as a pattern all day & Sam was somewhat removed, from his body pain, hardly protesting when the Carers had to turn him. He was more peaceful, smiling at moments, yet with a clear mind, conscious of his visitors. I had encouraged Sam's brothers & mother, to come before the weekend, since I agreed with Jane, our palliative care nurse, that they would probably be too late, if they waited till Saturday, as planned. Throughout the last months, Jane's been our most regular visitor from the palliative Care team. She has plenty of experience, with many on the Cancer journey.

Sam was fast approaching the day of leaving his body, having stopped eating for days, & taking less & less liquid. I gave him frequent sips of water, keeping his mouth moistened. Up in Ripon, North Yorkshire, Peter took his mother to her doctor's appointment, for more medication, to help her feel, less pain, on the long journey, then drove to Merseyside to pick up Neil, both having cut short their work, to be able to reach Sam, in time. Prem Dass & Narayan who had visited with Sam, earlier in the week, also came back from Glastonbury, alerted by my text. They arrived in the evening & sat with Sam. He greeted them with 'Om Namaha Shivaya,' his only words that day. His family arrived at 10p.m. & spent nearly 2 hours with him. After midnight I went to bed, slept through the thunder & lightning, but shortly after 3.30a.m.was woken by Sam's continuous rapid loud breathing. I spoke to him, stroking his face & body, but made *no attempt, to give him water as, he was not fully aware of my presence.* I went to the bathroom downstairs, did a few things, returned upstairs & found his breathing had stopped!! I called out to him, half believing he could come back. My body began to shake in shock. Of course, I regretted not coming upstairs sooner, to be with him as he left! - to remind him too, of the Love & Light he is. I sent Girish a text about 5.30a.m. & he set off to my home. About 6a.m. I 'phoned Durgadas &

Hari Sudha. Talking with Durgadas first, his voice & words helped steady me, Hari Sudha too, & when Girish arrived, his calm & logical reminder of all we must attend to that day, helped also, so I remained steady. I sent a text to Neil too, as the family was staying in a nearby hotel. They returned after breakfast.

That morning Girish took me, Sam's mother & brothers, to see the small lovely hillside cemetery. I walked up & down just below the designated tree-planted burial plots, by the wild flower section, & found a spot where I felt, the strongest energy, confirmed moments later by one, then several butterflies, arriving on the flowers in front of me. Girish continued to call relevant authorities & organize all arrangements, while relating with me, Sam's Mum & brothers with care, sensitivity & openness.

After Ruby, (Mum), Peter and Neil returned to North Yorkshire, I was left with Sam's cold, stiffened body, which I washed with warm water, perfumed with essential oils, massaged too, the skin of his fast-decomposing body, with lovely scented cream, as it seemed appropriate to honour, the physical service given by this real/unreal body. I was going to search next for his passport, medical card etc. but then thought, 'No! Time to stop, just sit, be, & tune in to surrounding energies. Quickly my whole energy field, my awareness, expanded, & I felt strongly the presence of many beings around me & felt lovingly supported by this. All was, is, good. At 4.30p.m. the mortuary 'chief' arrived first, to clear the way, for Sam to be carried to their Ambulance. With the continuing hot weather, flies had already begun to show interest, in the body. Sole had arrived too, & agreed to return to help me, the following morning, with whatever will be needed, especially for the altar she will prepare in the venue (the British School) for the 'wake'. I showed her the beautiful Shroud, lying by my bed &, we sat & shared thoughts, for a short while. She & I watched Sam's body removed discreetly, on a wheeled stretcher, to their Private white Ambulance, to wait in the mortuary till Wednesday. The morning after, Saturday July 19th 2014, my mind is grappling with the reality/unreality, of Sam's identity being no more. One third of my life in my role as Sam's wife, with our character traits, tendencies & interacting patterns, my ego self has related to Sam as such, being Real. My mind is having difficulty believing this is no more. Though if Time is an illusion, who knows what is true!

I do not know if I am adequately conveying the shock of, making sense of, or processing, this transience of form. Although it is part of every moment, day & night all around us, we stay somewhat removed, creating distance from really seeing the continual decay, 'death' & transformation, of all matter. I feel now, that in praying to come into deeper intimacy with Life, I have been gifted with more intimacy with Death. The decay process is in truth, just as much about life & movement, just the forms have changed.

I had felt, he zoomed off fast &, it was not till Sunday morning I got a sense of Sam being nearby. The impression I had of him, was of his dancing, light, more expansive self, a mirror of the photo's I had chosen for the Burial day leaflet, quickly being designed by Joshna & Rama. I guess he approved of my choice. (Joshna had arrived, the day after Sam had left his body, to pick up photos of Sam, when I had felt too tired, to properly focus. Rammiel arrived later, having given up his Swansea job & flat, prior to starting his new Bristol job on the Monday. He sent a more appropriate photo, since Joshna had chosen one, of Sam busy on his Organic stall, his (4yr.) job. I knew he had felt challenged & burdened, working so hard, with heavy crates, to lift. He would have found it a struggle, not to escape, for frequent tobacco & coffee breaks, his normal pattern.

I received so much support, offered so willingly by so many. Much of this is thanks to Girish, who played his funeral Director role with impeccable efficiency, in his organization of details, with real sensitivity & dedication.

Today Wednesday July 23rd 2014, Girish came with me to the Mortuary, to retrieve **Sam's body. The decomposition process was more advanced, green areas** around digestive area, blue nails, red areas where the blood has coagulated. (I asked David, taking care of the mortuary, about the colours, fascinated as I am, about the death process). As I watched the morticians dressing Sam, in the silk shirt & 'lunghi', I had chosen for this occasion, I was curious about how the main mortuary director, David Baker, had been drawn into this, relating with death as his work, as I felt a relaxed, good energy from him. It felt inappropriate to ask at that moment, but Girish afterwards showed me the book 'A Life in Death,' David had written about, his life as a mortician, which I later read.

We gathered up on Minchinhampton Common, sitting in the sun and grass, till Girish said the timing was right, to proceed to the cemetery, after which shuttle drivers, our neighbour James & my daughter Samantha, directed by Ish, brought the other waiting participants, from the Common to the Cemetery, in turn. What to say about the ceremony, which was very beautiful, simple, sacred, held in a very focussed way by Girish's 'know-how', & Hari Sudha's music from the harmonium, plus everyone being mostly very present, attentive, honouring of Sam & each other. For me it is wonderful, when so many people, from so many different life-styles & beliefs, can come together with common Purpose, plus an overflowing of Love & good will, without the barrage of the million distractions and habits. Relaxing into being oneself, & connected in common purpose & Oneness. Flowers, sunshine's warmth, yet high enough on the hillside for freshness of air. Narayan & Durgadas played a big role, in the ritual aspect, with Joshna recording many moments, with her camera. Some of these, I will add to this book. So many offerings from the Heart, by so many! Thank you, Girish, Ish, Rama, Joshna, Samantha, Peter, Neil & Ruby, Narayan, Durgadas & Hari Sudha, Rammiel, Prem Das, Sole & all of you. I gratefully acknowledge the amount of support for Sam & me, too, throughout his physical challenge with Cancer. For me, this came into its intense phase, in a more noticeable way, since mid-October 2013, when he became more incapacitated, & I was effectively needed in the Carer role. It has been a gestation of about 9mths. till his Birth into the Life he is now experiencing, wherever that is!! 5 to 6 yrs. later, I would be at Narayan's send-off, his daughter Joy present, in Glastonbury, with the Tor in the background.

In the process of sifting through a roomful of Sam's belongings, no longer of much relevance, since he has stepped away from playing that identity, I am aware of a parallel dismantling, of my own ego identity structure. Who am I now, what Life expression will emerge? A sense of release, relief, as well as appreciation & gratitude for Sam, & our long, testing journey, on our return to Love. We have been so lost in our roles, our identities & patterns, uncomfortably comfortable, forgetting we were limitless Being, playing out a human story, in dense physical matter, a transient universe appearing from Space, from the Quantum field. I learned to really love my body, my humanity, & our essential innocence as, we comply, fitting in rebelliously, with what is demanded of us, - in order to be accepted, as more loveable! Our parents or elders did the same. Time now to bring everything back to Love, into more resonance with less limiting possibilities. Both the transience, the fleeting, ephemeral nature, of dense illusory matter, (slowed down to appear as linear), yet the eternal never-dying creation, & real nature of it all, has been brought into my foreground at this time. What mind boggling, intricate games, we create in our divine interplay. Continual expansion, to continue bringing in, ever more possibilities, more of me to Love, play with, enjoy, living in a world of infinite having, of everything already manifest, & Source expressing, manifesting, whatever we are ready to meet or receive. Enough of believing in the old stories, the old dreams, yet, though I am stating my choice to come into limitless Being & Love, that which I truly am, everything that is not that, seems to be meeting me, showing up to be healed and released!! More about that later in the chapter.

*

On August 19th I drove to London to park by the mosque, & was at the Traders' fruit market by 5a.m. When I had bought fruit supplies for the month, I set off for Nubia's to take her the avocados she wanted. I was driving down the Western Avenue, in the right-hand lane, by the central barrier, approaching East Acton, with all due attention, in anticipation of the extra right turn lane. A big white van came alongside on my left, then attempted to cut into my lane in front of me, without my having any way of knowing, his intent. The result was 'his' breaking off, my front bumper & lights on the left, leaving them trailing. It felt shocking to my body that sound, of breaking car. (It did enter my mind, this might be a faster way of a new car coming to me, since my beloved 'car home' was beginning to show rust, & was becoming costlier to maintain, & I had been feeling a new car would soon be needed)! There was no point in stopping, since the driver had got in front, & kept going, ignoring my nearly continuous hooting. In fact, other drivers too, seemed to pay no attention! Many on their way to work. I certainly noticed all the stares directed at my car, after I turned to drive through, a pedestrianized area, to Nubia's home. There I 'phoned the Metropolitan police, & also called the A.A. rescue service, hoping the car might, be sufficiently fixed, for me to complete my visits to friends, do my 'Journey' 'work', spend nurturing, relaxing time in Kew Gardens, & visit Samantha's house on my way back. Instead, the A.A. man reckoned my car was a write-off! He took off the whole bumper, put it in the rear of my car. When I asked about being relayed home, he told me my breakdown cover did not include accidents, so I would have to pay £417. I had not realized I could have asked my insurance company to do this. The 2nd A.A. driver picked me up at a Service station about half-way (I was told 70 miles is the limit for each driver), but he, opted to tie the bumper back on the car, & told me to drive, & he would follow behind. We passed by my local garage. They agreed the car was not worth repairing so, that was my last journey in it! A few days later, when I had visited Sole, she had offered me a chance, to be the Journey practitioner, in a new healing venue, planned to open, near centre of Stroud at the end of September, (which never happened)! The very next day, I was going up my ladder, in order to bask in the bliss, of lying in the hot sun, on my shed roof, when a rung broke, exposing nails which, as I fell, tore into my leg. Rammiel took me to St. Luke's surgery, as I really did not want to go to the hospital. Luckily a new lady doctor, plus a nurse, were still there, & though it was past surgery hours, they were totally ready & willing to stitch up my leg. Life seemed to be saying 'Stop!'

*

One focus had been, a Self-Love Mastery Course, moving too, into an Advanced Self Love Course, which took me, into deeper intimacy & love, with the 'All' of my true Being, with my Body, & deep acceptance of my humanity, plus increasing disconnection, from my Illusory identity. My friends continued to offer me lifts to the surgery, twice a week, & wherever else needed. With all these recent body shocks, feelings of not being so safe, had arisen, so I felt very ready for a 'Journey' process, & Judith agreed to come the *morning of August 22nd*. We can enjoy the newly cleared space in Sam's room, no traffic noise, sunshine streaming in, garden, tree, & bird energy through the window. *My prayer is, to come deeply into Unconditional Love, Compassion & Intimacy with all of Life, & to meet & let go of anything in the way, of total love & acceptance of my body, my humanity, & living in love with my true being. The steps down are defined & black on the right, yet lacking in solidity on the left. Easy to go deep. The door is very large & has windows in upper part through which, I can see much light on the other side.*

*Interestingly, my guide turns out to be, a **tall, goddess-like being, with ornate clothing & head-dress, seeming energy-wise, to rest in neutral equanimity. No judgement of good or bad, or of emotional turmoil, & not even vocal, when addressed, though responsive in her gestures**.*

*The vehicle to transport me into my body is more of a car, & ends up in the left part of my chest. The ribs appear as, fragile latticework, easily broken. The two recent accidents, have shaken my body-sense of safety, & though I still feel how much, I am supported, yet the feeling of being exposed, to unknown danger lingers. Nevertheless, I easily drop from there, into an expansive darkness, though feel a little lost. I am aware a golden light is, reaching down, which is restful, so I deeply let go. A potent moving force draws my attention, and I have very little sense of any solidity, or form, but sense I am all this energy, vast beyond imagining, full of possibilities ever-birthing, in never-ending Presence. A great sadness arises, like my heart is breaking, at my sense of separation, but here in this vast presence of Love, judgement does not exist. I relax into simplicity, humility, & humour, no pressures here to be anything, nor prove my worth! I begin to sense form too, amazed by an unending kaleidoscope of forms, textures, colours, shapes, different temperatures, densities, all disappearing, letting go of one form, ever reappearing in, yet another form. Always I have been fascinated, by inner vision mandalas, & one facet of Source which I love, is this display of Divine order, symmetry, & geometric patterns, infinitely intricate, constantly shifting. All happening Now & Now & Now. Our human creations, seem to birth with struggle, resistance, effort, plus an illusion, of lasting endurance, as we hold on, exerting control, to try to make it so. In the 'camp-fire' part of process, my belief shows up that, I can never be 'right enough', yet I quickly realize, that also, I **do not have to display wounds**, to be noticed, or worthy of attention! Maybe important too, to cut the cords, of identifying with my last year as Carer, with the exhaustion, strains, accidents. Sam was no longer able, to offer any support nor, relate from his higher Self, caught rather in Pain & fear, seeking escape in food, tobacco & treats. Yet he **was** more able to accept support, as he could no longer pretend, to be independent &, not needy! Me too!*

I sense our programmed mind beliefs &, the consequences thereof, are already all forgiven, - everything is, in truth, already as it should be, already all right! My presence, is enough & matters, & is no more important than all 'other' Presence. It all simply is. I now state "Others love my simplicity of being & feel, more intimately connected with me" as, increasingly, I certainly do with them.

Such a miracle of constant re-creation infinitely, intricately, beyond physical seeing, sensing, or mind's understanding. Yet still we attempt to control, manipulate, trying to shape events, according to stubborn wilful intent, rather than let go, into the vaster flow & intelligence, of Creation. I have felt lighter since this session, the heaviness gone, more bubbling sense of Joy, Play & Humour, more present & accessible. Still more to come I sense.

*

I was rocked for a day or two, on receiving a copy of the insurer's letter (on my 74th birthday 25-10-14), regarding what his client alleges! He is telling blatant lies, which may mean, I will never recover, the thousand pounds or so, taken from me as a result of the accident, yet these thoughts just pull me, into victim mode &, the illusion matrix of drama. I surrender attachment to results, & stay in trust, of Life's support & love, & the truth of my expansive being, & so feel more empowered. By today, Oct.28th, as I have been releasing places in me, that still held sadness, anger & pain, at not mattering or, being loveable enough, I have now been able, to thank this unknown driver, for triggering whatever in me, was not wholly returned to Love. Once I am fully living as, expansive expression of Love, that is what will be mirrored back to me. I am glad the lessons are being resolved, very fast nowadays. How does this story of that year's events in my life, relate to the Chapter heading of '100% responsibility'? I believe it highlights, how choices made every moment, stem from Fear or Love.

*

Self-Love, is the most important Journey for me, for you. People have this strange or false notion, that Self Love is wrong or, conceited, as though it were better to, pour criticism or scorn, on ourselves. I categorically claim, one cannot love anyone, while we still live in a world of judging & comparing ourselves, or any 'other' self, as inferior. Whatever in us still resists, will continue creating scenarios or opportunities, where we can choose again! Choose Love! Will we choose what stems from Truth, or from Illusion stemming from, the belief we are Separate, from all else that is? Stuart Pierce, is a wonderful guide, Merlin, one of his mentors. He mentioned how it is the British Press, who tries to emphasize a rift, untrue - between Princess Diana's sons.

Our stories have been forged at times, in a crucible of pain, in the discomfort of emotional dramas, induced by, old programmes & beliefs. More peaceful to rest in knowing, that we are, & always were, enough, & sit in the neutrality, that judges nothing, as wrong or right, surrendering to, what meets us on our path. 'What's in the Way is the Way' - Mary o' Malley - the great title of a book I have read, long ago. Interestingly, approx.7mths. after the process where, my Goddess guide had sat in balance, an observer of 'good and bad' without judgement, three incidents happened within 24hrs. reminding me of her. I had watched the total solar eclipse, in Stroud, for over an hour, as the sky took on a darkening glow, until the sun's return, in full brightness, then travelled later that day Fri. March 20th, to the Somerset Levels, not far from Glastonbury, to Hari Sudha & Durgadas's home, for Navaratri. This is one of the oldest rites, & began, in tune with tradition, with the new moon. Ritual offerings are made into a special Fire, representing the mouth, of the 'Mother,' the smoke taking the Mantra prayers, into the Sky. It is a very focussed time of sharing sacred rites with others, with the Music, Love, mantras & prayers bringing many blessings. During morning Aarti, as I gazed at a picture of Babaji, I could see & feel, a swirling of cosmic energies &, felt so grateful for the immensity of Babaji's Love & Compassion. Sunday eve, after Hari Sudha & Durgadas had left, for their gardening work, in Tiverton, I stayed on (with their son Bhushan too), as Tuesday, I was to offer Journey sessions, to a couple of my friends, who were on a visit, to nearby Glastonbury. One of them, unable to willingly handle her pain, preferring to keep it stuffed out of sight, to better enjoy, her break from work, <u>got angry with, both me &, the process</u>, knowing anyway, I would not take it personally. That same night I had an unusually vivid, strong dream, of being in a Manor House, full of hundreds of people, in vast grounds. It was night-time, & whatever the event, it was over, and people were making their way towards exits. I had noticed tense groups of brown-skinned men, seemingly on the verge of, offensive action. I thought they could possibly, be Muslim terrorists, & decided to move away, as fast as I could, but was on foot, & though both my sisters were there, they had no car space. I tried to cross over, a well-lit small road, but noticed a group of these men, stopping cars, so turned to run across a vast dark lawn. Looking back, I saw a short, stocky, strong-looking, very dark-skinned man, in my pursuit. I turned empty-handed, to face my attacker, feeling somewhat impotent, as he caught up with me, in this 'kill or be killed' scenario, other than to possibly, aim a knee in his balls. **He swung a weighted sack round, which hit me hard on my lower back, causing so much pain**, that though I did not fall, it woke me up.

Again, I felt no animosity towards my attackers &, as I was taking Behru the dog for a walk, maybe an hour or two later, I was asking myself, "what would Love do?" My mind went, to Krishna & Arjuna before their big battle. Arjuna does not want to fight, his friends & relations on the opposing side. Krishna helps him be aware, of the true nature of the play, & that one does not have to feel hate, or hostility to fight well. Sometimes knowing how to be a good fighter serves, even as we may realize we are, in truth, all One. The human drama is a Dream, stemming from, our having forgotten, our divinity & eternal nature. Returning from my walk across the big field, I saw a very irate man striding towards me, who <u>berated me, in very strong terms, with trespassing on his private land & grass lane</u>, also for having no bag to deposit dog-shit. (I had not yet joined this dog-walkers world, where carrying bio-degradable pooh bags, is normal). This in a huge field, used by cows, sheep, rabbits, foxes, badgers etc. but he was insistent, his animals, could be infected, (by my animal's faeces), thus, having to be 'put down.' Clearly, I was not appearing, sufficiently cowed or subservient, as I stood observing, his angry stance, since at one point he said "this is no smiling matter!" I felt as in the recent dream, & Journey session, innocent of any crime, or hostility. A 'Test?' <u>these 3 events within 24hrs</u>.? I had stayed, I felt, centred in equanimity.

The best thing about coming into a new relating with me, especially my body & humanity, is that I have a new best friend, who is always here, if I do not abandon her! Where better to have a friend. I still find I need to remind my body, my human self, to relax, to know there is no-one, outside of me, I must tense for, or be different for. I have been on alert, for threats from outside, for most of my life. Given an environment of such tension, thankyou body, for serving me so well. I am more than OK, more than enough, in every molecule of my being, every facet of my humanity, to be here for me, let go into me with, relaxed unconditional approval. As is everyone else!

I was now regularly, looking in a mirror, to speak aloud consciously to my body, as if to an honoured & loved friend. To tell her, her body, personality & 'soul self, she can relax now. I love her… As a child I explored why I was not happy, but at 74yrs.old, when I was writing these words, my world felt transformed. It has been my conscious choice, to let go of the baggage, of programmes which, may have served me in the past, but no longer. Lifting, any lids of limitation in my life, cutting the cords with illusion, so, though I have taken but baby steps, I have been choosing to let go of suffering, rather, to know I am held in Love's arms, able to trust Life, & to enjoy the moment. Increasingly I am relishing both my time alone, aware how I can behave so much more freely now, plus the increased Connection & Love, I feel with others, since my Love with me, has deepened. No pull to engage in the emotional dramas, I see so many people immersed in, (except fleetingly maybe?).

It is amazing how we humans, imprison each other, with so many expectations around what choices, we, or others, should make, how we should look, dress, think, even feel, or which behaviour we can exhibit, in order to be more acceptable & loveable. In fact, we are broadcasting our beliefs, negative or positive, out to others, without even saying a word! These mores, considered essential, for survival, are passed down through families, tribes, communities, from ancestors, or, as in other species too, the new-born are taught by parents, leaving deep imprints, which may differ probably, from the Soul's blueprint encoded in our being. Being multi-dimensional, eternal beings, unconstrained by time & density, what a strange choice it seems, to have choose, to be contained in a body, with so many challenges & seeming limitations. It is fun to play in a body, with gravity, to climb, jump & dance, or to use our voices, in song, paint murals. We can develop so many skills, play as actors in so many roles, in one physical world, life-time. What a wonderful world, especially the magic of Nature, to explore, far beyond, what we thought possible. Bodies have their own consciousness & evolutionary cycles. In truth there's, only present time, yet we can be affected by, the shadows & emotions, of every time, by our ancestors' experiences too, so it is good to release, from our cells & memories, all that is holding us, in any limitation or pain, maybe allowing more exciting possibilities, - a deeper relaxation.

*

Back in Nov.2014, I had travelled to support 'newbies' as a 'trainer' for 3days, at a Brandon Bays Intensive, plus Satsang with Brandon the day before. I took time to enjoy Kew Gardens, afterwards, before gathering supplies in the Traders' Fruit market & seeing also, my 'Journey' clients/friends. At the Intensive, we trainers are given too, the space to swap processes with each other. I was glad to receive a more in depth one, on the *Sunday Nov 16th*, which mirrored changes I had experienced, since I came into different relating, with my body. *We chose to do a 'Physical' process, & my initial prayer continues, to be to meet anything, in the way of, loving myself more totally. I seemed to be very ready to go deeper, as I had to drop-jump down, even to reach, the top step, as if the stairway's, already suspended in the dark depths. Unusually, where the left side of the stairway has usually been, more ethereal, there were solid black bannisters, on both sides, a very safe stairway. I drop down deep very quickly, yet must drop even deeper, to a sort of underground cave, where I find a bright yellow doorway. For the very 1st time, it is opened for me. My Soul's a blaze of colourful lights &, to the right of these lights is Babaji, dressed in black, as my guide! Our magic vehicle, is a black-winged fly-like insect, which expands as we enter it. We travel into my upper chest, but I feel a strong energy link, with face & throat. The ground seems like, boggy peat-land, quite dark all around, in this part of the heart, I think of as, the universal love area. Also, my throat feels tangled up. Two images surface, at the same time, one of me as a baby, & in the other I am 2yrs.old, both screaming in the dark, for my mother, angry that she chooses, not to respond. We place the images up on a screen, to be seen later, meanwhile setting up, in this upper chest area, a Fire of Unconditional Love & Acceptance. At the fire, we have my present-day self, Babaji, my baby self in Babaji's lap, my 2yr.old snuggled at his left side, & my mother. My present-day self suggests which resources would have been good at the time: i.e., Relaxation*

Remember my Clear, strong Communication Protection

connection to Love Knowing I am totally Safe to be Me

My young selves, breathe in these qualities, return to the scenes on the screen, & report, how it is now playing out. My baby self can relax, in the Love, feeling her connection with, angelic energies & guides &, is happy 'alone'. However, my 2yr.old still needs to return, to the camp-fire, to express her rage at her mother. She wants to kick out, stamp her feet, to shout out loud in Spanish at 'Mama', that she does not love her, because her mummy's not listening to her. My mother explains why, she held herself in, such tight control, not always able to respond to what I needed. She was afraid of falling apart, losing control, terrified, near breaking-down point, - as a refugee from the Spanish Civil War, then alone with us, while our father, is fighting abroad, in World War 11. (Not only was my father fighting overseas, but she had been alone with me, later pregnant with Carmen, not speaking English well &, both the landlady in Scarborough & my father's relations refused real help. They were harshly judging her, because she was not an English mother, & certainly they did they want her, with one young child &, pregnant with the 2nd one, in their homes). So, remarkably for me, as that young child, when I ask my mummy whether she loves me, her response is an immediate real, warm, reassuring, loving hug, such as I never remember receiving, in so visceral a way. I felt so held & loved, by a real mother of flesh & blood, maybe because, now I feel so much more connected, with my body, & my vibrantly alive & sensitive 2yr.old. Reclaiming now, more of my real, alive, blissful state, which is my true being!

Our bodies serve us so well, never ceasing to restore us, to balance, if given the chance, given our choices. Yet we chose to live, in such defended, limited, contracted, ways. I am choosing, to open more fully, to who I am in truth, at the pace I allow myself! Also encouraging others, even more, to come back home, to this in themselves; who we always were, & forgot, getting swallowed into, the Dream of separation, thus suffering, grief & pain. Enough already! I asked Babaji to cut the cords with, the old story, spring-cleaning out of my body whatever, I am ready to let go of, including the War consciousness, (or dreams). Part of my prayer has also been, to come into fuller expression, beyond my present comfort zone, so Truth can be spoken with, full power & vibrancy, joy & play too, from my Heart. I find, as I look around my upper chest, the light's now here, & reaches up through my throat too. The boggy peat, has new young shoots, springing forth, with vigour & light. I feel my face is beautiful, & the final message is "Dare to be more fully yourself!" My body needs to be helped back, to full strength, exercising more, than happened recently, particularly in the last year, when I suffered so much strain, & 'accidents'. It became so habitual most of my life, to prove my worth, showing my capability, by treating my body, - with pride! (my car, too), like work horses! Such a hard time my body has had, (probably for many other lives too, as I have identified with, having lived many former, peasant lives!) Now I feel strengthened, by my mother's love, in a new way. I felt supported previously, by her generosity with gifts, food, money, but now it is as if my child self, is really mothered, for the first time, rather than my feeling, I had to take care of, her neediness. Sam's too. More balance restored.

I believe Rikka Zimmerman, **has** said that, all giving & receiving is 'manipulation'. Rather we simply, fully Be the Expansive Bliss & Joy of the All that we are, forever allowing Love's unique expression, through us, like a flower in perfect bloom. This, is the greatest gift to All!

Driving near London, Dec. 2014, feeling so grateful for Life, for Existence, aware of the Awesomeness of being alive in such a Multiverse, I became finally aware too, how habitual it **had** been, to wear a 2ⁿᵈskin of low-level depression, most of my life. This seemed so normal, I had not even noticed till now! Almost like a veil of fog. In tandem with releasing, my 'damp fog' of that low expectation, that I could find fun & love, in the adult human world, I had a nose-blowing kind of cold! This would usually be over in 24hrs. but this time went on for weeks, though I bore in mind, all the year's strains & accidents, plus some eating of congesting type, cooked foods, & less exercise, (Sam and I, used to enjoy days, of walking the old 'rights of way,' after Sandra & my long walk, across the land, but he did not have the strength, for the last couple of years). Now my Exhaustion is leaving, I am expectant too of magic, beauty &, all manner of things to enjoy. I let go quickly too, resisting & judging whatever! I have been cutting the cords with Illusion, to be free to create new possibilities, rather than being controlled, by limiting beliefs! I intend to open new doorways, for me & others, to abundance! Financial too? Not surprisingly, lightness, playfulness, joy, or fun has been somewhat low key, in my earlier reality. There is a magic feeling, of excited expectancy now. Whether or not, there is an immediate money flow, in my bank account I feel abundant. My Insurance claim for compensation, from the white van driver, is at a stalemate, what with his dishonest denial, of having trashed my car, police disinterest &, lack of witnesses to help. I totally felt the shock in my body, plus my mind's disbelief, as my car body, was being broken apart in front of my eyes, by that very van. I have also used my entire bereavement payment, plus any remaining cushion of funds, on the new car, so I have been left this Christmas, with an emptier bank account, sometimes overdrawn, & yet, how can I know the whys & wherefores! Concurrently with any lack of help from my 'Insurance company,' (on the contrary they contributed to my emptier bank account, to my astonishment) - serendipitously, my sisters & I, plus our Spanish cousins, are due it seems, to inherit funds from Maria Luisa, the Spanish Aunt I never met, since my fascist uncles, kept her locked away, from 18yrs.old till old age, in a home run by nuns, because of her crime, of having a baby out of wedlock. I could attach meaning, about my worth or love-ability, with either circumstance, (i.e., whether money goes from, or comes to, me), having since very young, expected disappointment, rather than Joy & Love. However, I have consciously been releasing, those sort of, judgements &, conclusions, choosing rather to allow my fun-loving, uncontrolled, joyful, child-me to surface, letting more suppressed excitement & laughter bubble up, to warm my heart & blood, & stir my aliveness. Nowadays, I enjoy so much, to see my playmate, best friend me, in the mirror, to Love, because Love is who I am. Knowing it, brings a growing delight in Life, and me. Thankyou Life. In fact, before my 75th birthday, October 25th 2015, the other driver's insurers finally, paid up, as did my insurance company, so all is complete, plus the inheritance just arrived, in time for my birthday! Now it is up to me, to allow Life's expression, to create new streams, of income. It is a relief, to be more of, who I am, no pressure to be anything different, allowing easier access, to higher planes of light, an accelerated opening of my heart too, & a deepening Peace & Stillness. Glory Be! I think I expected Love, to be deeply serious, not delightful & fun, as if our nature was not, to be playful! See any undamaged child, (not programmed enough yet, to be caught in beliefs), how they love, to have fun with others, with themselves, with leaves, grass, twigs, all of Nature. Nature's Intelligence is, intricately part of Creation, so never, ever, could we be separate, from her play in our bodies, in the elements, in all of matter. Without Nature nothing, including us, can be manifest! All of it, our very embodiment, starting with an idea, a zillion chemical interactions, mitochondria, stem cells, such magic weaving & co-operation, involving millions of cells in each body, by all Being, including Nature Intelligence. How can we treat Her, Gaia, with such ingratitude & disrespect, so little Love? Honouring Being me, as the All, is wondrous, while honouring too, the body I inhabit, the personality ego mind role, I play, plus every other varying personality, each with our peculiar programming, from family, ancestors, DNA, culture, religion, education, with our resulting Diversity & conclusions, our many, many co-creations, plus mistaken, constricting opinions. And yet, we are fearfully using such a small part, of our potential. sharing one another's left brain, limiting logical beliefs, not realizing how utterly Joyful & miraculous, Life could be! Once we are more aware of our multi-dimensional true nature, our life trajectory will be stirred, by more expansive vision. I feel no loneliness. It is enough now to be me, which includes everything & everyone, & thus so enjoy, my many friends, my sisters, daughter, my son, all my human family, all of Nature, & multiverses in ever-changing, expansive

Creation. It could be, I would one day invite the intimacy, of a Soul-mate physical lover husband, as a play-mate friend, yet not out of any idea of Lack! Next life is soon enough for me! This is not a priority in my life. I love my freedom! There is such a taboo about being truthful about our sexuality, with all the shame which has surrounded Women & Sex. I was slow to learn about, my own sexuality, & realize I have never truly felt intimately met, as I had not even honoured, nor ever communicated what I would like! In fact, I have lost interest in having another male partner! I feel delight, with myself & if, I suddenly feel or choose to pleasure myself, I do.

*

As incarnated Soul Expression, from the Love & Gratitude, in the Heart, of so many of us, who were awakening, in the Global Spiritual Community back in 2015, we were being called, in an increasingly purposeful way, to help the many, still caught in suffering, pain, & the drama of, the Separation Dream. Time to cut the cords with the Past, old repetitious stories, to restore balance & harmony on our Earth, for the good of All of Life. It had been such an exhausting and, stressful expression, of who we are (not)! The whole World is within Us! Love it All. There is an epic struggle & delightful awakening, happening for humanity, as we move from Fear, into Trust of the Love &, Support, in the Quantum Field. The Forces of Light, born from the Dark of the void, 'Let there be Light! It is expected by many, that by 2025, higher dimensional awareness & our approach of harmony in every country, will be apparent. This is a time of such rapid acceleration, we need to stay in balance by spending time in Nature, honouring our wonderful bodies, which welcome our total Love, deep rest, exercise, nutritious food, letting our action follow a path of Joy, expressing from Being, & knowing ourselves as One with All of Life. Thus, we move from selfishness to Selflessness, knowing Oneness with, every_molecule of existence, in every form! Maybe, maybe, it is time to wake up to the 'All', the full unlimited Potential, the Love we are, were, & always will be! Then we will tap into the other 75% of the brain!? In 2020, it was a time of extremes. The latest pandemic disease, labelled Corona Virus, or Covid 19, with all this internet hype, it is said many people world-wide, have been dying, though I suspect it is contagious through Fear, as well as the effect. of so much low-vibe processed foods &, of our destroying so much of our natural world, so many species of plants & creatures. Destroy Nature, we destroy Us! Our population was decimated by the Plague, so by 1400, it had halved, so I have read. Aids was another such time, of reducing the population, plus Ebola, at the appropriate time. There is no end to Life, just we move on to new experiences, new forms, yet because of people having, long given over responsibility, for their health to others, plus the power of belief, there's world-wide controlling measures, on free movement. It has been a crazy time, of having to wear masks, covering our air-passages, in more confined areas. I suspect all the craziness, is having to show itself, before we come into, a more enlightened cycle of time. I am expecting bigger shifts towards harmony & hopefully our Earth home more healed, of the damage done, by 2025.

I have mentioned how it took me, **till** my **70ᵗʰ Birthday**, to fully realize, I did not feel I was enough, nor loveable. This led me into knowing, how important it was for this to change. I would tell myself, daily, - body, personality as well as my infinite spiritual Being, with full focus, I love you, until finally, I truly did come to love me. As I have come to deep trust & surrender with Life, all is now truly deeply transformed. As this is constantly mirrored back, I feel deeply grateful & infinitely blessed. It is 2022 now &, I not only intend publication of this book, but I recently finished translating, Lolita & Kenneth's War-time letters, from Christmas 1937 until the first days of June 1946, from Spanish to English, & already have over 1,136 A4 pages on my laptop & have completed my task, - except to get the 5 sections, bound in folders. I know my parents much more intimately, than I ever did previously!

I do not know, if it was in order to heal, or bring more balance, regarding my deep rejection of the orthodox medical establishment, but in January 2017, I had manifested a worse accident, standing on the arm of a chair, jabbing at a smoke alarm, to try to stop the sound, which hurt my ears. As I found myself falling backwards, I was thinking 'This doesn't look good.' When I landed, I did not know, but my left hip was broken, (the opposite one to the hip I cracked, falling down a tree, when I was 12 yrs. old) &, I could not move my left arm. It did not seem to belong to me.

I managed to shuffle backwards, on my bottom, to lean against a chair, & reach my left pocket with my right hand, for my mobile. That very week, I had considered, not carrying it, on my person, as being preferable, health-wise. I hesitated about calling 999, but seeing no other recourse, I made the call, then thought of 'phoning Ish, (who works as an ambulance driver). I said, 'Ish, I'm in trouble.' He sent his downstairs neighbour Bea, plus his daughter Ananda. It was somewhat humbling or embarrassing, as what had happened was, that the only wood I had, to get a fire going, in the stove, was damp, from the garden, but I had attempted anyway, to get a flame going. Instead, smoke was seeping out, but I had needed too, to go to the toilet, yet before I had even finished wiping my bottom, or flushing the toilet, had rushed to open, the outside door at the back, to try to silence the smoke alarm. The last time the noise was set off by smoke, Maurice from next door, had stormed around saying, 'What's that terrible noise' in an annoyed voice, so I was rushing to avoid a repeat! I had to ask Bea, after she & Ananda arrived, if my bottom was alright &, would she please flush the toilet. She stayed with me all day & followed the Ambulance in her car, until Rammiel was able, to come to the Gloucester Royal Hospital, about 6p.m. after work. It took a month, before I was back home and, I then had to use a noisy 'Zimmer frame' for 2 months before I could walk around Stroud without. It had wheels only at the front, as they thought, I should ask for help for shopping, which meant the other two legs, scraped very noisily, along the ground. I now have a permanent titanium plate, put in place, to hold my left hip bones together, while they've re-bonded. My dislocated left shoulder, also healed during the 2 weeks in 'Gloucester Royal' plus a further 2 weeks, in Stroud Community Hospital, a much smaller & more relaxed hospital. So, I made my peace with, the medical world, though refused all medication except 2 tiny white bone pills, I thought would not do, too much harm. I learnt to walk as quickly as I could, with a tripod wheeled frame. I deeply honour all the nurses, from so many Countries, who are so over-worked, yet underpaid. I had a lot of visitors, as well as Rammiel, almost daily, who brought me plenty of raw food, so I ate only a limited amount, of hospital food. The doctor's last words to me, were, 'I know you'll please yourself anyway!' (- as regards taking pills' etc). The last days, they put me in a room with attached toilet, on my own, as I was quickly more independent, than the others in my Ward. One of them had died, while I was there. Maybe I needed this experience, to recognize, that the orthodox system has its' place &, does perform some necessary or helpful, procedures. Though still I believe the body's immune system, is compromised by synthetic drugs, & know from my many years, handing out drugs as a Carer, that taking these unnatural remedies, weakens the body's immune system, with many unpleasant side-effects. I still have never knowingly, taken any antibiotics, though after a day or so, of being admitted, to Gloucester Royal, I was wheeled to the Operating theatre doors, & though watching very closely, (on guard!), have no inkling, I received any injections, nor other medication, prior to entering the theatre, yet, only came to awakened consciousness, after I had been operated on! If they injected me with anaesthetic, prior to my being wheeled off, I saw nor suspected, anything! I woke up after the operation, in a recovery room, with a pleasant, Spanish-speaking male nurse, before being wheeled back to my bed, so how was I 'knocked out? I did receive blood transfusions the next days, so no doubt lost a lot of blood. I had some minor accidents in the following months until I said; 'Right! That is enough of accidents.' Well! Seems not, given the latest one!

I did enjoy living alone in no.18 Slad road &, was living very much, in Surrender & Trust, but was obliged to sell my home of 25yrs in September 2019, to become free of the yoke of the Mortgage & other money debts. However, living so deeply in Surrender & Trust, I was offered a home, the other side of my neighbours, a totally unexpected & welcome blessing, which moved me to tears. The only condition, (I think because Penny had seen, the mural, I had painted in my bedroom, on wall & ceiling), was to paint a mural, in their bathroom, which I was still completing, when life took a different turn. It was somewhat testing, & did take humility & continuing trust & surrender, to find myself beholden to Penny & Guy, whose house I found myself sharing, with Boosh a she-dog & Beatrice the cat, I really loved. I served & supported them the best I could, regularly taking Boosh for walks &, when Penny & Guy went off, on adventures, caring for the house, Boosh & Beatrice, plus whatever other support, I felt able to offer, whenever. I was deeply blessed myself, by that interaction.

*

I am coming maybe, to the finishing reflections of this book. Though my story is different from yours, still in truth, my story is yours, & yours mine, yet no more significant, than the story which might be told by any part, any molecule even, of the whole. Every cell has Conscious awareness, plus more or less light. The mind, in the world of duality, cannot even conceive of the magnitude, the wondrous mystery, of an infinitude of different planes, dimensions, microcosms & macrocosms, universes, galaxies, wonderful geometry, black holes, shining Suns, & planets, -The Quantum Field. Via Stargate energies, I have been connecting with other dimensional Beings, plus a huge family of Beings around this world, especially for our more recent, 'Becoming Super Conscious' gathering, & most recently in 2022, 'Journey into the Void', via 'The Stargate Academy),' (with whom I have connected for years). I am in a very new, seemingly permanent stage, - now approaching October of 2022. An expansive & warm, Heart love, felt strongly from sacrum, to throat especially strong from sacrum & solar plexus to throat, moving upwards I trust, to radiate out from pineal & pituitary glands. Having felt this now, for so many months, when I went to Olympia M.B.S., on Good Friday, I was happy to receive confirmation of this, in the Aura pictures, gifted to me, (once our re-vamped aura camera, was working)! One before the opening of the Show & the 2nd, more of a rainbow colour, at the end of the show, which though very different from each other, rather than the predominant pink & white of the 1st one, showed the shift, in what I can contribute, from my being. Thanks, from my heart, to all the Guides I daily connect with, for what has become a persistent warm Love & Joy, radiating out. It feels to be a true blessing. There is a 'Super' intelligence, which encompasses endless Creation, but given free-will, our ego-centric interpretations of reality, are led by such very limited concepts, better to avoid 'the News' other than 'Positive News' or 'The Light.' (I did watch the whole burial ceremony after the Queen, left her body. A very special event. I think she was aware, she was leaving for, a more expansive reality). Here we are! In a holographic 'reality'! Yet even so, the Illusion too, is a gift to ourselves. Plus, everywhere else, everything else is here too! Those maybe most widely known, who have mastered manifestation, in this Earth reality, are Sai Baba, or 'Yeshua,' - as the Essene Community, called the Christ), manifesting physical objects out of 'space,' with no difficulty! We are facets, of the One. We are playing with a 3rd dimensional duality or free will, experiment, plus beyond. There are even darker 'reality' worlds, than ours, I've understood, from my reading, but it is a holographic game. We do not really die! Recently, I have been connecting with, the Unicorn World, or the 7th dimension. I have connected with dragons, for a longer while. I am reminded of the 1st lessons in 'A Course of Miracles' workbook, e.g. "Nothing I see.......means anything" or "I have given everything I see......all the meaning it has for me." Our minds try to maintain control, to keep us safe, busily interpreting everything, based on, past conclusions & beliefs, doing the best job it can! It is my job to honour & reassure the mind, for doing its job so well, knowing too that any belief system, however 'logically good' or well proven by experiment, it may seem to be, given the nature of the mind, with its' logic, doubts & fears, is still by its nature, a limitation on, the infinite possibilities, within the All. Until enough of us evolve sufficiently to make more inspired choices, from compassionate wisdom. More women & men are learning to honour & nurture each other, co-operate, make choices that are beneficial for all of life. I prefer to live in Love, Joy, Fun, Ease &, Lightness, while fulfilling my Soul Purpose! I stay in a balanced, non-judgemental place, at least **almost** always, (though to my surprise, I had an unwelcome experience, a couple of days ago, with Jos...! I have not wanted to see her since &, resented her preaching)!

I am aware of the magical, rich beauty of Existence, yet not attaching significance to any circumstance, in the sense of making anything, mean that, I or any 'other,' is more, or less, of value or loveable, in the eyes of 'God'! No longer giving energy to the world of conclusive opinions, - (I like Kenji Kumara's phrase, 'enchanted neutrality).' I have mentioned often, our essential innocence, yet I will emphasize here, that until I came to truly Love myself, this acceptance of my total innocence & acceptability, was more shaken by challenges, or re-assured by 'preferred' outcomes. Now, the Trust that I am totally, unconditionally Loved, & am here to play my unique role in this world, stays steady. Cha Zey, left her body & returned, so many times, I wonder if she is still on planet Earth. Dr. Edwige Bingue, was existing on Earth, yet almost between worlds too, I love the dark as an equally potent force in the Creative Play or Dance of our dimension, equally a gift & blessing, on our journeys back to Love. I must add, that since in truth, my essence contains the whole Multiverse within, I am 100% of the time, 100% responsible for creating my Reality.

I will have taken 11years, by the Winter Solstice, 2021, fast approaching, to finish writing this book, except I am forever adding & deleting! As I contemplate why this book got written, I can come to no conclusions, other than, it was communicated to me, in my dreams, which I trusted.

It seemed the book asked to be written. Maybe I am 'singing my song'. *A bird does not sing because it has an answer. It sings because it has a song'.* - Chinese proverb.

No real ending to this book!

A Mayan guide, Ja Karuk, pronounced Ikarook, was introduced to me in one of the MBS shows, maybe 18yrs. ago. (His picture re-surfaced a few weeks ago, from my storage container). I am told, this delightful guide, has come to assist me remember, who I really am &, who I was before, I came to Earth. He links me to, an incarnation in his culture, the Mayans of South America and, whatever knowledge & wisdom, I acquired in that life-time, is a resource, I can tap into NOW. I am a deeply caring, compassionate individual with a powerful healing ability. I emanate, a healing energy from my aura, wherever I go &, to please feel good about myself for this! I am also highly psychic & intuitive, so to please TRUST, HONOUR & VALUE myself for these gifts. My guide wants me, to really nurture, my sense of self & well-being &, to do things that bring me Joy, for this is probably the most important thing I can do for the planet right now, for we are all one &, what I do for myself, I do for the whole! Become an expression of Joy & celebration of the 'divine' spark that is ME! I feel a strong link with him. He does look a delightful being!

Well, I am doing all this, these last months in a strong way. Celebrating & emanating the **Joy/Love/Healing I am**, & this, as an expression of the divine spark within. Ja Karuk *also* links me with my Star families, with whom I will re-unite after, the great 'shift' (Ascension). I think Ja Karuk, is impacting me now, more strongly, as my energy has become more powerful these months, in my impact in the World. He says each time I look at my guide, he will activate my own natural psychic ability, which can alter my perception of his face. I will see his expression change & at other times, other guides or loved ones in Spirit will reveal themselves! He will also transmit messages to me (often through my feelings) - so, to keep a diary of his transmissions. Enjoy my Guide! (Bright Blessings Nick Ashron). This picture was given to me in 2004, & only now in 2022, am I consciously receiving the blessings, from following the instructions given, &, though I have been living all the time, for many months now, physically feeling the impact beaming out, from my sacrum up through solar plexus, a huge warmth which beams outwards so strongly from my heart & my throat, my hands too as, whenever I raise them, the healing is pouring out. The day after I wrote this, I spent some minutes, looking at Nick Ashron's picture gift of Ja Karuk, & for the first time, felt my energy extend down, from my sacrum, first down to my genitals, then straightaway connecting me, with a 'whoosh' to my legs, & rooting into the Earth. So, he really is a gateway for me! I have felt this healing energy in my hands, for many years, now it is beaming out from my whole body.

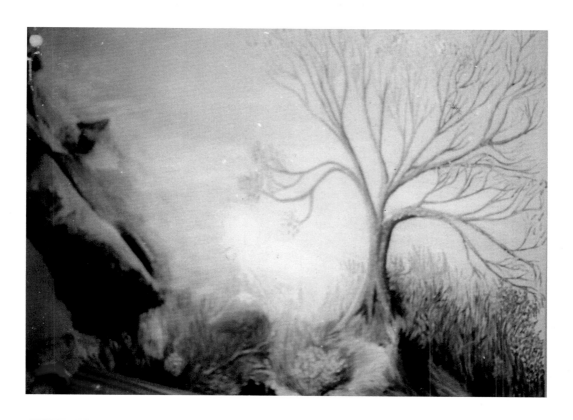

After-words or re-cap

Overview of what I have realized on the Journey

The Winter Solstice of 2012 was a turning point, where many of us were moving out of the 3rddimensional forgetfulness, of who we are, our bodies carrying cellular memories of the many traumas, not only from this lifetime, but from our mothers' lineage, our fathers' lineage, throughout aeons of the play of interconnected roles, & that is only on Planet Earth! Past Life traumas too! We have been playing many, many roles, as 'goodies' & 'baddies', in a dense, heavy vibration, with ideas of lack, fear & suffering, experiencing the whole gamut of emotions, based on the delusion, of our separate identities! Thus, so much comparison & judgement, greed, control of others, plus habitual recall of past pain, & focus on future suffering, kept us often, in self-attack & torment. Since there is only this moment, you & I, have the power now, to choose to surrender to. whatever emotional state is passing, whether, or not this feels pleasant. Fighting or avoiding, the emotion that is here, merely exacerbates it, or sends it underground, to gather hidden strength. Whether it is anger, joy, sorrow, tiredness, compassion, or fiery resolve, none of it is our identity, & all can be welcomed, with Love, allowing it to quickly dissolve, as it will, if not clung onto, nor resisted! The Journey's one way, to meet in perfect timing, whatever needs to be met. So many new healing systems too, are being directed to us, in these times more than ever, by so many beings of higher vibration & light, as many more of us, are waking or, are awakened from the Dream. For myself, I, plus thousands of us, around the Globe, consciously choose to connect via The Stargate Academy, for daily support, with each other, in meditations. The Alcazar group's wisdom, is offered daily, reminding us of truths about who we are. There has been increasing acceleration in the teachings, in the recent months-long 'Becoming Superconscious,' & the next phase, 'Into the Void,' has followed. I will add the following short Alcazar statements or quotes, (there is a daily quote sharing wisdom from the Alcazar group of Master Beings) - 'Creation happens from the

Quantum Field. Creation is in the Quantum Field. We are always in the Quantum Field, & are part of the Quantum Field, blinking constantly, in & out. As soon as we get to know our whole Reality, our whole ability increases, to have more influence, as our life experience gets stronger & stronger.' Alcazar has encouraged us, to periodically, connect with, floating in the void, & pause with hand on heart, upon waking & before falling asleep, & remember who we are. I am here, remember me. I am now truly in an ongoing remembrance, of warm, constant Joy/Love, always present. As we open to Love's voice, we awaken to our true nature, to who we have always been, and evermore shall be!

Also, the more aware we are, rather than driven blindly by our past Earth history & beliefs, the more we can consciously energize what fulfils our Soul Purpose. Approaching the mid-2020ies, this long, often painful God-play of experiencing ourselves in so many roles, is heading closer, to final completion! At least of these more challenging times, by at least 2025. I look forward to experiencing a time of Harmony, world-wide! It is time to realize, we are parts of the All, nothing solid & permanent, other than Love. Alicia Power too, is an in-depth guide, with her powerful inspiring, Spirit Creator Guides, whose words I enjoy hearing. 2032, the year Diana Coopers angelic messengers, have foretold harmony world-wide!

From 21-12-2012, increased Light began to pour in, with many further increases of Light since. Much letting go & releasing of the old, continued the next years. These recent years, many of us have come more firmly, into our sovereignty, & power, to play in the greater fullness as the Galactic Creator Beings, at One with this Source, we always are in Truth. The old games we thought normal, must end, before more damage is done, to ourselves, & all else, in our world, by fear-based, short-sighted linear ideas. Earth & Sky's rumblings are gathering strength. When we/I have enough inner knowing, that we are not our story, not our habitual identity, not our beliefs, nor past, nor, our passing often addictive, habitual thoughts & emotions, that rather we are One with a Vaster Ocean of Consciousness, the Void, the blackness of the Quantum Field, of all possibilities - deep inner commitment becomes possible, now in each present moment, to choose a happy, consciously empowering present, any attachment gone, to our unconsciously created past story.

It is essential, to come to truly Love my/yourself, without condition. Loving anyone else without judgement & comparisons, just will not happen, if there is an inner critic 'on my case'. I will feel less at ease, safe in my own body until, I first come to, an utter acceptance of myself, my body, & my emotions, my being exactly as I am, maybe pausing to remember, & direct loving thoughts to me, & when I do not, loving myself anyway.

We got used to trying to avoid ourselves more than anyone, in countless ways. It is a great gift, to extend loving kindness to ourselves, the more the better, as part of all of creation. A powerful practice is to speak appreciatively daily with ourselves, in a mirror! Until we recognize who is in the Mirror!! This, nurtures strength of Love for both oneself & all 'Other'. Recognizing too, my & everyone else's core Innocence. Be the Love! Supposing it is finally time to let go of the dream of separation in our Lives!!!? Maybe, ... May Be, it is the time to wake up to the All, to our full unlimited potential as Galactic beings &, be the Love, we are & always were. Knowing ourselves as Love would include total surrender to the choice we made, to play in the dream of separation, in order to experience all, & thus contribute to the Collective, the gift of gathered wisdom, from the many roles we have played. It is all perfect. Years ago, I stuck a quote up on my kitchen wall, I copied by hand from 'A Course in Miracles'... - ' The world around you is, exactly what you have had in mind. What you carry in your mind about your life, is exactly what you will see in your life---- Change your mind about what you hold in mind about the world---- Think about what you are going to think about. Think on things good and wondrous.

To be totally accepting means not to quarrel, with what is showing up right now. It means not to reject it, nor throw it back or walk away from it, but embrace it, hold it, love it as if it were your own. Because it is your own. It is your creation with which you are well pleased – unless you are not. If you are not, you will resist owning what you have created, and what you resist persists.

Therefore, rejoice & be glad, & should the present circumstance or condition be one which you now choose to change, simply choose to experience it in another way. The outward appearance, the outward manifestation, may not be altered at all, but your inner experience of it can, & will, be changed forever, simply out of your decision about it. Accept everything therefore, as the divine manifestation of the divinity within you. Then you declare yourself to be its creator, & only then can you 'uncreate' it.'

Being sad or horror struck at seeming 'tragedies' or 'unfairness,' adds to the horror & sadness, & sucks us too, into a dis-empowering belief in the dramas, the passing mirages. Choose compassionate equanimity, rather than the Fear, of seeing ourself as a victim. We are here to experience everything, &, love it All! Feeling one should not be happy while others suffer, adds to the world's misery!

It is perfect to radiate the Joy of the Love & Light we are, to help all return to Love. There is a gift in every present moment of our lives. Awaken to this moment. Our intimate relationship with Oneself, our inner world, nurtures this Love & our Oneness with the Heart of All, Here

& Now in the Present moment, which then reflects out to All. Love rather from Fullness, with oneself, than try to grasp this from another. Never can we relax in Joy of Being, if we are looking to be filled by, someone else's love, measuring whether to give or, withhold, receive or, defend, manipulate & control. Relax rather, delighting in the fullness of our own authentic, transparent expression of the Love we are, without apology, with nothing to prove, nor need to hide, nor posture. It does take the time it takes, to move out of believing we are separate beings. Often, we felt not able to trust anyone, any 'God', even anything outside, the limited scope of our senses. We take the time we take, to deeply know that Life, Source, whatever name you prefer, has always loved every created being without condition. Life very generously, gives us more of what we nurture. If it is debts, we will get more of them, if it is fearful thoughts, we will be given more to feel fearful about. If I truly wish to create another reality, this can be energized by a strong inner commitment, to choose focus on Love, & Gratitude, if I delight in having more to love & be grateful for! Knowing this is who I truly am, I can expect a Joyful Life, expect Miracles.

The more I Trust Life, the more I feel ever supported. Such overflowing Gratitude, Love &, so much more energy becomes mine. It is exhausting, takes so much energy, to resist and fight life, keeping life-negating habits in place. This neither serves me nor you.

Here is a great quote from Ramtha, from 'A State of Mind – My Story' by JZ Knight; She asks, "Does God judge us?"

"God, that which is the Is, is without judgement. God be that which is ongoing Isness. Eternal 'Everness.' God is the Isness which allows that which is creativeness. It be you, who judges you, entity. It is you who judge people. It be you, who must live on your own path. Everyone's path be that which is different."

"So, what you are saying is that I and each person decides whether something is right or wrong?"

"Indeed! There shall come a time when you will understand that all life is only an adventure which endows you with wisdom, and it is the wisdom that will make you as I am."

"And what are you Ramtha? I mean, really?"

Ramtha laughed. "I am God, as you are. Indeed, I am the manifestation of the Father, as you are."

"So, I've always been right in believing there is no such thing as the devil?"

"Indeed."

"So, the others who believe in the devil are wrong!" "No, entity, they are right in knowing that. That be their desire. God allows all desire, thus there be no wrong or right, or that which is good or evil…only there be experience."

"But what kind of world would we have if nobody believed anything was wrong?" I retorted. "Indeed, entity, what kind of world do you have now?"

*

Forgiveness is important, first forgiving oneself for, whatever happened in the past, & for whatever we resist, in the present. Holding on, to resentment or grudges, harms oneself more, than anyone else. Inevitably, sooner or later on this journey home to myself, I will realize that the way people react to me, the way my life is happening around me, **maybe** has something to do with my own attitude, behaviour & beliefs. Although it took me, years of inward Journeying sessions, to fully realize & know, that I created all my inner distress, affecting my level of abundance, health, & whatever happened in all my relationships, now is an optimum time, for much faster change & realizations. (Certainly, my husband Sam, began to relate to me in a very different way, (before steroids), because I was no longer the same person. He listened respectfully to me, and I to him). I always was 100% responsible, for co-creating my world of 'reality', more so, than I fully realize even now! Transformation could otherwise happen much faster, beyond measure, beyond anything yet imagined, even instantaneously, faster than I could maybe, integrate or, rationally comprehend. Yet I have learned to trust there is a right timing, of all events, bringing me to recognize the gift of each moment, that earlier I could not see was indeed, a gift! Meet what wants to be met, what longs to be accepted & loved. Let go, relax, enjoy. Be willing to allow even any self-created monsters, to lose their 'death grip'! All is Energy, endlessly dissolving & re-forming.

I like how 'Larry Crane' phrased this, the (delusional), ego-mind is simply a 'recording.' Because we embodied false programmes so long, from the womb onwards in this & many lives, it usually takes committed practise, to leave old rigid thoughts & emotions, where they belong, in the past, & be guided daily by a deeper, more conscious, choice. As the Heart opens, more energy is freed, & Life becomes 'wonder-full'. "Life is a Gift, enjoy the Present." Be Here, NOW! Taste the Nectar, the many flavours. All enjoys being met, & loved. Even after I was more or less, neither internally nor externally, creating suffering, painful, fear-based scenarios, still my birthing into, what feels to be a much more magical Life, opened wide, more immediately after, I had fully met Panic held in my body since before Birth. I could then, quickly let go & drop easily with the surrender of a new-born babe, into helplessness, compassionate acceptance, & Love, root deeply too, & relax into the Potent Creative power, the Ground of my Being, into the Safety & Ease of being One with Life's expression, growth & flowering. No longer now from a place of wanting to be in control, except to choose where & how, to direct my energy, which thoughts I prefer, - to be in alignment with my vast infinite Self, expressing from the Love, the Truth, the Beauty, the Fullness, of connection with All I am. Be more of who You Are, & always were, less of who you are Not!

No-one is an exception, no-one unworthy to be included in Life's Embrace. As soon as you know this, Life will reflect this back a hundredfold! Until you find & Love 'You', nothing can truly change in your life. Everything else outside is transient & will not bring lasting Joy nor fulfilment. We are looking for what is immortal that is only ever here, in this moment. Fun, Love & Joy can be found with others, but only when all you seek is already here within you! Truly we are, galactic, eternal beings. My life had transformed, three months after my powerful June 2013 re-birth, in so many ways. Since we are all One Body, this energy surge, is particularly powerful, when we are really meeting ourselves, with a strong intent & commitment, thus at the start of a Journey, I would feel how strong the process will be, my focus being, to bring each client to live, in the truth of who they are, leaving the illusion of wicked perpetrators of their suffering, & victim roles, of separation, self- judgement, self-hate, & lack behind. Much more fun to enter the real wondrous world of Joy, synchronous Miracles, Connection, Love, PLUS Energy! It is exhausting to keep patterns of resistance to Life in place, so much energy locked up in knots of contraction & tension! Yet still, if tiredness, panic, grief, despondence or WHATEVER, should arise, choose to welcome this moment & love it, rather than attach to, identify with, or push away what is here, or attach meaning about our worthiness to be loved! This allows faster change, faster dissolving of emotional states. Our daily exercises, focus, or practice, can remind us to stay aligned with more of the Truth of who we are, a Channel for Love, for healing Life 'Chi'.

I have included with my photos, & pictures, six of the men, of more significance in my life, from my first to last sexual partners, up until now, - my 81st year. (Or at least whichever ones my editor allows)! These days, I must say, I enjoy having no sexual partner. I am intent, on fulfilling whatever I feel is to be my Soul Purpose... so, - Miguel, shown with his steel drum, was a gentle, caring, first lover, whereas Bob, my 2nd boyfriend, seen next to my daughter Samantha, in her wedding photo, was quite a challenge. He was more damaged by his past. Martello my son's father, is a good man, seeking his true home, outside of himself. May he realize his true Source, while still in his Earth body! Max, was a long-time companion, in our deep exploration of physical healing & inner self-knowing. I introduced him to the widely known spiritual teacher, (in the sixties onwards), 'Krishnamurti, - who wrote books & offered his wisdom in person, in large gatherings, & introduced him too, to Luis Kuhne, regarding Nature healing, such as, - fasting, enemas, raw food, steam baths, living close to Nature sleeping out, swimming in natural lakes, eating wild food, fruit from the trees, before the days of, so much poisoning of the land, & Max remained my friend until his death. He failed to live without eating physical food, as he hoped to do. Berris, it seems was my deepest love. I periodically, still have significant dreams about him. With Sam, I experienced my most challenging relationship, from the end of 1990 until 2014, when he died. Maybe he best served me for inner growth!

(Jungleyes, a close friend till death, was rarely caught by a camera. We explored the world of psychedelics & read stories to each other. Durgadas is also deeply in my heart. Must be a lot of past life connection. These last 2 were not sexual partners). Of course, I must add Mo, Im or Mu, whom I now imagine, I have known in Lemuria. We both read my book 'The Land of Mu.' We have helped each other on our way, from the 70ties onwards, I believe, - yet. beyond the planned ritual, on the Winter Solstice, which included sexual intimacy once, initiating me, after 5years Celibacy, back to appropriate sexual relating, - our friendship is not a sexual partnership. Changes his name, every so often, as I have!

Asara Lovejoy's book 'The One Command' six steps process, is also a powerful tool, I enjoyed for a year or two, - (I had bought 4 or 5 copies of her book, of that title, to share, as it is an in- depth manifestation book, simply & clearly written). The 6 Steps are; - Ground, Align, Command, Expand, Go to Theta, Receive with Gratitude. As soon as I focussed even just on the 1st step, I'd feel deeply rooted, even embedded in the Earth, so blessed within her Love & support, my Love for Gaia, & quickly aligned too, with the 2nd step, (though over time these two steps quickly merge), so I feel myself part of, all the elements, sky light, Air, Fire and Water, connected too, with fertile nurturing soil, crystals, stones, with plant life, trees, the animal, insect and bird kingdoms, yet with stars, planets, universes, and Cosmos too, knowing I am all of it.

I briefly started to train too with Gerald O' Donnell, who is a powerful guide into limitlessness possibilities. To think that, before my sixties & 'The Journey', despite all my many previous trainings & explorations, I had never really accepted my being incarnated in a body, & though I felt safe with Nature, was very disconnected from my Being. It took many Journey processes of becoming more connected with my essential self, & finally too, with all other human beings, to be glad & grateful beyond measure, for Life on this planet, feeling part of all Existence &, really loving myself & all 'other'! All disconnection gone. I have noticed as my relationship with Life has come to feel so intimate, my very breath, & every passing desire or thought, is known, is Life in fact, & everything takes form faster, with the help from Love & Light! I truly marvel at how many 'nature beings' & other forms, we do not often see with 'normal' 3rd dimensional senses, must be constantly adjusting form, as every change of vibration & resonance in someone, brings immediate change in the Reality field!

Marci Shimoff, (who wrote 'Happiness for no Reason', & 'Love for no Reason'), suggests useful fast techniques for coming back to Love &, expansive Connectedness... such as breathing into the Heart, with hand on Heart for some moments (from HeartMath).

Allana Pratt reminds us to live in Fullness as part of our sexual nature, especially, as women, intimately receiving Life with every breath, as we move and interact, - 'making Love with every particle of 'God' energy' (my words). Becoming fully alive, feeling the deliciousness of being, and sensing the true nature of All. Coming to ever more Joy, Ease and Safety. Every Body a beautiful expression of Creation, enjoying each other because we enjoy ourselves! The end of Competition with others!!

Rikka Zimmerman, a delightfully, inspiring teacher for anyone preferring to live in Love, no longer willing to feed Illusion, ready to leave belief systems & discard limiting stoppers! Michael Beckwith, Matt Kahn, Panache Desai and Jo Dunning speak with humble simplicity, from Heart Being, in Truth. Increasingly more awakened beings, are here to help this shift to Harmony. Mahalia Michael, too from her home near the Pacific Ocean, & Ameera Atlantis. She mentioned a War which happened between Lemuria & Atlantis, which made me wonder whether that is why, I have always felt I was in Lemuria, yet I have not felt so, about Atlantis. You will find, which teachings resonate for you, whether from 'outside' or within. Lester Levenson's Release technique, then taught by Larry Crane, is a fast, helpful kind of 'Journey process', of surrender to emotions we are resisting or trying to get away from, or avoid in a thousand ways. A quick way of realizing, we are the creators of, our experience of it all! - either unconsciously, - many still live in this Reality, or consciously, which can lead to a life so blessed by Joy. As Souls from the Quantum field, having lived in many dimensions, the Pleaides, most recently went through, what Earth is now experiencing, so I have heard. Reading people's aura photos recently, in 2022, in the MBS show in Olympia, I notice a general shift to deeper inner focus, thus increased light, in their photos!

Meg Benedicte is, for me, an ongoing guide every month, to journey, with many others, to higher dimensions, Alicia Power, a favourite guide too, who for 30 yrs., has been a channel for, very high Creator Beings At present, I most often join the Stargate Academy meditations, guided by Alcazar, & the Elohim (council of Angels) through Prageet, Julieanne, plus support from, many high dimensional beings. Sometimes I listen to Kryon or, Asil Toksal, & sometimes they offer a meditation, where they have come together. Best of all, we can re-connect consciously with our own Quantum field multi-dimensional 'Self,' plus welcome close, those guides, whom we have felt strongly in our Hearts, on our path, such as, for me, Haidakhandi Babaji, Gezra, Lu Yin, Saint Germain, Dragons, Cobras, most recently, Unicorns, Nature Beings including too, Bees & insects **&, Ja Karuk**.

I was so blessed in London, (the last week -Dec.28ᵗʰ & 29ᵗʰ 2021, for a hundred or so of us to meet, for a week-end, free of masks, so much love, openness & gratitude between us. Deep beautiful meditations & sharing, hundreds more participating online globally, raising the planetary vibration, speeding a global shift

for our Mother Earth. For many of us, there is much less focus now on imagining we need fixing, aware rather, of miracles of Creation, overwhelming wondrous Beauty, the intricate, inter-related harmony & vast cosmic order, together with huge volcanic explosive Power, & immediate grand scale disruption, - all possibilities, especially re-connecting with, or remembering, the Source being we are! The game of playing victims & perpetrators, through countless lives, is coming to an end, thus we can stop feeding fear, being greedy for profit at Planet Earth's expense, though shadows of these may still arise. I have found myself healing, many victim scenarios from other of my lives.

Love, our source potential, really is, **Everywhere**, whatever illusory shows appear. Dis-ease or resistance to Life, comes from unawareness of our true Nature, which simply is, & depends on no doing, simply reflecting our relationship to Universes, to Love, to macrocosms & microcosms, -no-one else to be, nothing to get, or do, in order to Be, rather **remember**, the one Being we are!

'I finally understood that *being* was only possible when you can accept that it does not entail being anything in particular. That really this is the most beautiful way of being anything at all. That the abandonment of the eternal chase for recognition and confirmation is a decisive condition for the gaining of peace.' Quoted from 'The Seer' by Lars Muhl. I am aware too that, to fully reclaim our true galactic heritage, this does involve emerging into the unknown, from our cocoons, even as we glimpse the possibility of the freedom of flight! I was reading very recently, 'On Mortality', written by Atul Gawande, son of immigrant Indians, and a Surgeon. He writes with much insight & compassion, on how sick, mainly older people with challenging body symptoms & dire prognosis of expected outcomes, are treated as mechanical bodies, to be kept alive at all costs. Little attention paid to how, especially as Physical death might be approaching, or even if, they would prefer to live their lives. Some caring, imaginative people have had innovative ideas which have so improved the quality of, people's daily enjoyment, that they started to enjoy, to be alive, bringing healing results.

I will finish this chapter with a longer quote from 'The Messengers', a true story about Nick Bunick & his colleagues, written by Julia Ingram & G.W. Hardin, a powerful Tale indeed. - from (Chapter 5): - 'Of all that is held sacred about humanity, nothing is held more so than free will. In all human history, there has never been an incident, a story, or a legend in which the will of man has been usurped by Heaven. In fact, legends intimate, that the fallen angels rebelled against the divine plan, that put human souls bestowed with free will, in Oneness with Christ. It is said that the angelic realms constantly gaze towards the face of God, dedicated totally to Divine Will in all its manifestations. But humanity? Humanity can stand before God with an arrogant "No!" and leave the Creator with no choice but to allow us the consequences of our own decisions.

How many times have humans wailed in their own darkness over the horror of wars, over the inhumanity of humanity, over the fate of nations? How many times have we heard "How can God allow this to happen?" when the real question ought to be "How can we *not* recognize our own role, our own responsibility?" We are inheritors of the divine. That is how sacred our own free will stands before the cosmos. That is how powerfully we shine before Creation. And if we choose to destroy ourselves and the Earth in the process, then so be it. The divine experiment of free will shall simply fade into oblivion, forgotten like a bad dream.' I am deeply grateful, knowing myself as ever-present, ever-radiant, Heart-warmth of Love/Joy. Namaste. I bow to the Divine in you.

****

Resources

'The Journey'; - www.thejourney,com-infoeurope@thejourney.com
****

'A Course in Miracles' text and workbook, - (Volume Three is a manual for teachers) ... Inner Peace Foundation - a deeper look at what is Real.
****

'Anastasia' series; written by Vladimir Megre, originally self-published in Russia, (authorized English version published by Ringing Cedars UK Limited). Phone: 0115 9738 073
Online: www.ringingcedars.co.uk -Mind & Heart opening
****

'The One Command' by Asara Lovejoy - great manifestation support
****

Machaelle Small Wright -Perelandra 'Garden Book'- (originally books 1 & 2), for energy processes for working with Nature Intelligences. Her 1st book was 'Behaving as if the God in All Life Mattered'. Describes the beginning of her evolving relationship with the Nature beings.
****

G. Scott Sparrow ED.D. -'I Am with You Always'- True Stories of Encounters with Jesus
****

Haidakhan Babaji
UK link for Haidakhan Babaji news & practices: - pujari@ombabaji.org.uke
Jasmuheen: - 'Living on Light' - Breatharian
****

Michael Werner: - 'Life from Light'- Breatharian - described by Thomas Stockli
****

Michael Roads & Carolyn: - www.michaelroads.com, email: carolyn@michaelroads.com for news, Publications, CDs, Events schedule. Also: - enquiries@pinealpress.co.uk metaphysical journeys with Pan & Michael (Mixael). Mind and Heart opening.
****

Osho formerly known as Bhagwan Shree Rajneesh- great mystic, inspired teacher. (His initiates were called sannyasins, not the traditional sannyasins who renounce the world, rather encouraged to live totally, but with awareness, 'an initiation into innocence.' He wanted a religion that was free of superstitions). I was blessed to meet him on my Path.

****

Ho'oponopono...'Zero Limits' by Dr. Joe Vitale and Dr. Hew Len PhD - Taking responsibility for one's own part in creating the reality in one's world.

****

Louis Kuhne & Benedict Lust: new edition 'Neo Naturopathy' - The New Science of Healing or the Doctrine of the Unity of Diseases. Gave me the tools to Heal myself & continue to take responsibility for my own Health.

Gurudas: 'Gem, Elixirs and Vibrational Healing'.

****

Candace B. Pert, Ph. D: 'MOLECULES of EMOTION' WHY YOU FEEL THE WAY YOU FEEL

****

Barbara Wren, 'Cellular Awakening' -'How your Body Holds and Creates Light'
(College of Natural Healing) – healing in harmony with Nature in rhythm with Nature and our bodies. New book 'Our Return to the Light'

****

Frederick Leboyer: 'Birth without Violence' (first published in France (French ed.) in 1974, UK and Australia in 1975(English ed.) ...a gentler way to welcome souls into life in their new bodies, water births, allowing them to emerge into semi darkness, silence and peace – no slapping, bright lights, loud noises, nor cutting of the umbilical cord before breathing is established.

****

Edna Wright: pioneer of childbirth teaching, empowering women to again be more self-responsible, giving birth more easily, using breath etc. at a time when male doctors had taken over so much control!

****

Anaiya Sophia: Womb Wisdom. Honours the Divine Feminine Sexuality.

****

Baba Ram Das: 'Be Here Now', 'Be Love Now'. Shares his journey to Love.

****

Brockwood Park, (UK) co-educational school inspired by Krishnamurti's vision.

****

Stephen and Ondrea Levine: 'Embracing the Beloved' -Relationship as a Path of Awakening, also meditations, CDs, and many other books. I found 'Soft Belly meditation' good, surrounding pain, grief or whatever strong emotion shows up in the belly with a soft belly rather than contracting or avoiding. (Katie & Guy Hendricks)

****

'Rafael Medical Centre Ltd: (Address) - Hollanden Park, Coldharbour Lane, Hildenborough, Tonbridge, Kent TN11 9LE. Neurological hospital, both Steiner and orthodox medical procedures. Shamanism - Rebekah Shaman – 'The Shaman's Last Apprentice' & 'Beyond Illusion'

****

 T Centre www.thetreeoflifecentre.co.uk plus info@treeoflifecentre.co.uk - (Block Clearance therapy),

****

Scenar: Originally developed in Russia, by an elite team of doctors and scientists. An effective solution was needed for their cosmonauts to treat any condition that may have arisen. They needed a device that was lightweight, portable, would run on minimal power, be exceptionally medically effective and require minimal training. The result: S.C.E.N.A.R. Technology (Self Controlled Energy Neuro Adaptive Regulation). Scenar blueprint based on Acupuncture, Chinese zonal massage, and knowledge of the energy (Chi) flow, through the body. Soviet scientists who studied the Central Nervous system and the ability of cells to communicate via different pathways, began to formulate ideas that would lead to sophisticated electrical biofeedback devices. They are effective pain removers and stimulate healing in a vast range of disorders.

****

Milton Hyland Erikson -(05-12-1901-25-03-1980): 'Healing in Hypnosis' Milton Erikson specialized in family therapy and medical-psychotherapy. He drew attention by his approach to the Unconscious mind, as creative and solution-generating. I valued one of my teachers, Pamela Gawler-Wright, founder of the BeeLeaf Institute for Contemporary Psychotherapy. Its work is grounded in the ethical and therapeutic application of Neuro-Linguistic Psychotherapy and Eriksonian Hypno-psychosis. She is a sensitive, wise, and intuitive teacher.

****

Richard Gordon – 'Quantum Touch - The Power to Heal', 'Quantum Touch – The New Human', 'Quantum Touch – Core Transformation' – 'Hacking the Law of Attraction' - latest

****

Deepening Connection with one's true Essence or Source:

'The Journey' -Brandon Bays brought me & many, many more to this effective way of coming home to, remembering, the One-Self we always are.

Must mention Mary O'Malley and her book -'What's in the Way is the Way', also Larry Crane, (who learnt from Lester Levenson), - and Matt Kahn, Panache Desai, Amean Hameed, Jo Dunning, Maureen Moss, Alicia Power, Meg Benedicte, Richard Gordon, Michael Beckwith, Emmanuel Dagher, Gerald O'Donnell, Rikka Zimmerman, as exceptional teachers, & most powerfully for me, Prageet & Julieanne, channelling the Alcazar group of Masters, in their unique ways of teaching, plus so much more contact & a stream of teachings from galactic Beings, such as Pleiadeans, Hathors, Syrians, Lemurians, Venusians, Andromedans, Arcturians, The Brotherhood of Light and many more, as many portals open, from many different realms helping Humanity's transition to more evolved Living. We too are Galactic Beings who have experienced lives in many realms.

Channels for Galactic teachings - Omnec Onec, Ana-La-Rai, Robert Potter, JZ Knight, Dianne Robbins,

Amy Flynn, Nora Herold, Judy Call, Isira Sananda, Dr. Edwige Bingue, Miriam Delicado, Jim Self, Laurie Reyon Anderson, Shimara Kumara, Kimba Arem, Lisa Transcendence, Anrita Melkizedek, Prageet & Julieanne...............

Angelic Messages:

- Diana Cooper - 'Birthing of a New Age…Transition to the Golden Age in 1932'- The Magic of Unicorns & many more

- Doreen Virtue - 'Archangel Guide to Ascension'- plus many other books etc.

Cancer: -

Natural Burials - Jae Rhim Lee, -Mushroom spore Burial Suits, Anna Citelli & Raoul Bretzel, Biodegradable Seed Pods

Outside the Box - Liz Rothschild, Natural Death Centre, owner of Natural Burial Ground.

When I Was Someone Else - Stephane Alex

'Cancer is not a Disease, it's a Survival Mechanism' -Andreas Moritz

'Dancing with Cancer' - and How I Learnt a Few New Steps -Diana Brueton

'Dying to be Me' -Anita Moorjani

'Being with Dying' -Roshi Joan Halifax

'The Path of Practice' -Bri Maya Tiwari

'Grace and Grit' -Spirituality and Healing in the Life of Treya Killam Wilbur -Ken Wilbur

'The Tibetan Book of Living and Dying' -Sogyal Rinpoche

'On Mortality' -Atul Gawande

'Death and Dying' -Elizabeth Kubler Ross - plus many other Books

****

Mind-blowing Books:

- I'm Dying…Shit! Not Again! - Cha-Zey
- The Nature of Reality - (St.) Hilarion * (- harder to find these days - translator)
- Through the Eyes of Love (Book 3 especially), & -'Stepping…Between…Realities' plus all his books. - Michael Roads
- Behaving as if the God in All Life Mattered' - Machaelle Small Wright +
- Dancing in the Shadows of the Moon'
- The Mount Shasta Mission - plus her other books

Anastasia -Vladimir Megre - plus the other 8 books of the series

- Memories of Heaven - Dr. Wayne W. Dyer & Dee Garnes, plus many, many other lives after body 'death' books by many writers inc. Dannion Brinkley, Raymond Moody, Brian Weiss, Angie Fenimore, Elisabeth Hallett, Soozie Holbech, Andy Tomlinson and more! (We'll all have had these experiences many times)
- What's in the Way, is the Way - Mary 0'Malley
- My Stroke of insight - Jill Bolte Taylor
- Whole Brain Living - Jill Bolte Taylor
- Lost Knowledge of the Imagination – Gary Lachman
- Prince of the Skies - Antonio Iturbe

****

Spanish Civil War + World War 2 -(1936 onwards)

- Homage to Catalonia - George Orwell
- As I Walked Out One Mid-Summer Morning' - Laurie Lee
- A Moment of War - Laurie Lee
- A Rose in Winter - Laurie Lee
- Winter in Madrid - C.J. Sansom
- When I was Someone Else - Stephane Allix
- Only for Three Months - Adrian Bell-;
- The Spanish Civil War - Reaction, Revolution, Revenge - Paul Preston
- The Last Days of the Spanish Republic' - also, 'Franco' - Paul Preston
- The Spanish Holocaust - Paul Preston
- Franco - Paul Preston - (translator-bit heavy going)
- Fleeing Franco - Hywel Davies
- Fateful Choices: Ten decisions that Changed the World, 1914-1949' - Ian Kershaw

- People Like Us - Louise Fein - & 'To Hell and Back'? - (have not traced last book)
- No Place to call Home – Inside the real lives of gypsies & Travellers
- The Long Walk - (Escape from Russian (i.e., Stalin) Brutality - Gulag) - Slavomir Raisicz -
Prince of the Skies - also 'The Librarian of Auschwitz' - Antonio Iturbe
- The 'Tattooist of Auschwitz' - Heather Morris
- Little Bird of Auschwitz - Alina & Jacques Perreti
- Always Remember your Name' - Tatiana Bucci   *Lily's Promise: How I survived Auschwitz and found Lily Ebert*
- Love despite Hate Child survivors of the Holocaust & their adult lives' - Sarah Moscovitz
- In Spite of Oceans - Migrant Voices – Huma Qureshi
****

Internet Access to Global Spiritual Teachers and communities via, - live replays, teleseminars, videos, audios...

Prageet & Julieanne, (Stargate Academy): - Kryon, & Asil – interdimensional channels.
Cari Murphy, Kaia Ra - The Sophia Code,
John Burgos - http//Beyond the Ordinary show:
Jennifer McLean - http//www.mcleanmasterworks.com
Judy Anderson - http//Jazz up your Life with Judy: ... - Soul Talk Patty Malek: -
Lauren Galey - http://www.acoustichealth.com: Eram Saeed - http//From Heartache to Joy.com - (she seems to have disappeared from playing that role).
Cindy Kubika - http//EnergizedLivingToday.com/live
Darius M. Barazandeh - http//YouWealthRevolution.com
****

Restoring the Eco-system of our Earth

The Running Hare – John Lewis Stemple
Dancing with Bees – Brigit Strawbridge Howard
Global Hive – Horst Kornberger – (especially the last chapters, so relevant re. bees)! *
Biodynamic Beekeeping – Matthias Thun
The Secrets of Bees – Michael Weiler
A Sting in the Tail – Dave Goulson
Wilding – Isabella Tree
Bringing back the Beaver – foreword by Isabella Tree - Derek Gow
Rewilding - edited by David Woodfall
Rewilding and the Art of Plant Whispering - Rachel Corby
The Medicine Grove - Rachel Corby

Re-birding - rewilding Britain and its' Birds - Benedict

The Salt Path - Raynor Winn

The Wild Silence - Raynor Winn

The Hidden Life of Trees - Peter Wohlleben

Working with Nature - Jeremy Purseglove

Taming the Flood - Jeremy Purseglove

Irreplaceable - The Fight to Save our Wild Places – Julian Hoffman

The Sixth Extinction - & Field Notes from a Catastrophe,

A frontline Report on Climate Change - Elizabeth Kolbert,

Under a White Sky - The Nature of the Future - Elizabeth Kolbert

Prophet of Love - Elizabeth Kolbert

Last Child in the Woods, saving our children from Nature Deficit Disorder - Richard Louv

Abundance, Nature in Recovery - Karen Lloyd